Law, Government and Public Policy examines the relationship between law and public policy in Australia. Beginning with a study of legislation (which is a neglected aspect of legal learning), the author proceeds to argue that to understand legislation one must examine the conditions in which it is made, the legal form it takes, how it is implemented and what impact it has. He then turns his attention to the courts: who uses them? what issues are brought before them? how do the courts deal with cases? what impact do their decisions have on society? Social issues must be cast in legal terms to be litigated, is the message.

The remaining chapters deal with current and compelling aspects of law and society. 'Government' contains studies of how the courts review government decision-making (there is special mention of the role of the High Court in federal–state relations), constitutional conventions, and rules to prevent conflicts of interest; 'The Economy' has the first ever overview of the law of public finance in Australia. The final substantive chapter looks at how legislation and the courts have played a part in environmental protection.

There are three interweaving themes throughout the book.
- legislation is the most important and most effective instrument for establishing and implementing public policy.
- the courts have only a limited impact on politics, the economy and society generally (the argument is strongly put that the courts ought not to adopt an activist stance, because they do not have the capacity or authority to decide important issues of public policy)
- responsible and representative government is an extremely healthy system; the courts ought to be strengthening it rather than pursuing some notion that government should be accountable to them.

Ross Cranston is Professor of Law at Queen Mary College, University of London.

Other books in the series

Terry Carney and Peter Hanks
*Australian Social Security Law,
Policy and Administration*

Paul Finn
Law and Government in Colonial Australia

Law, Government
and Public Policy
Ross Cranston

OXFORD
UNIVERSITY PRESS

Melbourne

OXFORD UNIVERSITY PRESS
Oxford New York Toronto Delhi Bombay Calcutta Madras Karachi
Petaling Jaya Singapore Hong Kong Tokyo Nairobi Dar es Salaam
Cape Town Melbourne Auckland and associated companies in Beirut Berlin
Ibadan Nicosia

National Library of Australia
Cataloguing-in-Publication data:

Cranston, Ross.
  Law government and public policy.

  Bibliography.
  Includes index.
  ISBN 0 19 554848 5.
  ISBN 0 19 554850 7 (pbk.).

  1. Public law—Australia. 2. Australia—Politics and
  government. I. Title. (Series: Law and government
  (Melbourne, Vic.)).

342.94

Edited by Sarah Brenan
Typeset by Graphicraft Typesetters Ltd, Hong Kong
Printed by Hing Yip Printing Co, Hong Kong
Published by Oxford University Press, 253 Normanby Road, South Melbourne
OXFORD is a trademark of Oxford University Press

349.94
C852l # CONTENTS

ACKNOWLEDGEMENTS

This book began as a study of the law and politics of Australian federalism, but quickly grew to encompass broader themes. It is a product of my time at the Australian National University, both in the Research School of Social Sciences and the Faculty of Law. I welcome the opportunity to acknowledge publicly my debt to both parts of the University for their support during the book's preparation. Two of my teachers, Professors Colin Hughes and Geoffrey Sawer, deserve my thanks for stimulating an enthusiasm for the inter-disciplinary study of law and government. I am grateful to Mr Justice McGarvie, J.G. Starke, Q.C., and Professor S.J. Stoljar for their encouragement and support whilst the book was being written. My co-editors of this Oxford series; colleagues at the Australian National University, in particular Michael Barker, Dr Tim Bonyhady and Geoffrey Lindell; and certain officials of the Australian Treasury who must remain anonymous, made many useful suggestions and helpful comments on draft chapters. My greatest academic debt is to Dr Paul Finn. It was his vision which led to this series, and it was in his room that many of the ideas in this book were tested.

Christine Hogendijk and Glenda Wardell did a first-class job of typing the manuscript. Margot Jensen, Anita Kaney, Michael Kerrisk and Anne Walton provided very able research assistance. While most of the final draft of the book was being written, I was Associate Dean of the Faculty of Law. I would not have been able to perform the tasks associated with that job, and to write this book, without the superb secretarial and administrative assistance provided by Audrey Magee and Rita Harding. The librarians in the ANU Law Library cheerfully accommodated my requests for long loans and difficult references; Jenny Degeling, the reference librarian, deserves special mention. Parts of Chapter 2 appeared in a recent issue of the *Civil Justice Quarterly*; I am grateful to the editor and the publishers for permission to reproduce it.

Ross Cranston
London 1986

INTRODUCTION

SCOPE OF THE STUDY

As the title indicates, this is a study of the part played by law in public policy. I use the term 'law' in a broad sense, meaning a system of formal rules in society, the means by which society expresses and enforces the exercise of legitimate power. Legislatures, the executive and courts are recognized as having the capacity to make and administer law.[1] In this sense law is not simply lawyers' law—the rules considered by the courts or those the legal profession is involved with. An Appropriation Act of the Australian Parliament and a Dog Ordinance of the Wagga Wagga Council might never be considered by the courts, and the legal profession might never advise clients about either, but nevertheless both are law.

Public policy is an ill-defined term. As used in legal discourse, it indicates the non-doctrinal factors which might be used in some judicial decision-making.[2] In this book it connotes the 'product' of state decision and action, in other words the decisions and actions of government departments and agencies, courts, and other bodies able to allocate values authoritatively in society. A failure to decide or to act ('non-decisions' and 'non-actions') might also be perceived as public policy.[3]

Because the book is concerned with law and public policy, however, it does not address matters which never get on to the political agenda. Nor is attention given to those aspects of public policy which do not have a substantial legal manifestation. For example, excluded is the not uncommon response of government to particular problems, the establishment of avenues for complaint, where these do not entail new law. Also excluded from examination are the codes of practice sometimes encouraged by government for particular areas of business activity.[4] This self-regulation has legal ramifications (for example, because of its anti-competitive effect), but it is not regarded in this book as law.

Finally, the book does not have much coverage of administrative guidelines or codes, although these might be published or available under freedom of information legislation. While sometimes categorized as quasi-legislation, they do not have the status of law, although acts committed according to such guidelines may have legal force and be open to legal challenge.

APPROACHES TO THE TOPIC

One way of conceptualizing the part played by law in public policy would be to look at relevant social mechanisms and their associated techniques. The three mechanisms of greatest importance in this context are the market mechanism, the private law mechanism (whereby individuals enforce their rights against each other), and the public administration mechanism.[5] The three are of course interrelated. Various issues arise. For example, advocates of the market mechanism usually assume that it involves minimizing government interference in the market, although they may concede that legal measures are necessary against fraud, restrictive trade practices and monopoly power; however, using the market mechanism can also mean that state enterprises are created to compete actively with private corporations. Enhancing private law mechanisms might involve not only changing substantive law and procedural law, but also strengthening the legal competence of citizens so that they use them.

Another approach would be to examine the functions that law performs with respect to public policy. Perhaps a little can be said about some of those functions. First, law legitimates particular policy, or a change in a policy, by embodying that policy or change in a form accepted as authoritative by members of society. The policy may be to proclaim or maintain the symbols of government and society, as with the *Flags Act* 1953; it may be to establish a government institution, in which case legislation legitimates the institution's structure, composition, powers and financing; or it may purport to control the behaviour of individuals and private entities, in which case it legitimates an alteration in the legal significance of their actions or their relationships.[6] Although some members of society may object to the policy, and thus to the law embodying it—indeed, may actively seek to have the policy reversed, or at least modified—most accept that law must, in general terms, be obeyed. That acceptance follows because of the source of legislation—democratically elected parliaments—and the respect in which the judiciary is held. In other words, the first function of law is to constitute order.

Second, law details public policy. Many of the implications of a particular policy may be available in official documents of the governing political party, in the reports of a government committee or in the speeches of the relevant minister. But legislation spells out authoritatively, and in detail, how individuals can obtain the support or sanction of the law for private transactions (making a will, getting married, transferring land); what they must do (generally, under threat of penalties); and the obligations which government officials have in relation to them (for example, to pay a subsidy or benefit when certain prerequisites are satisfied). Of primary concern in this book is legislation which imposes duties on private individuals or institutions, or obligations on government officials, rather than that which facilitates private transactions. 'Delegated legislation' may also be relevant in filling out further the details of policy. (As well as specifying public policy in greater detail, delegated legislation deals with machinery matters—for example, when the legislation commences—and modifies legislation—for example, financial limits in line with inflation.) In specific areas the courts perform this 'detailing' function by interpreting legislation and developing rules independently of statute law.

Third, some law has an 'educative' function. In other words, while law may impose specific duties on persons or institutions, it may also be designed, or function so as, to change attitudes.[7] Anti-discrimination and equal opportunities legislation are examples of the first. They may directly deter discrimination, or provide opportunities, under threat of a sanction, but they may also have an effect, perhaps long-term and almost imperceptible, on how some people in the community perceive these issues. The legitimacy of law in general may enhance public acceptance of values incorporated in specific laws. Moreover, legislation may support those wishing to comply with certain rules to resist pressure to the contrary, and it may promote its underlying values by discouraging overt behaviour in conflict with these values. Educative law will not necessarily have these effects: it may, as with legislation directed against abortion, fail to change attitudes and drive the regulated practice underground.

Finally, law at a general level has what can be called ideological functions. There is not-infrequent public mention of the 'rule of law', but closely related to (or subsumed by) this are other ideological dimensions such as equality before the law and due process of law (one aspect of which in the Australian system is the principle of natural justice). Much has been written about how law acts to disguise power through a form of ideological hegemony.[8]

The approach adopted here, however, is more conventional than either of the two outlined above. It uses neither mechanisms nor functions as organizing categories. Rather, the first part of the book (Chapters 1 and 2) takes the two most important legal institutions, legislation and the courts. With both of them the issues addressed include who is involved in using them, what is the character of the rules made, how are they implemented, and what is their impact. Then the second part of the book (Chapters 3–5) focuses on selected aspects of society—government, the economy and the environment. (Clearly, the focus is selective; other aspects could just as easily have been chosen.) Here the themes of the first part of the book are given a practical application, although new issues are explored. Central to the chapter on government, for example, is a theory of responsible and representative government.

Although the book concentrates on the legal dimensions of public policy, I hope that the issues discussed make some contribution to the appraisal of policy. Specifically, the discussion highlights the extent to which the goals of public policy are achieved and how better public policy might be fashioned in practice. At a more general level, perhaps it throws light on some of the broader issues which historians, political scientists and sociologists are interested in when they study public policy. One such issue is power. Lawyers are only too aware that when private parties making law are unequal in a social or economic sense, the product reflects this. Standard form contracts, such as insurance contracts, are a classic case. In addition, a legal perspective can frequently reveal that persons claiming to exercise legitimate power are on shakier grounds than they admit. At various points, the book subjects to examination the claims of those with legitimate power, especially in judicial decision-making.

THEMES

To anticipate somewhat, a theme throughout the book is that legislation is the most important and effective instrument of public policy and that the courts have (and should have) only a limited role in the area. Yet legislation is a neglected aspect of legal learning, and evaluation of matters such as the efficacy of legislation and its impact is unsystematic. The relative paucity of discussion about legislation can be explained in various ways. The method of teaching law in most universities and colleges downgrades legislation, because it emphasizes cases decided by the courts. Legislation, when it is examined, is looked at through the cases which have interpreted particular aspects of it. Another factor is that much law is taught and expounded along conceptual lines instead of by analysis of how it relates to particular social phenomena. Were the latter approach adopted, the importance of legislation in each area, indeed, its overriding significance in many areas, would be more immediately apparent. Instead, it is all too common for lawyers to be prisoners of a mentality which regards legislation as an unwanted and unnecessary intrusion into case law. This attitude sometimes underlies the approach of the courts to the interpretation of legislation.

This attitude of lawyers to legislation is surprising when it is realized that legislation has always been central to Australian public policy. In the nineteenth century, legislation regulated the alienation of public (Crown) land, established the framework for state socialism, notably in transport (the railways) and communications (the telegraph), and controlled mining activity—all matters of critical importance to the colonial economy.[9] Twentieth-century Australia has seen legislation in these and other key areas of public policy—for example, the regulation of business activity, the marketing of primary products, the exploitation of natural resources, and the payment of social welfare benefits. By contrast, legislation has played less of a role in the social and economic order of other societies. For the first three-quarters of the nineteenth century, for instance, United States legislation was highly particularized and 'statutes of broad policy or general reach were relatively few and reflected little bold programming or implementation'.[10] Consequently the American courts figure historically to a greater extent than the Australian in allocative decisions.

The second major theme of the book has to do with courts. The courts have a relatively limited role in public policy compared with legislation. In Chapter 2 empirical support is offered for this contention by reference to matters such as the scope of social problems which are litigated. Reference is also made to the limited social impact of judicial decisions. While some cases, such as certain constitutional decisions of the High Court, have dramatic repercussions for politics, the economy and society generally, most will not cause even the slightest ripple in community behaviour. Later chapters consider the argument in specific areas.

A third major theme of the book concerns the theory of responsible and representative government. By this is meant that there is a chain of political and administrative accountability—the officials of executive government are answerable to the ministry, the executive government as a whole to the parliament, and the parliament to the people. If accountability in practice does not always match the theory, this an argument for its improvement, not its abandonment. Courts, so the book contends, have a duty to give effect to the theory, if it is relevant to the issue before them. In other words, their duty is to strengthen the mechanisms of political and administrative accountability, rather than to pursue any notion of the independent accountability of government through the courts.

CHAPTER ONE

LEGISLATION

To understand the efficacy of legislation as an instrument of public policy requires an examination of its emergence, its legal form, its implementation by the relevant government bodies, and its impact on behaviour.[1] To take the relevance of the first point, the way that legislation emerges shows that sometimes it is designed to reassure the community that measures are being taken, without much concern as to what their effects will be in practice. Even if the proponents of a measure intend it to be effective, the legislation which results may be defective because important economic and social interests force its modification. Legislation may also fall short of its goals because of the form used. Its provisions may be ambiguous, over-inclusive, conflicting, or simply not commensurate with its ostensible goals. These defects can occur because its provisions may reflect conflicts between different interests at the time of enactment; because those drafting the law did not foresee particular problems; or simply because not enough attention was given to drafting.

The implementation of legislation by the bodies charged with the task might be inadequate, so that the individuals and institutions to which it is addressed can ignore the law with impunity. Financial and human resources are crucial, for they determine matters such as whether implementation is adequately monitored and whether action is taken if non-compliance is detected. In turn, whether adequate resources are available to the body turns on political factors; the absence of resources may indicate that nothing was really expected of the legislation from the outset. However, it is well to recognize that certain types of legislation are inherently difficult to implement, even if relatively generous resources are allocated, for legislative sanctions are only one of the factors which determine whether private individuals and institutions comply with legislative requirements. Sanctions which attempt to change the behaviour of private individuals and institutions may be misconceived because it might be more effective for the state to allocate financial resources to pay a benefit or to provide a service. Public housing may be a more effective, if more expensive, way of ensuring good cheap housing for the less well off, than a system of rent control.

As well as the direct effects of legislation, when those at whom it is directed conform with its requirements, there are the independent and unintended effects.[2] Independent effects describe what is independent of any conforming behaviour, such as a change in political support as a result of a measure. Unintended effects are what is not foreseen by the law-makers. These independent and unintended effects may well be acceptable to the law-makers, even if they do not admit this. In practice there is controversy about whether particular effects can be causally linked to legislation.

I   THE EMERGENCE OF LEGISLATION

Legal interest in the making of legislation has been largely confined to institutional description and legislative procedure. Identifying and analysing the forces behind legislation have been left to political scientists and historians. Yet the operation of legislation can only be fully understood in terms of its background. Ideology, social values, political party and pressure group activity, and media publicity all play a part in law-making. Explaining how these factors combine is a matter of great complexity. What follows is nothing more than an outline of some aspects of the process. The focus is on situations where legislation has been made. However, a full understanding of law-making requires an explanation of the absence of legislation, as well as its emergence.[3]

Legal and related mechanisms

Legislation in Australia is made by the parliaments. Although this is not stated specifically in the Australian constitution in relation to the Federal Parliament, it is implicit in various of its sections. Section 1, for example, provides that the legislative power of the Commonwealth shall be vested in a Federal Parliament, which shall consist of the Queen, a Senate and a House of Representatives. The Queen's representative in Australia is the Governor-General (section 2). The constitution provides that questions arising in the Senate and the House of Representatives shall be determined by majority (sections 23, 40). Under section 53, proposed laws appropriating revenue or moneys, or imposing taxation, shall not originate in the Senate; in addition, the Senate may not amend proposed laws imposing taxation, or proposed laws appropriating revenue or moneys for the ordinary annual services of the government, nor may it amend any proposed laws so as to increase any proposed charge or burden. (However, it may request omissions or amendments in such cases, and there is authority that therefore it may reject or defer a money bill.[4]) Except as provided in section 53, however, the Senate has equal power with the House of Representatives in respect of all proposed laws. Finally, mention should be made of the Governor-General's role: a proposed law passed by both the House of Representatives and the Senate is presented to him for the Queen's assent and under section 58 he must declare that he assents in the Queen's name, that he will withhold assent or that he reserves it for the Queen's assent. (In fact, the Governor-General has no independent discretion to refuse assent; and there would appear to be no bills where reservation for the Queen's assent is now legally required.) Equivalent provisions in the States about the making of legislation are less detailed.[5] However, it is clear that legislation must generally be approved by each of the houses of Parliament (one house in Queensland) and by the Crown. There are exceptions; for example, in New South Wales legislation appropriating revenue for the ordinary annual services of the government may be presented for royal assent even though the Legislative Council has not passed it.

Australian parliaments have adopted standing orders, which set out the procedures for the passage of a bill. Section 50 of the Australian constitution empowers each house of the Federal Parliament to make such orders. In the Federal Parliament the ordinary stages are initiation, first reading, second reading, committal and consideration by a committee of the whole, report from the committee and its adoption, third reading, passing, transmission to the other house, and presentation for assent.[6] Instead of being considered by a committee of the whole, bills may be sent to a legislative or general purpose committee.[7] Since 1981, the Senate has referred all bills introduced to its Standing Committee for the Scrutiny of Bills, which reports on whether they require amendment because they trespass unduly on personal rights and liberties, make rights, liberties or obligations unduly dependent upon insufficiently defined administrative powers or non-reviewable administrative decisions, inappropriately delegate legislative power, or insufficiently subject the exercise of legislative power to parliamentary scrutiny.

As a general rule, it seems that the courts will not entertain a challenge to legislation on the basis that the procedures embodied in the standing orders have not been complied with.[8] Similarly, it seems that they will not be concerned with contravention of requirements such as sections 53–55 of the Australian constitution relating to money bills.[9] However, there are situations when the courts will inquire into the procedures which govern the way legislation is to be enacted. For example, section 57 of the Australian constitution sets out a procedure for the passing of

legislation where there is disagreement between the House of Representatives and the Senate; basically it involves a double dissolution, an
election, and a joint sitting of both houses to vote on the matter if the
election does not resolve the political stalemate. The High Court held
that one of six laws passed at a joint sitting in 1974 was invalid because
the procedures of section 57 had not been followed.[10] However, judicial
review in this instance was exceptional: there have only been five double
dissolutions since Federation (1914, 1951, 1974, 1975, 1983) and the one
joint sitting in 1974. Proposed State legislation has on occasions been
thwarted because it has not met existing legislative requirements as to
the 'manner and form' of passing it.[11] Again, such occasions have been
infrequent.

Bills in the Federal Parliament are public bills, that is, bills relating
to matters of public policy. The House of Representatives does not
recognize, and there has never been introduced into the Senate, what
are called private bills, that is, bills for the particular interest or benefit
of a person, public company or corporation, or local authority.[12] Private
members' bills, like public bills, deal with matters of public policy, but as
their name suggests they are not sponsored by the government. Such
bills are relatively unusual in Australian parliaments. For example, only
fifty-two private members' bills were introduced into the House of
Representatives, and 111 into the Senate, between 1901 and 1980. In
Australian practice, bills are divided into ordinary bills, money bills and
bills proposing an alteration of the constitution.[13]

Government bills formally originate in decisions of the Cabinet,
except in a minor matter, where the Prime Minister may agree on
alternative means, or for amendments of a purely drafting or formal
nature involving no policy, which need only the authority of the
Minister.[14] The normal procedure is that within five working days of
receipt of Cabinet approval for legislation, final drafting instructions
must be furnished to the Office of Parliamentary Counsel for drafting.
Within limits, Parliamentary Counsel can influence the content of
proposed legislation, for example, by drafting it so that it does not depart
from existing practices or impose what are seen as unnecessary restrictions on individual rights.[15] Once drafted, the bill must be approved
by the sponsoring department and other interested departments and
agencies. The legislation committee of Cabinet then determines whether
it accords with the Cabinet authority, ensures that 'legal policy' matters
such as onus of proof, penalties or administrative discretions are dealt
with appropriately, and may clear the bill subject to specific technical
or other minor changes being made. Party clearance can be obtained in
the development of the original Cabinet proposal, following Cabinet
approval of the policy, or following the decision of the legislation
committee to clear the bill. Private members have access to the Office of

Parliamentary Counsel for assistance in the drafting of bills and amendments, although the Attorney-General may decline to permit access if it would substantially prejudice the government's legislative programme.

Delegated legislation is made under the authority of already enacted legislation. By law, delegated legislation is 'made' when it is signed by the Governor-General, Governor, Minister or person specified, or at least when it emerges from the meeting of the Executive Council or relevant body.[16] In particular cases, the person or body empowered to make the delegated legislation may have to consult beforehand with another person or body, although the statutory language will be crucial in determining whether departure is possible from any recommendation of the person or body consulted.[17] Notwithstanding that the delegated legislation is made, it will not normally take effect until it has been notified in the government gazette.[18] (The justification for this requirement is that in a democratic society citizens must know the law if they are to be bound by it, but notification in the government gazette seems to be a highly artificial way of informing them. There is no requirement of antecedent publicity to enable citizens to make representations about proposed delegated legislation.) Moreover, delegated legislation will generally be void unless laid before the Parliament.[19] Parliament, or at least committees of the Parliament, may scrutinize delegated legislation with a view to possible disallowance.[20] An alternative approach, used for some delegated legislation in the United Kingdom, is that the delegated legislation does not take effect until there is an affirmative resolution by Parliament. In one decision, members of the High Court expressed a reluctance to become involved when it was claimed that procedures for parliamentary disallowance had not been followed.[21]

Explaining the social and political process

The legal and related mechanisms outlined tell little of the forces behind legislation. Indeed, they might positively mislead one as to the power of those such as members of Parliament. Moreover, they cannot show how legislation, or delegated legislation, is made (and unmade) over the years. Just as there may be an accretion of case law around a certain doctrine, so there may be an incremental, possibly slow or even inept, legislative building in important areas of public policy.

To explain better the reality of law-making, some writers have attempted to characterize the process by developing models of the process. These models reflect their conception of the nature of larger social forces. None of the 'models' of how legislation emerges adequately captures the complexities of the process.[22] What can be called the 'public interest' model, in which the state responds to an identified problem by establishing legislation for its orderly solution, is too naive, for it assumes that the state responds to ideas and popular concerns and that there is a consensus, or that the state acts as a neutral arbiter reconciling differences. The 'pluralist' model is more realistic, for it recognizes that there is a clash of interests, with the state itself being a separate interest or a surrogate for one or more other interests. For example, the 'pluralist' model argues that reformers might mobilize sufficient political support to achieve legislation, but on the other hand might have to compromise, or might be defeated in the face of opposition from other interests. However, the 'pluralist' model is defective in glossing over the asymmetry in power between interests and the existence of links between some interests and the state.

A third model of law–making, the 'private interest' model, conceives of regulatory legislation as being instituted at the behest of groups such as business to advance their interests.[23] It overlooks the fact that others with contrary interests are not without some power to effect social change, and confuses the functions served by some regulation with its origins.

There are a variety of Marxist models of law-making. One is that certain types of legislation are inherent in the development of a society, being necessary, for example, to avert social disintegration in the face of changing class relationships.[24] Conflict might be neutralized, for example, by legislating to have a matter dealt with by legalistic procedures (as is often done in industrial relations in Australia). One difficulty with this approach to law-making is that a particular result (averting social disintegration, neutralizing conflict) might have been as well achieved in a comparable society by quite different legislative arrangements (establishing a state agency rather than tribunals, encouraging collective bargaining rather than interfering directly in industrial relations).

While each of these models has deficiencies, each also contains some truths about the emergence of legislation—the 'public interest' model, in suggesting that the state, or at least parts of it, can be motivated by a conception of the public interest; the 'pluralist' model, in recognizing how different interests can have a hand in the emergence of laws; the 'private interest' model, in underlining the crucial role that powerful interests, their surrogates in the state, and dominant ideology, can play; and Marxist models, in emphasizing that legislating occurs within the limits set by the larger economic and social forces of a society. But none accounts fully for the process by which legislation emerges from the interaction of government, interest groups and the media, and against a background of public opinion (perhaps inchoate), institutional arrangements, community expectations and the economic, social and cultural inheritance. Rather than pursuing the models further, then, let us look in a more concrete way at some of the influences on the making of legislation in Australia.

Influences on legislation

It is possible to identify a variety of institutions which influence the shape of legislation. Centre stage are the Cabinet, ministers, the political parties and the Public Service. Little need be said about the first three.[25] However, it is important to underline the role of the Public Service, for it belies the popular view that legislation simply implements the policy of the political party in power. Much social reform legislation—legislation which materially alters concepts and rules which have for a considerable period governed social relations—originates formally in the Public Service and public authorities.[26] In addition, the Public Service and public authorities initiate a great deal of legislation to meet the regular needs of government, in particular money bills and the mundane amendments to existing legislation shown to be necessary by the everyday work of government. Proposed legislation also comes regularly from the Standing Committee of Attorneys-General, law reform commissions, and less regularly from parliamentary committees, royal commissions and committees of inquiry.[27] The processes are different in each case: one notable difference is that there is much less opportunity for public comment on proposed legislation emerging from the Public Service and the Standing Committee of Attorneys-General than on measures originating from the other bodies mentioned.

Beyond these more formal instigators are a variety of sources of legislation—interest (pressure) groups, trade unions, professional associations,[28] lobbyists, the media, public opinion and individuals such as professionals or academics who are familiar with an area and are able to obtain a platform for their views. Where a government is not committed to action, interest groups and others might still be able to have legislation effected through the political process. This might be through traditional channels such as lobbying ministers and public officials. Conversely, government regularly consults interests about proposals for legislation and delegated legislation. Formally, consultation may be undertaken by distributing a Green Paper or even a draft of proposed legislation.[29] Of course different groups have differential access through this process: business, farmers' groups and trade unions have privileged access with certain Federal government departments.[30] The present Australian Government has institutionalized consultation with the Australian Council for Trade Unions under the 'Accord' between the two. Close consultation between the present Government and interest groups, in particular by means of the two 'summits' (on economic policy in 1983 and taxation in 1985), has led to the suggestion that Australia is moving towards 'corporatism'.[31] However, it is a matter for debate whether interest groups in general have a greater influence than previously, and whether the role of established institutions of government has been downgraded.

Interests might be able to achieve change by attracting favourable media publicity or building political support through letter-writing, research reports, political protest or contacts in the Government or Parliament. For example, the South Australian Council of Social Service was able to achieve some of its proposed amendments to legislation in the mid-1970s by lobbying the Legislative Council, where the Government lacked a majority.[32] The task is facilitated if those seeking legislation can exploit a 'crisis', 'moral panic', a 'moral crusade', capitalize on what is widely thought to be undesirable, utilize government attempts to consult, or associate their proposals with values which are widely shared in the community (e.g., health, safety, possibly social justice). A number of examples are illustrative: the evidence of unethical and dishonest practices in Australia during the mining boom of the late 1960s and early 1970s built up a momentum for tougher companies and securities law;[33] community groups in Victoria had a significant influence on the *Residential Tenancies Act* 1980;[34] environmentalists have made some advances by highlighting especially serious threats to the environment;[35] and the advent of the women's movement paved the way for anti-discrimination legislation.[36] Direct action may sometimes achieve desired legislative change by arousing public support. However, the government response may be to resist change, and indeed to legislate to crush a direct action campaign. The response of the Queensland Government to the anti-uranium marches of the mid- to late 1970s is an example of this.[37]

It is by no means certain that interest groups will achieve success, for their proposals may be too adverse to other interests. For example, there may be outright opposition, although this can range from a concern with minor details to near unanimity that proposed legislation should be vehemently opposed, and threats to stifle its impact by political moves or through administrative pressure should it be enacted. Consequently, even legislation which is intended to bite on certain practices can be weakened as a result of opposition. The upshot of opposition may be purely symbolic 'reform', for its failure may be obvious from the compromises necessary to get the legislation onto the statute book.

The role of business

The influence of business in law-making is a matter of considerable interest, because it bears on ruling-class theories and on the models of law-making outlined above. There are instances where business has been instrumental in shaping legislation, or even been able to defeat proposed legislation impinging on its interests. The recent history of health and safety at work legislation in Australia provides an example, as does the defeat of the anti-smoking Western Australian Tobacco (Promotion and Sales) Bill 1983.[38] But there are also instances where business has been unsuccessful in its aims. For example, the history of the *Trade Practices Act* 1974 is of business vigorously resisting the legislation, but the Labor Government being totally unresponsive.[39] Again, the major contentions of the mining industry were rejected in the enactment of the *Aboriginal Land Rights (Northern Territory) Act* 1976.[40] However, defeat in particular instances does not mean that business is not overall a significant force, indeed the significant force, in law-making affecting its interests. Its influence need not be direct. The inter-penetration of business and law-makers, or the degree to which law-makers and the community are imbued with a business mentality, render it less necessary for business to take overt steps to protect its interests. For example, the quest for economic development and the fear that tight regulation will produce a flight of capital has made State governments chary of introducing tough environmental and health and safety laws. Business can identify with key values in the Australian ethos such as progress and development (and, in the case of property, home ownership).

The historical record makes clear that on many occasions businesses have been strong proponents of legislation imposing regulation, either singly or in combination with reformers. It will be rare for the business community as a whole to support such legislation, and there may well be divisions between small and large businesses, between different types of businesses, and between businesses in different sectors of the economy. In a few cases such legislation has actually been promoted by particular businesses as a means of inhibiting their competitors. Merely because businesses support regulatory legislation does not necessarily mean that it advances only business interests, for there is no logical reason why it cannot simultaneously serve both business and other interests. If business supports it, however, it is a matter for close inquiry whether it can also benefit other interests, and whether modifications can ever be made in the regulatory scheme to achieve such benefits. Arguments similar to these apply where the professions support regulation.

Business and the professions may actively support regulatory legislation because they anticipate that it will facilitate economic or professional activity, will rationalize an industry or profession and stabilize competition within it, or will attract government support (including financial support). Regulation often represents a victory for established sections of a business or professional community in their efforts to attain conditions of stability in periods of economic or technological change, when the newly established are entering the market and often competing success-fully. The professions in Australia have supported legal and other controls over fees and advertising on the basis that the latter undermine professional status and public confidence in the quality of professional services.[41] Factory legislation in Victoria in the 1870s and 1880s was advocated by some of the larger manufacturers—in common cause with the trade unions—who saw regulation as giving them protection against the unfair competition of their small trade rivals.[42] Commercial broad-casters supported legislation establishing the Australian Broadcasting and Control Board so as to take decisions about broadcasters' licences out of the political arena, to ensure security of tenure for licences and because of the precedent in America of the Federal Communications Commis-sion.[43] Business and professional support for regulation in circumstances such as these produces an obvious cleavage between the free-enterprise ideology most espouse and their behaviour.

In addition to supporting regulatory legislation which advances their immediate interests, businesses may support, or at least not oppose, regulatory legislation which damages their immediate but promotes their long-term interests. One situation is where regulation will curb the behaviour of 'marginal' businesses which are lowering the reputation of an industry as a whole, for the reputable may hope that this will forestall more far-reaching regulation or adverse publicity. For example, larger manufacturers and retailers have tended not to oppose much modern consumer protection legislation, partly because some of it is generally directed at 'fly-by-night' traders, and partly because a good deal of the remainder does not impinge greatly on their business practices which match, or are in advance of, the standards laid down in legislation. A second situation is where business or a profession realizes that it is politically inopportune to be seen opposing regulation outright, and so accepts its inevitability but pushes for amendments to reduce its effectiveness.

A third situation is when business or a profession proposes self-regulation in an effort to forestall regulatory legislation. For example, the Australian Federation of Travel Agents proposed self-regulation for the industry in the early 1980s, when there was a great deal of talk of legislation along the lines of the New South Wales *Travel Agents Act* 1973.[44]

II LEGISLATIVE FORM

A knowledge of legislative form tells a great deal about legislative efficacy.[45] First, the study of legislative form draws attention to barriers to the operation of a statute inherent in its very provisions. For example, the lack of efficient implementation may actually be foreshadowed in the 'law in the books' (that is, formal law) by the failure to solve obvious problems of implementation.[46] Second, the focus on form can indicate where a law has its impact. For example, with the licensing of businesses, the aim is to prevent wrongdoing before it occurs, either by requiring approval of a relevant business before it operates or of its products before they are marketed. If licensing is successful, undesirable activity should not occur because the opportunities are either non-existent or severely limited. Detailed control at the level of the 'law in the books' minimizes wrongdoing at the level of the 'law in action'. Third, the form used in legislation plays a role in determining who is to implement it. A basic distinction exists between private law, which operates when individuals take action to enforce their rights, and public law, which relies on the machinery of the state. But enforcement agencies are often set in motion because individuals complain to them rather than because they have taken the initiative in uncovering offences. The extent to which enforcement agencies depend on complaints or on their own initiative varies, in part, with the form of the relevant law.

Finally, the form of a statute determines in several ways how it is applied. The agency enforcing it may be entrusted with wide discretion. Since an agency founded on one set of premises can acquire a different perspective from that originally envisaged, discretion may enable it to substitute its policy for that of Parliament. To avoid this, the legislature sometimes casts legislation in a form designed to prevent excessive discretion and to acquaint officials with its aims. Moreover, as a general rule the more precise a law, the more effective its implementation. Nevertheless, a precise law may be uncertain because it is too complex. A point of diminishing returns can be reached, where to increase detail in legal terms is counter-productive because of the consequential increase in complexity. However, this need not occur if, for example, law can be condensed in simple language in explanatory publications. Uncertainty may also result if a legal standard is ambiguous. The application of a general standard—requiring, for example, that food not be 'adulterated' or that a factory adopt 'reasonably practicable measures' to avoid pollution—can be problematic, since such terms are subject to varying interpretations.

Three major techniques are used in legislation to ensure compliant behaviour: broad statutory standards, administrative regulation, and licensing. The simplest form of legislation is that which announces a standard of behaviour in broad terms and imposes penalties on any deviation from it. In some cases the standard is taken from private law, so that it is simply the remedial law (the mechanism for obtaining redress) that is changed. Administrative regulation overlaps with legislation containing broad statutory standards, but there is the difference that it operates preventively and is more selective in its field of application. With administrative regulation, for example, businesses are specifically directed as to the nature of their products, practices or processes, and are usually prohibited from acting if they do not attain certain detailed standards. An attempt may also be made to control conduct which, although innocent in itself, could lead to objectionable activity. A third variation of public policy legislation is where those responsible for particular practices or processes are directly controlled, through licensing, on the assumption that this will indirectly control their practices or processes. A yet more detailed method of control is where persons must obtain prior approval for what they produce.

Broad statutory standards

The most common form of a broad statutory standard is a legislative fiat forbidding an activity and attaching imprisonment or a monetary penalty to its performance. Broad statutory standards usually operate so that official action is deferred until wrongdoing occurs. In this sense they are self-regulating, because the person has the choice of complying with the standard or of violating it and incurring a penalty.[47] The assumption is that the majority of those being regulated will choose to comply with the standard. Public compliance is assisted if the standard corresponds with societal values and is precise and well known so that individuals can bring their behaviour into line without much official guidance. The major difference between broad criminal standards and other forms of public control is usually that the former need fewer resources for enforcement. The drain on enforcement resources increases, however, if the standards are not sufficiently precise to allow compliance without much guidance, if specific exemptions from the general standard can be made, or if breaches are difficult to detect or to prove.

Broad statutory standards, backed by criminal sanctions, are generally an unsophisticated instrument and not always a satisfactory method of controlling undesirable activities. They may prohibit all forms of a particular activity, including what may be desirable, on the assumption that the latter is outweighed by what is objectionable. Not only may economic analysis seriously undermine this approach, but the fact that many more law-abiding people than evil-doers are thus affected may be thought to dictate a policy of relatively low maximum penalties, which clearly lessens the deterrent effect.

Enforcement problems also attach to the use of broad statutory standards as a legislative technique. First, their edge is blunted because they compete with each other for enforcement. A method of counteracting this tendency is to entrust the enforcement of a particular type of standard to a specialized agency, the success of which is then identified with its vigorous application. In Australia, trade practices law, companies and securities law, environmental law and so on are enforced by separate agencies, not the police. Second, if there is some uncertainty as to the application of a broad standard, there is a temptation for enforcement authorities to refrain from taking any action because of the possibility of not being successful. Third, broad criminal standards are not interpreted liberally because as a general rule courts construe criminal statutes narrowly. While this may be justified where individual liberty is at stake, it is different with regulatory offences where the typical punishment is a fine. Fourth, criminal procedure is inappropriate when applied to intricate regulatory offences.[48] Existing criminal procedure evolved for discovering truth in straightforward crimes such as murder or theft, where evidence is relatively simple and is capable of being assessed by ordinary citizens comprising a jury or a bench of lay magistrates. By contrast, some regulatory offences are relatively complex and only readily understood by experts. The burden of enforcing broad statutory standards is somewhat eased because the great bulk are 'strict liability' offences.[49] (The crucial question then is whether the elements of the prohibited act have been committed, and it is irrelevant whether there is *mens rea* ('guilty mind'), that is, intention, recklessness or criminal negligence. The assumption is that offenders can always re-order their affairs to avoid breaches of statutory standards. Strict liability makes for convenience in law enforcement, for it would be virtually impossible to penalize undesirable business behaviour if it were necessary to establish criminal intention in each case.)

It would be wrong to downgrade broad statutory standards as a legislative technique. As discussed above, the more precise the legislation, generally the more effective it is likely to be. Yet the uncertainty inherent in some broad statutory standards may be used to advantage by an enforcement agency where the cost of clarification, by the legislature directing its attention to the problem, would outweigh the benefits likely to result from easier enforcement or greater self-regulation. Within limits, uncertainty can be manipulated by an agency to secure compliance with its enforcement policy.[50] If those to whom legislation is directed are uncertain as to whether an agency will invoke sanctions against a particular activity, they may prefer to avoid the risk and desist from the activity. Agency policy with respect to a particular activity will often be obvious from the pattern of enforcement, but this will not be the case where individual enforcements can only be compared with the standard and not with each other. An agency may adopt a deliberate policy of fostering uncertainty by sporadic and random enforcement if the resources needed to enforce a law fully are excessive. Such a policy can have undesirable effects. Uncertain and random enforcement are generally objectionable on the ground of fairness, for discriminatory treatment of those in identical situations is inevitable. Futhermore, regular enforcement is crucial with broad statutory standards, for it is only by constantly bringing proceedings in the courts that enforcement agencies can bring home the need to ensure compliance with legislation. Numerous studies indicate that certainty and severity of punishment are the factors significantly influencing compliance with statutory command, and that, of the two, certainty is much more important.[51]

An important correlate of broad statutory standards is that a fairly wide discretion reposes in the relevant enforcement agency. Some discretion is always present with law enforcement, partly because of the vagueness of language and the need to apply legal categories to specific circumstances. But generally speaking an enforcement body will possess greater discretion if control is neither detailed nor specific. Discretion involves flexibility, and it may be that the legislature chooses a general standard in preference to other forms of legislation to allow adaptation of the law according to changing social conditions. In other words, Parliament feels incapable of dealing with the details of a matter and deliberately entrusts the task to an enforcement body which, it assumes, will have the advantages of flexibility and accumulated expertise. Of course broad and vague standards may also result from a failure of legislative drafting, because a statute incorporates competing and inconsistent values, or because of the cost of adopting another approach.

Administrative regulation

The growth of administrative regulation reflects the complexity of modern society and the fact that in the last century the state has assumed greater burdens. Although broad criminal provisions are perhaps sufficient in preventing all members of the society from committing acts that are widely regarded as morally reprehensible, detailed and individualized legislative action is more desirable if the state wants particular members of society, such as an industry, to perform certain affirmative acts. Historically, another consideration in the move to administrative regulation was a feeling that the judiciary was not handling the existing broad statutory controls in a manner consistent with legislative purpose.[52] Moreover, too onerous a burden was involved in extracting principles of law from a series of individual and often conflicting judicial interpretations of broad statutory standards.

Three basic techniques of administrative regulation will be analysed: compelled disclosure of information, imposition of detailed standards, and control of trade practices.

1   Compelled disclosure of information[53]
Actually forcing the divulgence of information about products, practices, processes and operations, under threat of criminal sanction, is now

a popular technique of modern administrative regulation. The assumption is that once information is disclosed citizens will use it to protect themselves. Disclosure regulation is relatively inexpensive when compared with other forms of regulatory control. Compliance can be readily checked where it is simply a matter of determining whether advertisements, contracts in standardized form, documents officially lodged and so on contain the requisite disclosures. Nor need information be conveyed directly for it to have impact. The justification for disclosure regulation in the economic sphere is that it facilitates competition, one of the necessary conditions for which is that citizens possess a high degree of knowledge in the market. Businesses are deterred from providing information voluntarily because of self-interest, since ignorance furthers oligopoly power by impeding the market.

Closely related to disclosure regulation is moral suasion, which is said to be 'the attempt to coerce private economic activity via governmental exhortation in directions not already defined or dictated by existing statute law'.[54] To back up its exhortations, government may threaten to introduce legal measures or it may publicize unsatisfactory behaviour so that citizens will take retaliatory action. Because the public's response is important, moral suasion is at its most effective when those at which it is directed are few in number, dependent on public goodwill, and highly 'visible' so that non-compliers are readily identifiable. Moral suasion can be used as an excuse for a government's failure to take more definite action.

A number of reasons can be suggested for the ineffectiveness of disclosure regulation. First, citizens may not have a strong desire for information. This derives partly from habit and partly from a deficiency in education. Another factor is that citizens may not regard as important much of the information presently the subject of disclosure laws. Next, certain types of disclosure are more effective than others. For example, information in contractual documents may be incomprehensible to ordinary people. There is a dilemma in communicating technical information to a non-technical audience. Information must be capable of being understood by citizens, but at the same time it must be accurate and that can mean use of technical expressions. Moreover, even when bold and simple warnings are set out in contract documents, for instance, persons may no longer be psychologically disposed to take them into account because in most cases they have already committed themselves to go ahead with a transaction. Thus even simple information may not have an impact on citizens, depending on its manner of presentation.

Another factor in the relative ineffectiveness of disclosure regulation is that citizens may have no choice but to behave in a certain way, whatever their state of knowledge. Thus many poor consumers have no realistic alternative to paying high interest rates for credit, because they are regarded as bad credit risks by established financial institutions. Other factors are also involved. Thus, even if poorer consumers know of cheaper prices they may prefer to do business with familiar, if more expensive, institutions. A related point is that the impact of information disclosed can be counteracted by other aspects of a transaction. Advertising, for example, may be a force so strongly influencing choice that it offsets detailed, objective information available to consumers. Finally, citizens can make a rational choice to disregard available information. Opportunity costs and the time and effort associated with using information may not be worthwhile, especially if small amounts of money are at stake.

2 Imposition of detailed standards

There are detailed statutory standards in various areas: product standards, environmental standards and behavioural standards. Detailed standards for particular products, for instance, differ from broad criminal standards in that the legislative material actually specifies what is required. Such standards are confined mainly to products where safety is at risk, as with the standards made under section 62 of the *Trade Practices Act* 1974 for motor vehicle child restraints, protective helmets for motor cyclists, portable fire extinguishers, pedal bicycles and children's night clothes. Policy-makers have been compelled to legislate in these areas because physical harm and not just economic detriment may occur. Experience demonstrates that competition, disclosure of information, and even the broad prohibitions of the civil and criminal law are inadequate in preventing physical harm. The setting of standards in such circumstances is facilitated because of the central aim of preventing harm.

There may be practical difficulties in fixing standards.[55] If, say, a product standard is too high it may prevent an activity which has an acceptably low incidence of risk, or raise costs without providing any corresponding benefits to citizens. On the other hand, a standard set at too low a level will achieve little. It may actually operate as an inducement to degrade quality to or near to the standard, if the market is non-competitive and higher quality does not result in as profitable an operation.

Without enforcement, standards have little effect because there are always those who will not comply with the law. Enforcement agencies may not posses the requisite manpower or technology to assess compliance with standards.[56] Enforcement authorities may need additional powers, such as the power to issue recall notices for unsafe products or 'stop' orders for polluting factories where there appears to be an imminent danger to public health. Civil and criminal penalties by themselves are quite deficient in these circumstances because the damage will be done before a matter is dealt with.

3   Control of trade practices

In the past, governments were reluctant to control trade practices other than by private law or by broad criminal prohibitions if these would interfere with the substance of market transactions. Apart from the administrative costs of further legal requirements, it was said that trade practices were so varied that widespread control was impracticable. A major objection advanced was that the great majority of citizens were sensible enough to protect themselves and that their range of choice would be restricted if controls were introduced for the benefit of the minority. It was said that on the rare occasions when difficulties arose, citizens had certain rights at civil law and there might even be a criminal offence involved. The great majority of businesses were assumed to be reputable, one piece of evidence being that many had agreed voluntarily to high standards of behaviour.

The last fifty years have witnessed a change in this attitude and a growth in government regulation. Individuals failed to institute civil proceedings against businesses under the private law to secure redress for their grievances, and many prejudicial trade practices were not caught by the broad criminal prohibitions on the statute book penalizing fraudulent practices.[57] The very complexity and range of trade practices, and the need for considerable resources of investigation and detection, are now seen as positive arguments for preferring public control to other methods.

Over the years legislation has been enacted to control specific marketing and promotional practices particularly obnoxious from the point of view of ordinary citizens. Controlling prejudicial trade practices through legislation has the self-evident disadvantages that trade practices change and new ones develop, yet legislative measures may be delayed or in some cases never enacted. With this in mind parliaments have given regulatory agencies powers to permit more frequent and flexible action to be taken against particular trade practices. In addition to rule-making power by delegated legislation, a regulatory agency may have authority to issue directives to specific businesses.

The regulatory control of trade practices overlaps with that involving broad statutory prohibitions, with the difference that it is more preventive because it is more selective in its field of application. Businesses know what is expected of them with greater certainty because they are specifically directed as to the nature of their trade practices. But whereas violations of these laws may ultimately give rise to the imposition of penalties, businesses that fail to meet the regulatory requirements may actually be denied the right to operate.

Despite the advantages of closely controlling objectionable behaviour, critics argue that there are a number of limitations which attach to the regulatory control of trade practices. It calls for a disproportionate amount of scarce resources in drafting and then in enforcement. Like all legislation, uncertainty may result from too much complexity or detail, as well as too much imprecision or ambiguity. Legislation can retain its effectiveness, however, despite its complexity and detail, if it is effectively communicated to the regulated group by being condensed, expressed in ordinary language, and given wide distribution. Many regulated groups have ready access to information in the form of loose-leaf publications detailing services and trade associations. Lawyers play an important part in communicating and explaining laws to their clients.

Licensing

Licensing is sometimes used to impose limits on an activity, as with liquor licensing. Governments use licensing to develop natural resources or to allocate scarce resources such as television frequencies.[58] These types of licensing have repercussions for the ordinary citizen in that they impinge upon competition and involve the government in distributing wealth to particular groups in the community. Licensing may also serve primarily as a type of prior approval. The theory is that prior approval permits beneficial activity but at the same time prevents its harmful consequences. Prior approval varies in the ambit of its control. Approval may have to be sought if a person is to engage in an activity, but may also be needed for, say, the products sold.[59]

Distinctions can be drawn between registration, certification, and licensing proper.[60] Registration is where persons must simply list their names in an official register. Registration is best illustrated by the requirement that companies must file certain documents and be officially 'incorporated' before commencing business.[61] The assumption behind such a requirement is that information filed will reach the citizens affected by the activity, in this case most notably the creditors. Certification goes one step further, since persons must demonstrate that they have reached a certain standard if they are to identify themselves in certain ways, but does not prevent similar activity on the part of others if they do not have a certificate.[62] Licensing proper is much more restrictive, for once a person meets certain criteria he or she is given the monopoly right to engage in a particular activity.[63]

Licensing is a powerful tool of control. Instead of the occasional private-law proceeding or prosecution if a person breaches the law, a person is faced with the possibility of being denied the right to continue an activity altogether. For this reason licensing is sometimes used in areas where fraud or exploitation are rife. Conditions attaching to licences vary in their generality. A licensee or potential licensee may simply have to meet the criterion of good character or may have to comply with quite detailed specifications as to the business's mode of operation. An incidental benefit of licensing is that the information provided might prove useful in enforcing other legislation.

Choosing whether to adopt licensing turns, in part, on the difficulty ordinary citizens have in making decisions. Occupational licensing of medical practitioners and others in the public health field to ensure competency is justified on this basis. Potential danger is another factor, as in the case of prior approval for hazardous industry. The severe consequences of an error in judgment explain why drug manufacturers need approval both for themselves and their products. Closely related is the consideration that it is frequently easier to prevent an activity than to undo the undesirable consequences associated with it. In this regard building regulations have a long history, and the principle underlies more recent legislative efforts in the environmental field as in the disposal of waste, the discharge of effluent and the operation of certain industries. Sometimes financial solvency is the most crucial factor in licensing. Not only must a business be run by persons who are competent and of good character, but it must also have sufficient financial backing to compensate persons if, despite this, things go wrong.

The scope for control through licensing can be limited because of the cost of administering it. If individuals or particular activities have to be approved, a substantial bureaucracy may be necessary, or there will have to be heavy reliance on information provided by licensees, the accuracy of which is ensured by imposing heavy penalties on non-compliance or for providing false information. Should insufficient resources be allocated to the administrative side of licensing, there will either be a delay in issuing licences or the agency evaluation procedure will be perfunctory. Likewise, licensing can become futile if not supported by adequate enforcement machinery to ensure adherence to the standards set.[64] However, licensing can be financially self-supporting if the fees charged for licenses are high enough to cover the administrative cost.

Another consideration militating against licensing is that it frequently acts against the public interest because it restricts competition, inhibits innovation or operates as a cartel in the interests of existing licensees. The adverse monopoly effects of occupational licensing have been a cause of complaint and are especially pronounced where the state hands over administration of the licensing to the occupation itself. If pressure for licensing comes from the members of a business or occupation, this raises an inference that its aim is to restrict entry or raise prices.

Once established, a licensing system is deficient if it does not contain a gradation of sanctions ranging from the mild to the severe. If a sanction is too mild it will not deter; if a sanction is too severe the agency will be reluctant to have it imposed. If suspension or revocation are the only penalties for non-compliance with a licence, licensees will probably be able to commit minor transgressions with impunity because such severe sanctions cannot be justified. Suspension or revocation are especially unlikely with larger organizations because innocent employees would become unemployed. In cases such as this the hope of policy-makers must be that there will be a deterrent effect because of the possibility, albeit remote, that the licence can be suspended or revoked. In addition it might be thought that the threat that a licence can be suspended or cancelled will encourage informal resolution of disputes. Since both these outcomes are uncertain, it is better for an agency not to be restricted to the sanctions of licence suspension or revocation. Instead, it should have recourse to a range of disciplinary powers, for example, the power to reprimand licensees or impose fines for abuses which do not merit a more extreme penalty.

Other legislative techniques

Not every form of legislative action has been considered here. Mention should be made of the use by government of its powers as a consumer and as a source of credit and supply. The power can be used to pursue broad economic policies such as industry modernization, or on a more limited scale as where an attempt is made to have businesses meet certain standards regarding workers or consumers. Standard government contracts are a well-known technique in the United States for achieving fair employment practices, safe and healthy working conditions, fair wages, a reduction in pollution, and support for small and minority businesses.[65] This method of control hinges on the extent to which a particular company is dependent on the government for the purchase of its products or for the supply of its finance or raw materials. In addition, the need to purchase particular goods may override the collateral purpose of controlling their quality or method of production.

Economic inducements may be used to influence behaviour. The most widely used economic inducements are the subsidy and its functional equivalent, the tax incentive.[66] The advantage of such economic measures is that they maximize individual choice and reduce the need for an overarching supervisory agency. But their effectiveness is doubtful and the evidence suggests that in the past persons have not changed their behaviour greatly as a result of a subsidy or a tax incentive. Instead, they have often benefited economically from these measures after having decided to pursue the course of action favoured by the government for other reasons. Moreover, there are the theoretical arguments against economic inducements. They may encourage disobedience and may imply that fidelity to law is optional rather than obligatory. In addition, it is less easy to predict the effect of an economic inducement than of that produced by a coercive sanction. Another approach is grants or payments varying with the attainment of standards.

III ENFORCEMENT

Enactment is only one aspect of the relationship between legislation and public policy. Just because a bill has passed into law, or because delegated legislation has been made, does not mean that their goals will be achieved. While many will invoke or comply with the relevant provisions, others will fail to do so. Without mechanisms for implementation, legislation will have only limited effectiveness. Moreover, legislative effectiveness turns on factors such as the nature of those subject to its mandate and the economic and social underpinnings of the conduct involved.

Legislation is, in some instances, not intended to produce any immediate legal consequences. Rather, it might simply evidence a governmental commitment to a particular goal or give legitimacy to that goal by incorporating it in statutory form. Again, it might be intra-governmental in character, in that it might set out the procedures to be followed before government money can be spent or it might constitute a body which will advise government or educate the public about an issue. Another example is the legislation which establishes procedures for producing criteria which will inform public and private decision-making. Only these decisions have legal force, not the legislation itself. Examples of this type of non-justiciable legislation are referred to in Chapters 4 and 5.

Then there is legislation which is self-enforcing. If individuals or institutions invoke its provisions, they benefit from the rights the legislation confers, although they must also comply with the obligations it imposes. Sole traders or partnerships need only to satisfy the prerequisites of the companies legislation and they can incorporate. Persons wanting to convey land need to register the transaction under the registration of title (Torrens) legislation. Those wishing to marry need to satisfy the relatively straightforward provisions of the Commonwealth *Marriage Act* 1961. In each case individuals or institutions must take the initiative, but once they do so certain legal consequences flow such as, in the case of companies, the advantage of limited liability but the disadvantage of having to file annual accounts.[67] Legislation may also be substantially self-enforcing in conferring certain rights and benefits, once its provisions operate. In the event of non-compliance (for example, a failure to register), another person may be able to avoid having to make a payment or other obligation, or may gain an advantage such as having a right recognized in priority.

If legislation is not self-enforcing, it may be capable of being enforced privately. The *Aboriginal Land Rights (Northern Territory) Act* 1976 establishes land councils, the members of which are Aboriginals chosen by Aboriginals living in the area of a land council, and then confers on the councils certain functions in the pursuit of land rights recognized by the legislation. Generally speaking, however, private persons and bodies are not specifically identified as being capable of enforcing legislation. Rather they must rely on the general rule that anyone can launch a private prosecution, unless this is barred.[68] Similarly, a private person or body may be able to enforce public rights conferred by legislation by means of a declaration or an injunction, provided they can obtain the fiat (approval) of the Attorney-General or have standing themselves.[69] Exceptionally, the *Trade Practices Act* 1974 enables any person to seek an injunction restraining a breach of its provisions.[70] There is some authority for the view that the courts will grant mandamus (a court order to compel performance of a public duty) against an enforcement body which is refusing to enforce the law.[71] Finally, mention should be made of breach of statutory duty, that is, that the courts sometimes regard a breach of legislation as giving rise to a civil action for damages or an injunction. Private enforcement is discussed in greater detail in Chapter 5.

Public enforcement of legislation is the focus of the present discussion. Public enforcement underpins the self-enforcement of legislation, for typically the legal obligations which flow once legislation is invoked are supported by criminal penalties. Futhermore, private enforcement of legislation is exceptional. Cost is one inhibiting factor, delay another. The dearth of private prosecutions is probably explained on these grounds.[72] There may also be legal difficulties. The problems of establishing the right to seek a declaration or an injunction in public law (the issue of standing) are examined in Chapter 5. As to breach of statutory duty in private law, the courts say that the test is whether the legislation intends to provide for a civil action. In fact there is judicial choice as to whether a remedy will be given. In practice, the courts act inconsistently but have confined the doctrine mainly to breaches of health and safety at work legislation.[73]

In the popular mind the main mechanisms of public enforcement are the police, the directors of public prosecutions, the courts, and possibly royal commissions.[74] However, there are many areas of public policy where the task of enforcing the relevant legislation has been entrusted to government departments or specialized agencies. As befits the focus of this book, it is to their activities that most attention is given here. In particular, what form does this type of public enforcement take? How do the relevant enforcement bodies obtain their cases, what are their resources, and what are the backgrounds of their officials? How do they respond to their political, economic and social environment? And what of the courts, when these bodies institute proceedings before them?[75]

Design of public enforcement

In the United States considerable attention has been given to the form public enforcement should take. A considerable body of opinion has tended to favour entrusting the task to the independent regulatory agency rather than to the executive. As formulated in Landis' classic statement, the case for the independent agency was to concentrate and nurture expertise and to free administration from political and judicial pressures.[76] Expertise was said to be vital because intelligent enforcement involved the interpretation and application of a wide range of scientific knowledge and social facts. Freedom from political pressure, through a broad mandate, was to enable the agencies to respond flexibly to current developments, but without the threat of being diverted from a planned course of action by political expediency. Excluding the courts from detailed oversight followed because of the fear of legalistic approaches, applied by judges without a real appreciation of the context in which enforcement occurred.

It is a matter of debate whether the institutional location of public enforcement makes a great deal of difference, whether public enforcement involves all that much expertise, and whether it ought to be insulated from political control by elected representatives. In Australia the independent regulatory agency is not as common as in the United States. At the national level the Trade Practices Commission and the National Companies and Securities Commission are examples. In the States there are bodies such as the Environmental Protection Authority in Victoria. Little systematic thought has been given in Australia to the most effective manner of public enforcement.[77] For example, the form of the National Companies and Securities Commission reflects the philosophy of co-operative federalism espoused by the Federal government responsible for its establishment.[78]

What of the discretion entrusted to public enforcement bodies?[79] Wide discretion might render departments or agencies more exposed to undesirable influence from the regulated, one reason being that the regulators and the regulated come into contact over where the boundaries will be drawn to discretion in practice. Wide discretion can be criticized as violating the legal ideals of certainty, for those to whom a legislative command is addressed might not know what is expected of them, and of formal equality, because a standard applied to one might not be applied to others in similar circumstances. Moreover, democratic theory demands that primacy should be given to legislative purpose, so consequently wide discretion stands condemned inasmuch as it permits departments or agencies to substitute different goals from those contemplated by the legislature.

Apart from these qualifications—the need for certainty, formal equality and the implementation of legislative purpose—it is difficult to say on the basis of legal principle how wide discretion should be. Rather, the scope of discretion must be formulated in the light of the circumstances. In some cases public enforcement needs comparatively wide discretion, as where the situations being regulated are relatively unlike; where the enforcement task is novel, so that the only way to develop a standard is from experience or after detailed investigation; or where the context of enforcement demands that standards be moulded to the particular circumstances. In such cases a legalistic approach by the enforcement body would deprive it of flexibility to assess all the relevant factors, and would undermine legislative purpose.[80] But in other cases the legislature may decide that specifying how those regulated should behave, rather than setting performance standards, is the most effective means of reaching the desired goal, or it might decide that certainty and enforceability outweigh any advantage that performance standards theoretically have in achieving legislative purpose.[81]

Some legislation expressly prevents enforcement bodies from taking economic factors into account in the setting and enforcement of standards; in other cases the courts have held that on their interpretation of the legislation enforcement bodies must not do so but should simply apply the statutory standards.[82] The exclusion of economic factors from consideration cannot be condemned, however, since a legislature can legitimately decide to make other values paramount, such as health or clean air.

Although it is difficult to derive from principle the optimum degree of discretion, what can be said is that the manner in which enforcement bodies exercise their discretion should be systematized and open to public scrutiny, subject to the limitation that this should not unduly inhibit their effectiveness.[83] In some cases it may even be possible to embody the manner in which discretion is being exercised in statutory form, without threatening its flexibility, for example, by specifying the criteria which the enforcement body ought to take into account. Generally speaking, however, legislatures have no great interest in structuring discretion: the political pressures to do so are comparatively weak, and there is little kudos for legislators if they take the initiative themselves.

Wide rule-making power in the field of legislative regulation is a crucial issue in the United States, where it is sometimes in the hands of independent regulatory agencies; but it is not as important in Australia, where formal rule-making power lies mainly with the executive, and delegated legislation is subject to some legislative scrutiny.[84] However, it is as well to recognize that enforcement bodies in Australia engage in rule-making indirectly or informally by advising on delegated legislation, drawing up conditions for licenses, and drafting manuals on the enforcement of the relevant law. In an effort to make rule-making in the United States more public and more accountable, the process has been 'judicialized': proposed rules are notified and it is then difficult to modify them; a hearing is conducted in accordance with adversary principles; and appeal can be taken to the courts.[85] There is an obvious tension between fairness and efficiency when rule-making is judicialized in this manner. On the one hand judicialization gives an air of fairness to the process, for interested groups have an opportunity to present their views about proposed rules. It seems that in the United States public interest groups prefer the judicialization of rule-making to informal procedures because it provides them with a forum they would otherwise not have, leads to greater publicity for the issues, and builds up a record for appeal to the courts. However, excessive judicialization builds in inflexibility and delay, generates division rather than compromise, and does not always seem appropriate to exploring all possible courses of action, or assessing certain types of technical evidence. Although rule-making has not been judicialized in Australia, interested parties are usually consulted by government or governmental agencies about proposed delegated legislation—although there is generally no obligation for this to occur—and the draft is not infrequently modified in the light of their representations. The advantages are greater flexibility and the recognition that rule-making is part of the political process; but the disadvantage is that only established interest groups tend to be consulted as a matter of course.

Nature of public enforcement bodies

Public enforcement is typified by laxness in the formal enforcement of the law. For example, the evidence in Australia is that in a range of areas enforcement bodies institute relatively few prosecutions compared with the amount of wrongdoing uncovered.[86] Their approach is justified on the basis that there are more effective ways of implementing the law informally than prosecution. More will be said of this later in the chapter. The present task is to explore key factors in the nature of public enforcement bodies which affect their enforcement work.

1 How cases are obtained

Enforcement bodies must strike a balance between being reactive (obtaining their cases through complaints) and being proactive (taking the initiative themselves to obtain cases).[87] Complaints are a particularly important source in drawing a body's attention to problems, especially when it lacks the resources to engage in widespread detection work itself. However, some enforcement bodies do not obtain a representative sample of complaints because they do not publicize their existence or disseminate information about their work, while others positively discourage complaints, possibly through fear that their slender resources will be over-stretched. Complaints put pressure on an enforcement body to take some sort of action, although they push an enforcement body in the direction of negotiation and mediation, rather than law enforcement, if redress is obtainable for complainants.

While complaints are important for enforcement bodies, it is fatal for them not to engage in proactive work. First, problems may be complex, diffused over time or hidden from ordinary view, so that not many people complain. Second, in general those who have most cause for complaint complain least, with the result that enforcement bodies may be unconsciously biased because they respond unduly to particular sections of the population. For example, even if poor people are knowledgeable about those charged with overseeing particular problems, they might lack the confidence or contacts to initiate and carry through with complaints. In addition, those such as poorer tenants and low-paid workers may be reluctant to complain to enforcement bodies because of their vulnerable position, for they might fear losing their housing or their job through vindictiveness. Finally, over-reliance on complaints can lead enforcement bodies to concentrate on trivial matters, without any thought as to how these fall into the overall strategy mapped by legislative purpose.[88]

Many enforcement bodies have a patchy record in proactive work. Inadequate resources are an obvious explanation, but within this constraint a crucial factor is that such bodies often seem to lack an aggressive attitude in monitoring their field of operation and in securing compliance with the law. Moreover, many do not seem to have established a sense of priorities for using limited resources in the most efficient manner. Information needs to be accumulated to set priorities, depending on factors such as how seriously people view particular problems, the harm these cause, the vulnerability of those involved, and whether enforcement action is likely to have any impact. Complaints have an obvious role here in identifying patterns in relation to particular practices, institutions or laws.[89] Bureaucratic structuring can ensure that an emphasis on proactive work is incorporated into the routine work of enforcement. For example, officials can be required to give reasons why they do not recommend further legal proceedings when a breach of the law is detected, although a danger with this is that officials will overlook breaches so that they are never recorded in the first place. Another possibility is to establish specialist units within regulatory agencies which concentrate expertise and induce officials to demonstrate their activity in that aspect of work.

2   Bureaucratic features

The historical development of an enforcement body can influence its behaviour: for example, if a body begins small and poorly endowed, it might continue to adopt a restrictive view of its powers. A body might use precedent or certain physical or accounting measures as a basis for decision-making, but the result is to inhibit its effectiveness by causing it to pursue certain types of cases (perhaps trivial cases) to the exclusion of others.[90] There might be different bodies covering the same field, with little co-ordination between them because of jurisidictional divisions or bureaucratic jealousies—a particular problem in the Australian federal system. Ease of enforcement might induce a department or an agency to favour a particular policy, such as to require design standards over performance standards, even if this leads to unnecessary rigidity. If lawyers predominate in an enforcement body that might incline it to pursue a litigation strategy, regardless of effectiveness. Of necessity, enforcement bodies have links with the regulated—to obtain information, to advise them about compliance with standards, and to enforce the law—but as a result of these contacts and through other channels such as the trade press may become unduly sympathetic to their viewpoint.

The relative paucity of human and financial resources available to enforcement, in relation to the magnitude of the task, are further factors in the implementation of any statutory mandate. In discussing how responsibility for 100 000 establishments was transferred at the one time from local authorities to the factory inspectorate, Marx noted that 'care was taken at the same time not to add more than eight assistants to their already undermanned staff'.[91] The fewer the resources available to an enforcement body, the more its decisions must be reached with inadequate information, unless it relies on those it regulates for information, whereupon it is more susceptible to unacceptable influence. Law enforcement capacity is dependent on adequate resources, especially to investigate complex wrongdoing and then to pursue it through the courts. Limited resources lead many enforcement bodies to pursue the less complex (and less significant) cases, while some virtually abandon law enforcement and instead concentrate on seeking a cessation of wrongdoing in other ways (for example, by voluntary action) and perhaps also restitution for its victims.

3   The background and attitudes of enforcement officials

The background of officials is a central feature of the 'capture theory'— that regulatory bodies are 'captured' by those they are supposed to regulate—for it is said that regulators may have served in the relevant industry and will have been indoctrinated with its views, or that those who intend to join it later temper their actions so as not to jeopardize their careers. An empirical study in the United States found that the appointment of former employees of a regulated industry to a regulatory agency increased the likelihood of decisions favourable to the regulated industry, such as whether to impose a sanction for violation of regulatory standards or whether to allow a greater concentration within the industry.[92] While the 'revolving door' phenomenon is important, it should not be over-emphasized. First, the phenomenon is not uniform across enforcement bodies—those responsible for social regulation might be staffed by officials with far fewer links with the regulated—and does not affect all officials equally (e.g. political appointees vs. career public servants). Second, any measure of the extent of the revolving door phenomenon depends on the definition of prior or subsequent employment and whether it includes employment in enterprises working to further industry interests such as law firms or lobby firms. Third, the prior employment of officials might not affect their behaviour and their behaviour might not affect their future careers: for example, a short period in an enforcement body might be an accepted route for a lawyer to acquire experience, while industry interests might prefer to recruit 'tough' officials, for this is taken as an indication of their ability. In any case, the phenomenon is not as prominent in Australia, where government service is relatively prestigious and the concept of a career public service is taken seriously, although there may be other avenues of 'capture' in Australia such as government–industry committees.

The behaviour of officials, in particular of senior officials, sometimes reflects an unduly narrow view of their role. Partly this is forced on them by factors such as the political context or by a shortage of resources, but partly it derives from other factors such as an excessive concern for their own security or from a reluctance to create conflict with those they are supposed to regulate.[93] Among the causes of the latter are the blandishments to which officials are subjected from the regulated; the constant exposure of officials to the viewpoint of the regulated; and the philosophy, shared by key sections of the community, that business is basically law-abiding, or at least as law-abiding as possible in the circumstances, with only a small minority of 'bad apples', and that consequently it will comply with regulatory standards automatically, or if it is not doing so needs only to be informed of or reminded about its obligations.[94] Apart from structural design to minimize conflicts of interest and to strengthen public accountability, it seems that all law-makers can do if they wish to lessen this tendency is to choose senior officials carefully.

Environment of enforcement bodies

Clearly enforcement bodies do not operate in a vacuum, but are subject to influence from a number of sources. One is that much regulatory legislation, unlike the traditional criminal law, deals with issues over which there is a considerable conflict in society. The clash between economic growth and environmental protection is an example. The fact that many regulatory statutes deal with behaviour which is not widely recognized as evil or dangerous has led some to argue that breaches of them ought not to be punished severely. They hark back to the distinction drawn in Blackstone between crimes *mala in se* (wrong in themselves—e.g. murder) and crimes *mala prohibita* (merely prohibited by society). Certainly it is the case that many regulatory offences are shielded from the full process of criminalization. In other words, because the requirement of fault is dispensed with, the offences are regarded as morally ambiguous and hence the effectiveness of the law is weakened.

The attitude of enforcement bodies, in particular the absence of prosecution, is partly explained by the moral ambiguity of breaches of the legislation.[95] Wrongdoing is seen as a problem, rather than as a crime. Moreover, it is mainly the work of organizations, rather than of individuals. Enforcement bodies therefore take legal proceedings only in instances where the behaviour of the wrongdoer is blameworthy, as where there is substantial negligence, severe harm, a negative attitude on the part of the regulated, or persistent wrongdoing about which warnings have been given. However, other factors are also the cause of lax enforcement of the law in these areas. The high status of business interests is one reason that those who commit offences are generally not condemned by the community.

Three specific elements of the environment surrounding enforcement can be highlighted: political pressures, the influence of the courts, and the role played by the regulated and those supposedly benefited by legislation.

1   Political pressures

Political pressures are not always, or even mainly, formal, since enforcement bodies can be influenced by the general political climate of a society as reflected, say, in the mass media. Environmental protection agencies were established, or strengthened, during the 1960s and 1970s when the political climate seemed generally to favour environmental protection, but since then they have had to operate during a decade when Australia has experienced an economic crisis, and have consequently been under pressure to sacrifice environmental protection in the interests of cheaper resources. Economic prospects, in particular the unemployment outlook and its political repercussions, are behind some enforcement bodies' approach to their task, in influencing them to adopt a promotional attitude to a regulated industry if it is under economic threat, or to be lenient in enforcing regulatory standards against it if full compliance is beyond its economic capacity. The popularity of deregulation, as a political catchcry, is another pressure on enforcement bodies at the present.

However, there are instances of more formal political pressures, possibly at the instance of the regulated, where the specific decisions of an enforcement body have been aborted, or where they have had their legislative powers or resources curbed.[96] Attempts have also been made to affect the behaviour of enforcement bodies by appointing persons having a particular political persuasion to key positions within them. Political interference with the behaviour of enforcement bodies is sometimes exercised in more subtle, and hidden ways. No doubt officials also defer to what they anticipate or believe to be the attitudes of their political masters. Generally speaking, however, those holding political power have not had a great interest in mundane details of enforcement, and have only expressed general support or disapproval, unless there has been a dramatic event, there have been representations from the regulated industry, or the concerns (or at least the perceived concerns) of their constituents have demanded it. The keener interest which those in political circles have demonstrated in the details of regulatory legislation in more recent times follows because regulation has been linked to larger economic and political issues.

2   The judicial process

The courts also influence the behaviour of enforcement bodies, in particular the extent to which prosecution is undertaken. What aspects of their behaviour and attitude are especially salient for enforcement bodies? First, the rules of evidence and procedure are not always appropriate to complex regulatory matters. Then, organizational pressures and time constraints are other factors which militate against courts always giving proper consideration to matters. Unlike enforcement bodies, judges will generally not build up any expertise in particular areas because of the diversity of their work and the nature of their professional lives and training. Assuming that legal proceedings are not aborted, years might elapse before all appeals are exhausted and a matter is finalized by the courts. The regulated can take advantage of these delays if they wish to avoid or minimize the effects of legislation, although delay will work to their detriment if they desire to obtain approval for a course of action. Other institutional limits on courts include the episodic way that issues arise, the emphasis on the individual circumstances of particular cases and the nature of court remedies, all of which have an adverse effect on the development of a coherent and effective regulatory policy.[97]

Apart from whether courts are suitable in an institutional sense to handle certain matters, the attitude of the judges to regulatory legislation might also be a source of concern. There have been cases when judges have been unduly restrictive of the powers of enforcement bodies, have been too favourable to the regulated, have overlooked the interests of beneficiaries on appeal or in judicial review, and have not treated non-compliance with standards seriously enough in enforcing the law.

These defects have been attributed partly to the common background which judges share with the regulated, partly to legal education which emphasizes procedural concerns at the expense of the substance of public policy, and partly to the professional life of judges before their appointment to the bench, which many spend representing the regulated and possibly enforcement bodies rather than the beneficiaries of regulatory legislation. Without detailed studies, however, it is difficult to make blanket statements about the attitude and behaviour of judges or about how these determine judicial outcomes. Just as there are decisions in which judges have cramped enforcement bodies or overlooked the interests of beneficiaries, so there are decisions giving a generous interpretation to regulatory powers.[98] Similarly, the evidence on law enforcement is not clear-cut, for judges have both supported and undermined the activities of enforcement bodies, and have imposed both inordinately small and quite substantial sanctions for breaches of standards.[99]

3   The regulated, and the beneficiaries of legislation

Mention has already been made of the 'revolving door' phenomenon and of other links between enforcement bodies and the regulated. Coupled with other factors, such as the favourable conception held of commercial and property interests by important sections of the population, these links can cause enforcement bodies to accommodate to the regulated. In addition the regulated may deliberately attempt to subvert enforcement bodies either directly (by blandishments, say, or constant presentation of their viewpoint); or indirectly (by exerting political pressure through politicians or the mass media). It ill behoves some commercial and property interests to attack regulatory failure when they themselves are an important cause of it. Accommodation and subversion obviously produce weak standards and a lenient enforcement of the law.

Political mechanisms, which favour well-organized interests, are an important factor in the influence which the regulated have in relation to enforcement bodies, and in the frequent absence of countervailing forces. Those who advocate regulatory legislation often lose interest once it is enacted because they are satisfied with its symbolic passage, or because they assume that the legislative mandate will be automatically implemented. Potential beneficiaries of legislation are generally not organized, for those such as consumers and users of the environment have diffuse interests and little individual incentive to combine on these issues, although their stake might be high in the aggregate.[100] An exception is trade union activity, for workers have the incentive to act collectively in relation to issues such as health and safety at work. Enforcement bodies themselves can do much to stimulate beneficiaries to organize and to oversee enforcement activity by encouragement, financial grants, training, and so on.[101]

If the potential beneficiaries of legislation are generally not organized, part of the gap might be filled by political entrepreneurs and public interest groups who monitor the activities of enforcement bodies, adopt an advocacy role in public forums, and advance the cause of regulatory reform. However, political entrepreneurs and public interest groups generally have limited resources and in many cases their interest- or life-span is short.

IV   IMPACT OF LEGISLATION

Legislation is a means of social control, yet there is no definitive body of knowledge about how effective it is in influencing behaviour and how it compares with other social controls. Legislation frequently appears efficacious and has been used successfully as an instrument of social change. Yet legislation in a number of areas seems an insignificant instrument of control when compared with other social forces and needs to be supplemented by extra-legal sanctions. In seeking to explain how legislation can be effective, the social and economic dimensions need to be taken into account.

With some legislation the positive effects cannot be gainsaid: to take just one example, the reduction in air and water pollution, at least visible pollution, is readily apparent in many areas since clean air and clean water legislation have been introduced. However, it may be that there are unintended and perhaps unexpected side effects of legislation such as economic inefficiencies which, if taken into account, seriously detract from its intended impact. For example, the reduced pollution mentioned may be counter-balanced by greater pollution in other areas and, in any event, the gains may have been achieved at considerable cost.[102] The impact of other legislation is similarly contentious. There are studies which purport to show that health and safety at work legislation has not brought about a significant or widespread reduction in accident rates or an improvement in worker health.[103] Critics point out that these studies do not always take into account factors such as the low intensity of enforcement or the difficulty of obtaining adequate data, while their focus on overall activity swamps any effects that specific measures might have. Thus studies which have concentrated their attention on specific industries, notably, the very hazardous industries, show that health and safety at work legislation has caused a substantial decline in injuries and illness.[104]

There are many conceptual problems in assessing the impact of legislation. The intended effects of legislation may be ambiguous or conflicting; the actual effects may prove beneficial to those who initially opposed it; and even partial implementation of legislative goals may be a considerable success in light of the difficulties of achieving them. A real difficulty in assessing the impact of legislation is in isolating the relevant causal factors. Legislation is one among a number of instruments of social control, and it may be impossible to isolate its impact on behaviour from that produced in other ways. Any impact may not be immediately identifiable, especially if it occurs in social attitudes rather than in behaviour. Moreover, there may not be any obvious effects that one can identify. For example, legislation may not have any visible impact because it is not enforced, because the regulated ignore it, because it is technically impossible for the regulated to change their behaviour beyond a certain point, or because its effect is simply to hold the ground against a deterioration in behaviour. Then there are the independent and unintended effects of the legislation. With these qualifications in mind, it is possible to advance some tentative assessments of the impact of legislation.[105]

Evidence of impact

Australian historians have sometimes charted the effects of specific legislation. To give one example, Forbes writes of how the Victorian *Legal Profession Practice Act* 1891, which fused barristers and solicitors into one profession, became very much a dead letter following the 'barristers boycott', in which leading barristers undermined the law by refusing to deal with 'amalgams' (those who used the Act).[106] More characteristically, historians have assessed the impact of certain types of legislation, without distinguishing individual details. In his *A History of Australia*, Manning Clark remarks on the fate of the selectors, who claimed under the selection legislation:

> ...the selectors were sandwiched between Capital and Labour. This cut across the economic tendencies of the age to form two classes struggling for power—capitalist and worker. It ended with the selector either rising into the ranks of the capitalist or being pushed down into the class the acts were designed to help him out of—the class of hirelings for wages on the land. This class war raged all over the countryside. It was fought in the colonial parliaments, where both sides used bribery, persuasion, blackmail, any method either inside or outside the law to have the lands they coveted or were trying to keep declared either open to or not open to selection.[107]

Contemporary studies of legislative impact divide into what can be termed the statistical and the investigative. First, some examples of statistical studies. Compulsory seat belt wearing, first adopted under the Victorian *Motor Car (Safety) Act* 1970, has been shown to have significantly reduced the number of deaths and injuries for car occupants involved in motor vehicle accidents (with no offsetting increases for pedestrians, pedal and motor cyclists).[108] Another study has demonstrated that drink-driving legislation in Victoria reduced the number of night-time fatal accidents and serious casualty accidents following publicized enforcement campaigns in 1977 and 1978.[109] Non-compliance with health and safety at work legislation seems widespread from several official studies.[110] For example, of 2381 power presses surveyed in 159 premises in metropolitan Melbourne in 1982, fifty-one per cent were in need of attention to bring them to a standard set by law. Thirty-five per cent of 1095 dust samples taken in Queensland in 1983 failed to comply with the standard prescribed by the State's *Coal Mining Act* 1925.

Non-compliance is also clear from the more investigative studies of legislative activity. Evidence drawn from real estate journals, tenants' campaigns and the like show the extent to which landlords have been able to circumvent landlord and tenant law in New South Wales.[111] In recent times, massive evasion of Australian tax legislation has come to light.[112] But such studies also show that legislation and its enforcement can positively influence behaviour. For example, interviews with companies convicted under the *Trade Practices Act* 1974 found that organizational defects were the major factor in fifteen of the nineteen convictions investigated. Such defects included failure by management to check the accuracy of promotional material. Of the fifteen companies, nine made significant changes in their operating proceedings as a result of the conviction, two made minor changes, two made none and information was unavailable for the remainder. Overall, enforcement of the Act had a valuable impact in most cases.[113] An obvious difficulty with such findings is the heavy reliance on information provided by those affected by the legislation; also they do not reveal the effect, say, of enforcement on persons other than those directly involved, and they are not located within a particular economic and social setting.

Social factors in legislative impact

Various social factors can be identified in the impact of legislation. Public attitudes, the behaviour affected and the nature of those being controlled are the three examined below. It should be emphasized that the relationship between legislation and each of these is dynamic, in other words, that attitudes, behaviour and the nature of the regulated might change in response to legislation, and that legislation in turn might be amended to take these changes into account. Moreover, cutting across such factors are others such as knowledge, timing, sanctions and enforcement. And further refinements are necessary, such as differentiating between the knowledge and attitudes of elites and opinion-makers on the one hand and those of the general community on the other.

A favourable attitude towards legislation does not result inevitably in compliance, for laws can be broken accidentally. On the other hand, obedience to legislation may be the outcome of factors such as inertia or the lack of visibility of alternatives. But in general, the more acceptable legislation is to those to whom it is directed, the more easily it is applied. Attitudes toward specific legislation are not determinative, however, and those vehemently opposed to it may obey it to the letter. Opinion about legislation depends partly upon an evaluation of its attributes and partly upon pre-existing dispositions towards the legal system.[114] Often the mere fact that a statute makes certain behaviour illegal influences moral opinion about it, because citizens have internalized the habit of lawful behaviour. Whatever their attitude to the specific legislation, some comply with and in some cases go beyond its requirements, because they believe that in general laws should be obeyed, or because they wish to avoid legal proceedings.

The notion of socialization can be applied to the legal system and refers to the process by which members of society internalize attitudes toward law. The socialization process is complex, for individuals are members of groups within society, as well as of society itself, and a desire to conform to the norms of a group may lead them to accept or reject the norms which society has embodied in legislation.[115] For example, close connections with an area, membership of professional associations, or a high public profile might make persons or institutions reluctant to damage their reputation by engaging in unlawful or disreputable practices. In general, to the extent that legislation is consistent with widely held values in the community, it will be effective.

Nonetheless, some are indifferent to legal obligations, and others deliberately breach them, taking the risk that legal proceedings will not be instituted, or if instituted will prove unsuccessful. In legal terminology the latter go beyond avoidance to evasion of the law. For example, there are businesses which do not see the objection to maximizing profits by whatever means possible, and which regard court proceedings as a normal business hazard, or as a risk attached to their way of doing business.[116] A popular perception without, it seems, evidence to support it, is that smaller businesses are less likely than larger organizations to comply with legislation, possibly because smaller businesses have more intense feelings that the law is unfair because it unduly burdens them, or because they find it too complex to implement. In all cases where businesses fail to comply with regulatory standards but could do so, the direct cause of regulatory failure is obviously not legislation but subversion of its intentions by business.

Legislative efficacy also depends on the nature of the behaviour being affected. For example, there would seem to be difficulties in achieving an impact through legislation when a large number of persons or institutions must be persuaded to modify their behaviour, without their having any direct economic incentive to do so. It can be hypothesized that behaviour to which individuals are not committed as a way of life is deterrable to a greater extent than behaviour which is morally supported or connected to other behaviour, and that instrumental behaviour is more easily controlled than normative behaviour.[117] Max Weber wrote that economic behaviour was particularly difficult to control because of the strong commitment to it. Weber observed:

> The inclination to forego economic opportunity simply in order to act legally is obviously slight, unless circumvention of the formal law is strongly disapproved by a powerful convention, and such a situation is not likely to arise where the interests affected by legal innovation are widespread.[118]

Legislative regulation may therefore be more effective if it operates *before* economic incentives develop for a course of action.

The nature of those being controlled is another factor in the calculus of legislative efficacy. For example, larger corporations may be controlled more easily than smaller ones. Once a decision has been made to comply with legislation, the bureaucratic needs of the larger organization demand that the policy be applied systematically and consistently.[119] By contrast, smaller corporations retain a flexibility to evade legislation by varying their procedures. In addition, other things being equal, the fewer entities to be controlled, the more effective the legislation because the amount of monitoring is reduced and the relevant enforcement agency can develop an expertise.[120] The number of entities to be controlled is not as crucial to the effectiveness of legislation to the extent that it is possible to concentrate on the leaders or pace-setters in an industry. When production is being regulated, the point at which legislation impinges may be relevant. Regulatory legislation may be more effective at the manufacturing stage than at some subsequent level in the process of distribution, simply because it is possible to concentrate enforcement.

Forces within organizations are also relevant. For example, the possibility that at some time in the future, perhaps years hence, a business will be brought before a court because it disregards regulatory standards is not a pressing consideration when ordinary decisions are being made within the organization. Businesses which are under pressure to reach their profit goals are quite likely to ignore regulatory standards.[121] However, the impact of legislation varies with the nature of the business involved, for some organizations implement regulatory standards more effectively because they have the necessary bureaucratic procedures for implementation and feedback. Moreover, some organizations have a sense of social responsibility.[122] The development of new technology can also be an important factor in enabling compliance with regulatory standards, or reaching the goal towards which legislation is ostensibly aimed.

Lawyers have some role in the impact of legislation, since they mediate legal requirements to their clients, and for this reason might be regarded as one of the agencies of social control in the community.[123] But lawyers are not always effective as agents of social control, for their advice may be ignored: their clients may take advice that legislative standards are uncertain as an invitation to ignore them, and in some cases lawyers may assist evasion of the law.

Economic implications

Undoubtedly, some legislation has adverse economic repercussions for those at whom it is directed. It may lead to a fall in demand for certain products or to a depression in property values in an area.[124] To the extent to which costs can be passed on to customers, however, there might not be economic disincentives to comply with legislative standards. Indeed, in some circumstances there might be significant economic pressures to follow legislative requirements. For example, non-compliance with health and safety at work regulations might lead to accidents and thus to a loss of production and to dissatisfaction in the workplace. Failure to observe hygiene standards might lead to an outbreak of food poisoning, with disastrous consequences for the reputation of a restaurant or food manufacturer. There might also be market gains in being perceived as a socially responsible institution. Of course an economic incentive to obey legislation will not necessarily prevent breaches occurring, for instance, if the internal controls in an organization are inadequate. Moreover, short-term market pressures might outweigh long-term economic gains, as where the hard-pressed entrepreneur takes the risk that non-compliance will remain undetected.

Free-market economists argue that in interfering with market processes legislation causes economic inefficiencies, and at the macro-economic level inhibits growth and leads to inflation. The criticism concentrates on areas such as regulatory legislation, occupational licensing and government services.[125] An aspect of the criticism is that legislative standards inevitably restrict the variety of products and services marketed and thus deprive consumers of the choice they would otherwise have of obtaining less expensive products and services. The poor are said to be especially prejudiced. The critics also say that legislative standards lead to monopoly practices on the part of producers. Innovation is discouraged because particular products and services must comply with the standards set by law. Standards are said to render products and services substantially homogeneous and thus minimize the possibilities of competition between producers as to quality. Standards also establish a baseline for costs and thus limit the amount of price competition. Producers must use advertising to improve their market position, it is contended, but this in turn establishes barriers for new entrants.

There are difficulties with such arguments.[126] First, the faith that markets will always lead to the efficient result seems largely to overlook that markets are distorted in practice and that the economic world is one of second-best. Moreover, the criticism of legislative standards rests on the questionable assumptions that standards increase prices, even accepting that they increase costs, and that certain sections of the population, notably the most vulnerable, should constitute a market for, say, unsafe products or exploitative services. To what extent, if any, legislative standards promote monopoly practices is difficult to gauge, a fact which even the critics concede. Overall, despite its drawbacks, legislative intervention might be no less efficient in its effects that what would obtain under an improperly functioning market.

Second, there are deficiencies in the type of technical economic analysis which concludes that legislative intervention leads to economic inefficiencies. This type of analysis frequently takes the form of a model built on simple (and often unrealistic) assumptions, from which are drawn conclusions which are then supported by reference to empirical data. Quite apart from the problems associated with this methodology —is it a complete answer to say that the test of a model lies not in its assumptions but in its results?—the empirical evidence used is generally open to conflicting interpretations, and there can be genuine differences over the allowances to be made for the different variables.[127] Third, there is the problem at the macro-economic level of separating the effects of legislative intervention from other causal factors, as well as the difficulty posed by the casual observation of strong economic growth in countries such as Japan and Singapore which have significant regulatory legislation.

At a practical level, the cost of business regulation is a favourite target for attack. One estimate of the cost of Federal government regulation in Australia was in excess of twice the cost of maintaining the regulatory bodies.[128] However, the survey on which this estimate was based was not large or representative. Clearly there are also problems in business estimates being at the base of these calculations: distortion is possible, and businesses might also include costs, such as the cost of subsidy applications and tax returns, which are hardly regulatory costs. Indeed businesses might have to incur certain so-called 'compliance costs' irrespective of regulation, for the paper work required may be part of any efficient accounting system. Critics of such estimates have produced substantially lower figures by excluding the costs associated with certain types of regulation (for example, that which clearly benefits business), and by taking into account the fact that many businesses would meet the regulatory standards adopted, irrespective of regulation.[129]

Most important, attacks on the cost of business regulation frequently ignore its benefits, which is ironic when the benefits of certain types of regulation flow predominantly to business. At one level this neglect of benefits is because costs are more easily calculable than benefits. Insofar as the benefits of regulation can be assessed, they seem to exceed the costs. One United States study calculates that in the areas of air and water pollution, car safety, and worker safety, the benefits of regulation are five times the cost attributable to all forms of social regulation.[130] An Australian study of the anti-competitive aspects of the *Trade Practices Act 1974* concluded that 'the indications appear to be that if a full cost-benefit study were undertaken, the observed benefits would significantly out-strip the costs'.[131] Even if business regulation involved net costs, they would not be a conclusive argument that it should be abandoned, for people might be prepared to incur the costs because of their preferences or values. None of this means that business regulation is costless, or that where the benefits of regulation outweigh the costs the net benefit cannot be increased by regulatory reform.

Despite its limitations, economic analysis has a role in designing the scope and shape of legislation. It cannot be denied that there are instances where, say, regulatory legislation, or at least the form it takes, is un-desirable when its social and economic costs and benefits are weighed in the balance with other factors. Where it is desirable to change existing legislation, however, transitional arrangements must be designed, since the distributional consequences of change (e.g. deregulation, privati-zation) adversely affect many people and undermine their justifiable expectations.

V CONCLUSION

Legislation in this chapter has been examined in terms of its emergence, its actual form 'on the statute books', its implementation by the relevant enforcement bodies and by the courts, and its impact, given its social and economic context. It quickly becomes apparent on examining these four aspects why particular legislation has succeeded or failed. As we saw, an examination of the way legislation emerges might show that it was designed to advance particular interests, or that there were conflicting goals, so that it should not be surprising if it fails to achieve a more general public benefit. As regards the form taken by legislation, we also saw there that issues arise such as its over-inclusiveness, the techniques used, whether the substantive provisions of legislation are commensurate with what is generally conceived of as its purpose, and whether the discretion devolved to the relevant enforcement bodies is so wide that they can subvert the legislative purpose.

The implementation of a great deal of legislation is entrusted to government departments and specialized agencies. In theory this has an advantage, in that a law does not have to compete with a range of other laws for enforcement. The success of the particular department or agency is identified with its implementation of the relevant law. But the department or agency might be entrusted with limited power, endowed with inadequate resources, and undermined by the regulated. Moreover, the courts may not give adequate support to the implementation of legislation. That many regard regulatory offences as morally ambiguous is one factor, since it makes it difficult for courts to distinguish between the unscrupulous and the less serious offender. Consequently, this supports the tendency to impose uniformly low penalties, which are not a burden to the former.

Assessing the impact of legislation requires that attention be given to its social and economic context. Legislation might simply 'ratify' existing practices, so that it does not appear to have any visible impact. An examination of public attitudes, the nature of the regulated and of the behaviour to be regulated might well lead to the conclusion that legislation will be very hard-pressed to achieve change. Indeed, what is termed legislative failure might on reflection be better regarded as a substantial legislative victory in relation to a particular problem. Inasmuch as legislation has an impact, it might be unintended. Unintended results are not necessarily undesirable. For instance, legislation which compels motor-cyclists to wear helmets might have reduced motor-cycle theft, because a thief riding a motor-cycle without a helmet is likely to be stopped by the police. There has been much discussion of the undesirable economic consequences of regulatory legislation and of the need for deregulation. But arguments about regulatory failure based on the economic impact of regulation are often spurious (e.g., concentrating on costs to the exclusion of benefits), neglect other values to which economic ends might be considered subservient (e.g., equality, health), and fail to consider the distributional consequences of courses of action such as deregulation.

On the assumption that legislative purpose is meant to be implemented, a number of possible reforms are touched on or suggested by the previous discussion, for example, stronger substantive legal provisions in keeping with legislative purpose;[132] more adequate resources for enforcement bodies; the appointment of senior officials committed to and capable of implementing legislative purpose; controls to minimize conflicts of interest resulting from the 'revolving door'; and greater co-ordination among enforcement bodies and more committed political support for their actions. One key public policy issue is the role of legal proceedings in the implementation of legislation. There is a body of opinion which argues for the very widely used compliance strategy of negotiation and persuasion, with only the occasional prosecution where blameworthy behaviour is involved.[133] Proponents of this approach offer no evidence that it is more effective than law enforcement through instituting legal proceedings. It is of little assistance to say that it must be effective, given that many obey the law at present, when the issue is its *comparative* efficacy. Nor is it of much use to point to the resentment of the regulated when they are prosecuted, unless this magnifies significantly the costs of enforcement because of unco-operativeness or leads to an increase, rather than a decline, in wrongdoing. Indeed negotiation and persuasion as a strategy can appear to produce quite arbitrary results, since the way enforcement bodies structure their discretion to take legal action is generally unknown to outsiders. Moreover, the strategy of negotiation and persuasion conflicts with the rule of law, inasmuch as the latter demands the equal application of the law. Finally, legal proceedings on a regular basis are necessary to maintain the integrity of the law in the eyes of the general population, whether or not there is any effect on compliance.

A frequently mentioned reform is greater public participation in and scrutiny of legislative implementation. One reason that enforcement bodies are susceptible to the influence of the regulated is because the public is not as organized as the regulated. Participation can take various forms ranging from the public making representations, through their assisting to monitor performance, to their taking part in the decision-making process. An Office of Public Advocate would be one mechanism for strengthening the public interest point of view before government bodies.[134] Practical difficulties occur if the general public is to participate formally in decision-making. If mass participation is out of the question, how are the representatives of the public to be chosen? At what level should they operate, in existing structures or specially established review councils? Should they share in major policy-making or at the level of daily operations? The experience with participation in public bureaucracies is that the law-makers may not intend it to be genuine but see it as a symbolic gesture to assuage public opinion, and that it might not be effective because the public's representatives are co-opted.

Greater publicity about the nature, operation and impact of legislation is another reform. Publicity is said to further public accountability and hence effectiveness. 'Freedom of Information' legislation now operates at the Federal level and in Victoria, but a crucial limitation is that it is confined to the sphere of government activity and there is not a great deal of information available about the regulated.[135] Another effective approach might be to oblige departments and agencies to publish on a regular basis an account of how they operate, in particular, how they exercise their legal discretion. As well as furthering public accountability this might improve their efficiency, because they would have to direct their collective mind to what they did in practice. Enforcement bodies should not be required to publicize how they exercise discretion in all cases, for this might seriously threaten their effectiveness.

Are legal actions by private citizens a means by which the implementation of legislation can be furthered? Even were they to be favourably disposed, it is doubtful whether the courts could contribute a great deal in this way to more effective implementation because they only operate intermittently and lack executive power. In addition someone would need to seek judicial review of relevant government activities or institute legal proceedings directly for breach of legislative standards. Restrictions on the right of the public to take such proceedings have been liberalized in a number of jurisdictions,[136] but there are still important obstacles in others. It is important for legal action by the public to be effective when it is permitted, and finance is crucial in this regard. There are a few examples of departments and agencies being able to finance public participation from their own funds,[137] although in practice this has not occurred. 'Treble damage suits' under United States anti-trust law strengthen the deterrent effect of the law by providing an incentive for the individual victims of unlawful activity to institute legal proceedings, since they may obtain three times their losses. Of course the technique is inappropriate where unlawful activity causes a small amount of harm to each individual as with certain consumer protection and environmental offences.

More recent proposals for reform have as their main concern the cost of regulation. American proposals include the introduction of more extensive evaluation of proposed and existing legislative regulation so as to analyse benefits, costs and alternative courses of action; the establishment of a Regulatory Council or Ministry of Deregulation to review regulatory programmes; the adoption of a regulatory budget; and the enactment of 'sunset' legislation, to give regulatory agencies a fixed life, subject to extension. Deregulation has had an impact in Australia in certain areas of the economy. An attempt to approach the issue more generally is the Victorian *Subordinate Legislation (Review and Revocation) Act* 1984. As a result of the legislation, all statutory rules in Victoria are subject to a sunset provision, and statutory rules must usually be subject to cost-benefit analysis before they are made.[138]

While in principle the evaluation of regulatory legislation is commendable, in practice there is the dilemma of either entrusting the task of evaluation to the department or agency responsible for a programme, with the consequent risk of distortion, or of entrusting it to a central body, with the chance that it might be completed either superficially or only after considerable delay. The experience of evaluation in practice has been mixed: in some cases it has had clear benefits such as the removal of redundant regulations, but in others it has been obsessed with reducing costs, whatever the consequences.[139] The notion of the Regulatory Council or a Ministry of Deregulation would be less objectionable as a method of evaluating proposed regulatory legislation and reviewing existing programmes if it did not seem premised in favour of deregulation. The same bias seems inherent in the concept of the regulatory budget, although with it the practical difficulties loom larger, primarily, how the ceiling on total costs would be established. Sunset provisions could lead to a department or an agency devoting a considerable portion of its budget, and quite a substantial part of its time, to defending its continuation, given the assumption in favour of termination.

Finally, there needs to be a close assessment of whether there are alternative methods to legislation.[140] A popular suggestion is for a greater reliance on market mechanisms, reserving legislation for occasions when the problems are serious or the benefits substantial. Governments can do a certain amount to foster market solutions by promoting the disclosure of information, strengthening trade practices enforcement, encouraging technological innovation through the provision of incentives, and selective deregulation. There is also scope for greater enforcement via private action, as under section 80 of the *Trade Practices Act* 1974.[141] If there is a role for the market as an alternative to regulatory legislation, other approaches cannot be ignored in public policy-making. For instance, in Australia government participation in industry is not an uncommon avenue of public policy: government participation may be a more effective and efficient instrument than regulation in fostering competition, encouraging private industry to improve the standards of its products and services, and setting the pace in the conditions of health and safety at work.

CHAPTER TWO

THE COURTS

Inasmuch as writers on jurisprudence are concerned with what the civil courts do, their focus is on adjudication and law-making—matters such as the exercise of discretion in judicial decision-making, resolving trouble or hard cases, and the role of morality and policy arguments.[1] Another strand of writing, influenced by legal anthropology, places disputes centre stage: disputes or controversies which cannot be settled between the parties or their friends may be referred to a court. In this view the civil courts deal with disputes by the application of doctrine, a method of operation which distinguishes them from mediation and arbitration.[2] Influenced by the notion of politics as who gets what, when and how, a number of American commentators have regarded the civil courts as part of the political process. This third approach focuses, for example, on how interest groups use the courts to attain their goals, just as they might use the legislature or the executive.[3] More radical writers see the civil courts as agencies of the state, reinforcing the position of commercial and property interests in society. One study, for instance, concludes: 'Effectively what the court is doing is continually re-stating the rules, re-stating those entitlements and obligations which constitute the legal basis of use rights ("property") in our society.'[4] Finally, lawyer-economists see the civil courts as performing allocative functions, as does the market, and examine matters such as the efficiency of the procedure used and the rules made.[5]

None of these approaches necessarily provides an answer, in broad terms, to the question of what Australian civil courts do. Each may provide a persuasive account of particular aspects, and each may focus on critical or intellectually difficult parts of their operation. But none paints the whole picture—the matters going to civil courts, how they are handled, and with what result. This chapter attempts to do this. It adopts a 'systems' approach, examining the 'inputs' of Australian civil courts, then how decisions are made in relation to these inputs, before turning to the results of these decisions (the 'outputs').[6] The approach taken also throws some light on the questions which the other approaches address, for example, the nature of rights, how legal rules are applied, and the functions of law in society. Moreover, it identifies important areas in the operation of civil courts of which there is presently a significant ignorance.

As institutions of the state, courts make authoritative decisions about certain matters presented to them. The social, political and economic environment influences, possibly indirectly, the nature of these matters. Granted this truism, the issues which arise for examination include how this environment produces particular 'inputs' for courts, and the nature of these and the character of those advancing them. Comparisons can then be made with the inputs of, say, the political system or the market. What happens to these inputs? First, they are converted into legal issues in accordance with procedural and substantive rules of law. Second, they are disposed of at different points and in different ways in the process of litigation. Whereas jurists concentrate on complex adjudication, however, courts dispose of the majority of matters in a routine, mundane manner, or the parties settle a matter before—often well before—exhausting the legal process. The decisions of civil courts are not automatically implemented; enforcement may be necessary. In addition, there is the larger issue of the impact that decisions may have on other than those directly involved. Consideration of these aspects of court 'output' throw light on whether courts are central to Australian public policy-making.

I INPUTS

Courts operate within a particular social environment. Across societies, what are called courts do not necessarily handle the same matters. Within the one society, changes in the social environment may affect the civil courts.[7] Over recent decades, for example, changing social values have been at least partly responsible for the increasing number of applications for divorce. It is well-known that depression in the economy produces an upsurge in insolvency work. Even political change can produce a not inconsiderable volume of litigation, as with the constitutional litigation resulting from the advent of Federal Labor governments in Australia. For convenience, this part eschews historical analyses to concentrate on the present-day inputs of Australian civil courts. The focus is on litigation, although Australian courts perform a range of other functions, from issuing warrants and subpoenas, through granting probate on wills, to keeping records. In particular, how do social and economic problems become grievances which in turn are taken to courts as legal proceedings? And who litigates what types of issues?

The sources of litigation

Ostensibly, the operation of the courts is based on the assumption that people know their rights and will take the initiative to enforce them if they expect to be successful. Success in these terms is immediate, by winning the case, or long-term, by leading to greater pressure for change through legislation. In this sense the courts parallel the 'free market', which assumes that self-interest will motivate rational activity. In fact, social and economic factors mediate legal action—for example consciousness of rights, community and group norms, capability, the nature of the relationship between the parties, the desirability of publicity, certainty of outcome, the type of problem (what is at stake, its complexity, its legal dimensions) and the perception of, and access to, legal assistance. To put it another way, before parties take legal action they must perceive that there is a problem, that the problem is capable of remedy, that the problem is sufficiently serious to justify doing something about it, that self-help is inappropriate, and that involving the law might offer a satisfactory solution. Because these prerequisites are not always satisfied, the result is that many problems are 'lumped', many claims abandoned, and many disputes compromised or avoided by the parties without outside assistance (let alone legal assistance).[8] For example, residents of an area affected by environmental decay might not conceptualize this as a grievance but regard it as an aspect of life which must be tolerated. Consumers might not realize that a transaction has not satisfied legal requirements (e.g., to be in writing) or not think it worthwhile, given the cost of an item, to do anything about it. A retailer might not want to engage in legal action against suppliers because of the risk of disturbing harmonious relations with them, and so might prefer to settle disputes by steps such as appropriate adjustments to price.

First, then, let us look at the issue of whether problems are perceived of as grievances, that is, as being the responsibility of someone else. There is a recent study which tapped the nature and extent of personal grievances in the Australian community.[9] In it members of households in Victoria were asked if anyone residing in the household had experienced one of a range of possible problems entailing injury, harm or loss within the previous three years. The study then ranked the grievances and found that tort (accident) and landlord-tenant problems were the most reported. Problems related to schools and voluntary associations were relatively unusual. The figures are subject to important qualifications. The method of survey required almost instant memory recall, persons might not have revealed certain problems (e.g., debt), and certain of the grievances were admittedly minor (e.g., neighbourhood disputes). Moreover, the survey was confined to personal rather than organizational grievances. Nonetheless, the findings show the relative significance of grievances about certain matters, which rarely make an appearance in the courts, in particular about discrimination and relating to government and neighbours. Interestingly, there was an apparent lack of association between income and education, but not age, and the number of grievances experienced.

Now many such grievances would have been quite trivial and better forgotten or resolved informally. However, it seems fair to say that there were a substantial number of grievances, objectively significant, which were not pursued to litigation. The study showed that only a proportion of respondents made a claim against the person perceived of as being responsible. Claims in turn did not always give rise to disputes; in some cases the other party provided satisfaction. In only a small number of disputes did people seek legal assistance, and in even fewer did they institute legal action. Graphically, the results of the study can be presented as a pyramid, showing the number of claims, disputes, times that lawyers were used, and court cases instituted, per 1000 grievances. Not all litigation would progress step by step through such a pyramid. The person who challenges a prosecution on the basis of an administrative law or constitutional law doctrine would proceed directly from a grievance to civil litigation. More detailed analysis for the study showed a variation with the type of matter; for example, grievances post-divorce gave rise to most litigation, grievances about tort gave rise to the next most litigation, whereas grievances about discrimination led to the least litigation.

The limited involvement of courts can be further demonstrated in specific areas. One is taxation, an area which is also useful in showing the propensity to challenge government action. As with grievances in general, there is a pyramidal structure, although the base in this case is provided by the number of tax returns filed. For the financial year 1983–84, the following are the figures reported by the Federal Commissioner of Taxation in his annual report:

Table 1   Objections to tax assessments 1983–84

Tax cases heard: High Court of Australia	6
Federal Court of Australia	26
State Supreme Courts	47
References heard by boards of review	544
References transmitted to boards of review	767
Complaints to Ombudsman (requests for written comments)	155
Written objections to Commissioner decided in 1983–84 (income tax only)	245 241
Written objections to Commissioner lodged in 1983–84 (income tax only)	236 127
Tax returns assessed	8 201 484
Tax returns filed 1983–84	9 541 861

Motives are one factor underlying such patterns. Take litigation. Towards one end of the spectrum of litigation are relatively mundane motives such as the collection of debt, the pursuit of compensation, inducing compliance with the terms of a contract, and preventing further dissemination of a publication (by issuing a 'stop writ' alleging defamation). At the other end of the spectrum a business or government defeated in the political arena might turn to the courts for a remedy. A string of constitutional cases could be mentioned such as the 1948 bank nationalization case[10] through to the Tasmanian dam case.[11] Along the spectrum are many motives, such as delaying the other party, seeking a decision in a forum not overtly affected by political considerations, threatening the other party, revenge, vindicating a principle, gaining a tactical advantage in a continuing relationship, and obtaining a competitive advantage.

Various social and economic influences underlie decisions to pursue grievances through to the courts or not. Cost is well known as an inhibiting factor—from the direct cost of legal action (e.g., court fees), through the cost of legal services, to the opportunity cost of pursuing an action (salary/wages forgone, time expended, etc.). Legal aid has had some effect in mitigating the direct costs of legal action, but the grant of legal aid is usually subject to a relatively severe means test and is limited to certain categories of matter.[12] Some law firms are prepared to fund legal action in accident claims (except, possibly, for direct disbursements) on the basis that in most cases plaintiffs will eventually recover something and be able to pay legal fees. Wealth is also associated with knowledge, skills, education, consciousness of rights, social contacts and confidence, and all these may help to decide whether individuals exercise their legal rights. Generally speaking, poorer people are likely to be less 'legally competent'—less knowledgeable, less skilled and less confident in relation to the law. Accordingly, they are more likely to become victims of injustice, but less likely to use the legal system to their advantage. In many ways, then, wealth—or rather the lack of it—inhibits legal action in a direct or indirect way.[13]

Another aspect is whether some sections of society fail to take the initiative over matters capable of legal resolution because they are intimidated by what law is usually associated with (e.g., the police, the courts and prison). As a result of their experience and the experience of others, they might feel—perhaps unjustifiably—that a matter will be brushed off by those in authority. There might also be the fear that if people take action their employer, their insurance company, the social welfare department and so on will in some way retaliate. While the law tends to assume that granting rights to weaker parties neutralizes differences in power, many people will regard acquiescence, avoidance or tolerating a situation as a more rational response than asserting legal rights. There also seems to be an attitude among some that certain problems are 'private' and 'personal', and that they should find the solution within the network of family or friends rather than in the law.

There is little empirical evidence about the extent to which group and community norms affect legal action. One aspect is whether the propensity to litigate varies between jurisdictions. The conventional wisdom is that New South Wales is more litigious than the other States, a product, possibly, of a more individualistic culture and the more aggressive attitude of the New South Wales legal profession. Disputes, in other words, may occur more often, and lawyers may be more inclined to encourage litigation as a way of resolving them. In fact the number of civil cases commenced in the Supreme Courts in Sydney and Melbourne are comparable, more so if per capita figures are used. The conventional wisdom would still be true, however, if there were more disputes in New South Wales than in Victoria, but different institutional arrangements channelling these to bodies other than the courts. Certainly the conventional wisdom holds for civil cases which are heard to completion, with this occurring about three times as often in the New South Wales as in the Victorian Supreme Court.[14]

The tendency to take legal action also turns on institutional factors. Commercial and property interests may have a different propensity to litigate compared with individuals, not least because of the different transactions entered and interests to be protected. Certainty of outcome is also important. Professor Colin Howard has written:

Almost invariably the constitutional cases which reach the high court are only one tactic in a wider and more complex situation. Governments in particular are frequently reluctant to take their disputes to the high court because of the uncertainty of the outcome. It is often politically more advantageous to leave a dispute undecided, or to be decided by negotiation, than to rush into litigation which may settle the issue against you.[15]

Then there is the capacity of the courts to handle litigation—the more resources available to the courts, the more likely that if other things are equal claims will go there rather than be abandoned or channelled elsewhere.

Indeed, other institutions might offer acceptable avenues for the resolution of a matter. For example, private arbitration occurs in commercial and building disputes, and Australian governments have established a range of tribunals and bodies to handle certain matters— fair rent boards, committees on discrimination in employment, the administrative appeals tribunals (Commonwealth and Victoria), the Australian Conciliation and Arbitration Commission (and comparable State bodies), ombudsman offices, the social security appeals tribunals, consumer affairs bureaux, taxation boards of review, valuation boards, builders' licensing boards, residential tenancies tribunals, small claims courts, the Privacy Committee of New South Wales and more recently, community justice centres. Many of the matters which the latter bodies

deal with could go to the courts—although in some cases government
has attempted to give these other bodies exclusive jurisdiction—but the
cost of litigation acts as a deterrent, quite apart from perceptions about
the quality of adjudication offered. The courts still act as a long stop for
such disputes, for parties dissatisfied with these bodies might begin
afresh in the courts or seek judicial review of a decision if there is no
privative clause preventing it (that is, a clause which specifically excludes
the courts from reviewing a matter). However, the vast majority of such
matters are handled without resort to the courts.

Further, there are the gatekeepers to litigation. For example, lawyers
identify avenues for litigation of which lay persons are ignorant. On the
other hand, even if individuals seek legal assistance, lawyers might
inhibit litigation by screening out particular types of claim. An American
study found that lawyers did not regard litigation in relation to consumer
claims as being worthwhile or in some cases worthy, had little or no
knowledge of the applicable substantive law, but attempted to mediate
some claims informally with the relevant retailer, manufacturer or
finance house.[16] These findings are likely to be replicated in Australia and
would probably extend to other matters such as disputes with neighbours. Then there are the courts, for what they say influences perceptions
about what are grievances, claims and disputes. Courts might discourage
litigation through developments in procedural and substantive law.[17]
Examples of the courts explicitly encouraging litigation are rare,[18] but
courts can indirectly encourage litigation by doctrinal developments
which make it worthwhile to pursue a claim. Finally, legislation can
affect litigation. The introduction of new legislation might multiply the
occasions for disputed interpretations, but it might also resolve points of
legal contention and so discourage litigation.

Who uses the courts?

The nature of those involved in litigation has a profound influence on the
issues courts address, the involvement of lawyers, the development of
doctrine and outcomes. To take an example: if a particular type of
litigant constantly brings claims against another type of litigant, and the
latter typically does not defend or does not obtain legal representation, it
would not be surprising if outcomes tended to favour the first type of
litigant. Without any conscious bias on their part, judges would simply
be more exposed to the arguments favouring the first type of litigant so
that these attained a more 'natural' quality. Beyond any impact on the
courts, the nature of litigants might have ramifications for society. For
example, if plaintiffs were typically commercial and property interests
claiming against individual defendants, the courts would be functioning
to reinforce other institutional outcomes in society rather than acting as

an avenue for redressing the balance. By contrast, there is a widely accepted notion in the United States that minority groups ought to look to the courts for social reform if the legislatures are unsympathetic.

There is some evidence on the types of parties using the Australian civil courts. In a survey of cases commenced over a three-year period (1977–80) in three State supreme courts—those of New South Wales, Victoria and the Australian Capital Territory—it was found that about one half of both plaintiffs and defendants were individuals.[19] The results are set out in Tables 2 and 3 in the columns titled 'Commenced sample'. Analysis of the plaintiff cases involving individuals (not shown in the table) reveals that overall about half were personal injury claims. Of the defendant cases involving individuals, 30 per cent in New South Wales involved personal injury claims, 34 per cent mortgage default claims and 9 per cent money owing claims. The comparable figures for Victoria were 15 per cent, 29 per cent (for 'possession' cases) and 32 per cent, and for the ACT 28 per cent, 5 per cent and 52 per cent.

Once cases are commenced in the courts, the next stage for many (but not all) would be to enter one of the court lists ('listing'). The types of lists vary between jurisdictions but may indicate, for instance, whether a case is to go to trial with a jury or without. In fact many cases which would in the ordinary course of events enter a list do not do so because, as we will see below, they are settled or otherwise disposed of without having to go any further. For present purposes, the point to note is that at listing, the proportion of cases with individuals as plaintiffs increases. Of a representative sample of cases which entered a court list in the New South Wales, Victorian and the ACT supreme courts over a year in the late 1970s or early 1980s (depending on the jurisdiction), more than four-fifths had individuals as plaintiffs (see the columns in Table 2 titled 'Listed sample'). Most of these were personal-injury cases (not shown in the table)—73 per cent in New South Wales, 62 per cent in Victoria and 84 per cent in the ACT. By contrast, the proportion of defendants who were individuals generally fell as cases progressed through the courts (see the columns in Table 3 titled 'Listed sample'), since almost all mortgage default cases and many money owing cases were quickly settled or went to default judgment. The most important cases in the listed sample involving individuals as defendants were categorized as follows (not shown in the table): 62 per cent personal injury and 15 per cent realty (New South Wales); 52 per cent personal injury, 12 per cent money owing and 10 per cent testators' family maintenance (Victoria); and 78 per cent personal injury and 17 per cent money owing (ACT).

Hasty conclusions ought not to be drawn from the high proportion of plaintiffs and defendants who were individuals in the study referred to. First, the fact that individual plaintiffs constitute an important, indeed sometimes the largest, category of users of the higher civil courts is

Table 2   Nature of plaintiffs*, Supreme Courts NSW, Vic., ACT, 1977–80

	NSW		Vic.		ACT	
	Commenced sample	Listed sample	Commenced sample	Listed sample	Commenced sample	Listed sample
Individual	405 (54.7%)	253 (92.0%)	315 (44.1%)	239 (80.5%)	151 (45.1%)	122 (87.1%)
Business	197 (26.6%)	18 (6.5%)	275 (38.5%)	46 (15.4%)	127 (37.9%)	15 (10.7%)
Government	50 (6.7%)	2 (0.7%)	54 (7.6%)	2 (0.6%)	45 (13.4%)	1 (0.7%)
Miscellaneous	87 (11.8%)	2 (0.8%)	69 (9.6%)	10 (3.3%)	12 (3.6%)	2 (1.4%)
Other/unknown	1 (0.1%)	—	2 (0.3%)	—	—	—
Total	740	275	715	297	335	140

* first named party

Table 3 Nature of Defendants*, Supreme Courts NSW, Vic., ACT, 1977–80

	NSW		Vic.		ACT	
	Commenced sample	Listed sample	Commenced sample	Listed sample	Commenced sample	Listed sample
Individual	406 (54.9%)	127 (46.2%)	442 (61.8%)	169 (56.9%)	234 (69.9%)	97 (69.3%)
Business	239 (32.2%)	99 (35.9%)	219 (30.6%)	93 (31.3%)	72 (21.5%)	25 (17.9%)
Government	47 (6.3%)	36 (13.1%)	30 (4.1%)	28 (9.4%)	22 (6.6%)	17 (12.1%)
Miscellaneous	16 (2.2%)	11 (4.0%)	16 (2.2%)	6 (2.0%)	3 (0.9%)	1 (0.7%)
Other/unknown	32 (4.3%)	2 (0.7%)	8 (1.1%)	1 (0.3%)	4 (1.2%)	—
Total	740	275	715	297	335	140

* first named party

partly attributable to the importance of personal injury litigation before the higher civil courts. Second, there are many individuals with legal problems who do not get to court. Third, the individuals who sue are not necessarily representative of the population. Fourth, groups may stand behind some of the individuals who sue or are sued. It is difficult to uncover in a systematic way the extent to which this occurs. It is probably little on the plaintiff's side, although in theory the derivative suit is possible in the commercial context and individuals claiming on behalf of groups are not unknown in administrative law.[20] More significantly, with regard to defendants, although individuals appear as such in personal injury motor vehicle cases, in practice the third-party insurers conduct the defence, often without any assistance from those against whom the action is nominally being brought. Fifth, the results might not obtain for all Australian civil courts. In the Melbourne Magistrates' Court in 1982, while only 3.7 per cent of default summons were instituted by individuals, some 75.8 per cent of defendants to such summons were individuals. Ninety-six per cent of summons issued in the court in that year were default summons, and some 83 per cent of these involved debt claims. Of the special summons issued, however (the other 4 per cent), three-quarters of complainants were individuals issuing process to recover damages against defendants, of whom 80 per cent were also individuals.[21]

However, it is clear that Australian civil courts cannot universally be characterized as a forum where commercial and property institutions successfully claim against individuals. Of course there are many proceedings before the civil courts which involve businesses instituting debt or property claims against individuals. A great number of these proceedings are undefended and many are disposed of by way of default judgment, whereby a plaintiff can obtain judgement in the absence of any moves to defend a case. But many, indeed most, of such cases are legally unanswerable, for example, where the defendant has failed to pay the debt or rent or has fallen into arrears with a mortgage. In other words, the courts are simply perfecting what the law permits, so that in this area of litigation attention needs to be given primarily to the substantive law rather than to the role of the courts.

Further analysis of the data from the survey of the New South Wales, Victorian and ACT Supreme Courts of parties involved in the different cases is in Table 4. Again information is included from representative samples of both commenced and listed cases. Clearly the largest category of cases involved individuals claiming against individuals, this fact reflecting the importance of personal injury motor vehicle claims. A large number of the individual v. business claims were personal injury industrial accident claims, while the business v. individual cases were mainly debt collection and mortgage default matters. What might be surprising is that the figures suggest that business interests use the courts little, comparatively speaking, for dispute settlement amongst themselves. One answer may be that other institutions provide a more convenient forum for commercial matters: for example, they may be referred to arbitration. However, in Australia this seems not to occur regularly except over building contracts. Perhaps more importantly, the relative infrequency of disputes between businesses might testify to sound planning, with legal help, thus avoiding their arising in the first place, and to the desire to maintain continuing good relations with those such as suppliers, customers and financiers. Occasionally business sues government, presumably in relation to regulation of some aspect of their activity. Such cases are an important component of the work of the Federal Court arising under the *Administrative Decisions (Judicial Review) Act* 1977 and as appeals from the Administrative Appeals Tribunal.

Government is rarely a plaintiff in the State superior courts, except in the guise of the Federal Commissioner of Taxation (as in most of the government v. individual and government v. business cases in Table 4). Many individual v. government cases are claims against the Government on the basis of vicarious liability (as with motor vehicle accidents) or as employer (as with industrial accidents). In State supreme courts there is a low incidence of individuals seeking judicial review of administrative action or constitutional review. Similarly, there are few cases involving private groups such as associations, clubs and religious groups. Where they occur, however, such cases may have important political and economic consequences, as with faction fights in various political parties and churches.[22]

Subject matter of litigation

In the absence of historical information, it is not possible to say whether the matters handled by Australian civil courts now are different from those dealt with in the past. It would seem safe to say that there are relatively more family matters before the courts than at the turn of the century: for example, there were 378 divorces and 21 judicial separations for a population of 3 826 286 in Australia in 1901, but 44 088 for a population of 15 178 400 in 1982. Personal-injury claims must comprise a larger percentage of matters than at the turn of the century—how large will be seen in a moment—with the advent of cars and trucks. But although family matters and personal injury claims loom larger than they did, it would be too hasty to assume that the courts are now less oriented than they were to commercial and property claims.

Categorizing the subject matter of litigation is far from straightforward. Choices need to be made, for instance between legal and social categories. Using mainly social categories, Table 5 shows the breakdown

Table 4　Major configurations of parties, Supreme Courts, NSW, Vic., ACT, 1977–80

	NSW		Vic.		ACT	
	Commenced cases	Listed cases	Commenced cases	Listed cases	Commenced cases	Listed cases
Individual v. individual	28.6%	43.9%	26.4%	49.8%	29.6%	58.6%
Individual v. business	16.6%	32.4%	12.4%	19.9%	8.4%	15.7%
Individual v. government	5.5%	11.5%	3.4%	8.4%	6.0%	12.1%
Business v. individual	12.6%	1.8%	21.7%	5.1%	24.2%	10.7%
Business v. business	11.5%	3.2%	15.4%	9.8%	12.5%	—
Business v. government	0.7%	1.4%	0.7%	0.7%	0.6%	—
Government v. individual	2.4%	0.7%	4.6%	0.7%	12.8%	—
Government v. business	3.6%	—	2.2%	—	0.3%	0.7%
Other	18.4%	5.0%	13.1%	5.7%	5.7%	2.1%
Total	100% n = 740	100% n = 278	100% n = 715	100% n = 297	100% n = 335	100% n = 140

of case type for representative samples of cases commenced in the supreme courts of New South Wales, Victoria and the Australian Capital Territory over the period 1977–80.[23] Personal injury claims were a large category of the cases commenced, but so too were commercial and property claims (mortgage default, landlord and tenant, realty, money owing, company matters). Since 1976 family matters have been handled mainly in the Family Court. The 'other' category in the table includes public law cases; I have already said that such cases are very few in the State supreme courts.

Table 5   Types of cases commenced, Supreme Courts NSW, Vic., ACT, 1977–80

	NSW		Vic.		ACT	
	N	%	N	%	N	%
Personal injuries	238	32.1	136	19.0	87	26.0
Mortgage default	143	19.3	⎰142	⎰19.9	12	3.6
Landlord & tenant★	13	1.8	⎱	⎱	15	4.5
Realty	39	5.3	10	1.4	3	0.9
Money owing (liquidated claims)	72	9.7	231	32.3	167	49.9
Damages (unliquidated claims)	19	2.6	67	9.4	7	2.1
Defamation	11	1.5	10	1.4	8	2.4
Family matters	5	0.7	12	1.7	2	0.6
Estates	25	3.4	15	2.1	—	—
Company	74	10.0	32	4.4	8	2.4
Other	101	13.6	60	8.4	26	7.8
Total	740	100.0	715	100.0	335	100.0

★ In Victoria there was no breakdown for mortgage default and landlord and tenant cases; the court compendiously categorizes both as 'possession'.

An overview of the types of cases commenced in the three courts shows similarities, as might be expected given their nature as superior courts of general jurisdiction. However, there were distinct differences in the mix of matters, which may be explained by two major considerations. First, there is the extent to which particular problems are not present to the same extent in the communities served by the courts. For instance, in the ACT there appear to be proportionately fewer mortgage default cases and fewer company applications. The first may be explained by the high average socio-economic position of ACT residents, and the second by the low level of commercial and financial activity in the Territory. As might be expected, the number of possession cases in

Victoria was about the same as the number in New South Wales. However, there were approximately twice as many company matters in New South Wales as in Victoria, a phenomenon difficult to explain, when the ratio of companies registered in New South Wales to those registered in Victoria is some three to two. Defamation cases seemed to be proportionately most common in the ACT, which may be related to the political activity in the national capital or its more favourable judicial climate.[24] Second, and it would seem more importantly, the explanation for the differences may lie in the jurisdiction of the intermediate courts, the District Court in New South Wales and the County Court in Victoria. The lack of an intermediate court in ACT, and the relatively low upper jurisdictional limit of the Victorian County Court at the time of the survey, seem to have resulted in a large number of money owing matters being commenced in the supreme courts of these jurisdictions as compared with the Supreme Court of New South Wales.

Evidence such as this puts paid to any suggestion that there is a 'crisis' in the courts caused by the development of new doctrines and remedies. Product liability actions, challenges to contracts on the ground of unconscionability, claims that the state has interfered with human rights— matters such as these constitute an insignificant burden for Australian civil courts. However, a comparison of the subject-matter of litigation in Australian supreme courts with the nature of grievances experienced in the community shows that the higher civil courts play only a marginal part in resolving many of them. Such grievances are resolved, if at all, in other ways. Intermediate and lower courts play some part, as well as tribunals. For example, Table 6 contains information on the type of matters commenced in the Victorian County Court in 1981 and the Melbourne Magistrates' Court in 1982.[25] Clearly these courts have a role in the resolution of some of the ordinary day-to-day matters which arise between individuals and businesses, between landlords and tenants and between the state and the citizen. A note of caution is in order, however, since many of the claims were by way of routine debt collection. In other words, business, landlords and government departments with money claims instituted proceedings which were either not proceeded with (presumably the amount was paid or the matter settled) or were undefended (and so in many cases went to default judgment).

II THE CONVERSION PROCESS

Procedure has long been recognized as playing a central role in the administration of civil justice. Jeremy Bentham's concern about 'the burthens of judicial procedure' takes form in current interests such as widening access to the courts and reducing delay and expense. Substantive

Table 6   Types of cases commenced in the County Court, Victoria, 1981, and Magistrates' Court, Melbourne 1982

| | Percentages | |
	County Court	Magistrates' Court
Personal injuries	38.6	0.1
Debt: goods sold and delivered	16.7	22.7
commonwealth tax	12.2	18.2
local government rates, etc.	—	7.6
State tax	—	3.8
work and labour done	4.5	27.0
contract in writing	2.5	12.5
hire of goods and chattels	1.5	1.5
other debt	13.0	1.5
Vehicle property damage	3.5	3.2
Other property damage	0.5	0.1
Breach of agreement	2.7	0.3
Cheques, etc.	4.2	1.4

law, too, channels civil litigation. Of primary interest here is the extent to which the substantive law means that social issues can be converted into legal problems so that the courts can deal with them. To put it another way, only if there is a cause of action is it worth suing. A further aspect of what can be termed the conversion process in courts is the extent to which the majority of cases commenced never go to trial. Mention has been made of the many debt and property claims going to default judgment, but in addition substantial numbers of cases settle, often as late as at the door of the court and sometimes during trial.

Court procedures

Procedural law has an influence on those resorting to the courts, the matters litigated and the results obtained. Technicalities, anomalies and complexities in procedural rules discourage claims, delay them unnecessarily, or distort outcomes by preventing meritorious defences being heard. Consider, for example, how court procedures facilitate delay in cases in which the outcome is reasonably clear-cut. Certain parties have an obvious motive to delay: activity in violation of the law, for example, can be continued up to the hearing, unless interlocutory (that is, anticipatory) relief can be obtained. Similarly, a person might be induced to abandon a claim, or a case might be weakened with time because witnesses are no longer available. The rules of evidence also throw up barriers to establishing a case. Statistical evidence, for example, is not admissible to show, say, that a surgeon has a much higher wound infection rate than average.[26] Yet if only one case is examined, it will be much easier for the surgeon to argue chance and to have any inference of negligence rejected.

Areas of current debate in Australia concerning court procedures include the standing of a person or group, class actions and, to an extent, the 'Brandeis brief'. The first two are discussed at some length in Chapter 5. What of the third? In the United States the parties to litigation can file a Brandeis brief, which may include government reports, research by social scientists and laws in other jurisdictions. The brief broadens a court's perspective by introducing it to wider policy considerations. By contrast, argument before Australian appellate courts is generally confined to evidence admitted at any hearing and to competing contentions as to the relevant law. Yet courts might benefit in some cases where an important public policy issue is raised if they systematically collected information about the potential economic or social implications of their decision. Even in constitutional matters, Australian courts object to the submission of such information, although there is no criterion except relevance limiting facts in constitutional adjudication.[27]

Transformation of issues

Categories for the subject-matter of litigation, such as the description 'personal-injury claims' used above, coincide roughly with an everyday understanding of cases. If cases were to be categorized by the relief requested (damages, possession, injunction, declaration, etc.), there would be some move away from that everyday understanding. And if cases were to be analysed according to legal categories, the masking of social issues might be even greater. At one level this transformation is relatively straightforward and widely recognized, as a motor vehicle accident becomes a claim in negligence for money damages, a quarrel between two neighbours changes into a dispute over planning approval, and a marital contest takes form as a child custody case.[28] And at least on the surface, certain standards in civil law, notably that of the 'reasonable person', draw on community notions of proper behaviour.

But the transformation might be more fundamental as regards the number of parties involved or the issues addressed. Thus conflicts over economic resources, political principle, the exercise of government power or use of the environment become conflicts over the meaning and application of legal doctrine. *Johnson v. Kent*[29] involved the issue of whether the Australian government could build a multi-purpose tower on the top of Black Mountain, in the Australian Capital Territory, without parliamentary approval. Objection was taken to the tower on environmental grounds, but before the High Court the issue was disposed of on the grounds that the Commonwealth had executive power over activity on its land, that the *Post and Telegraph Act* 1901 empowered the Postmaster-General to erect structures for telegraphic, telephonic and other like services, and that this Act did not limit the exercise of the Commonwealth prerogative power in the Australian Capital Territory. As Jacobs J commented in his judgment:

[W]hat was at base a dispute involving community attitudes and purposes, a political dispute in the broad sense, had perforce when it was brought before the Court to turn itself largely into a technical legal dispute on the question whether there was legal authority to erect the structure.[30]

An illustration of how an economic issue can be substantially transformed is provided by the collapse in the market for home units on Queensland's Gold and Sunshine Coasts in the early 1980s. A certain number of people who had been purchasers before the crash sought to renege on their contracts. That was the economic context, but the litigation which followed unveiled legal arguments removed from the simple economic reality that some people could not, or did not, now want to pay—whether individuals had been induced to purchase by misleading or deceptive conduct within the terms of section 52 of the Trade Practices Act;[31] whether contracts were 'investment contracts' under what is now section 171 of the Companies Code, in which case enforcement of them by specific performance would be illegal since the vendor was not a public company as required by that section;[32] whether a by-law of a body corporate in relation to car-parking was valid;[33] whether the contracts were in writing as required by section 49 of the Queensland *Building Units and Group Titles Act* 1980;[34] whether mortgages given were in breach of section 73 of the *Property Law Act* 1974 of Queensland;[35] and whether the pendant jurisdiction of the Federal Court was such as to make it the appropriate forum for resolution of all the issues in some of the cases.[36]

The transformation of social into legal issues is facilitated by detailed regulatory legislation. In addition to relying on broad common law and equitable principles, a party might be able to invoke a range of statutory law relevant to a particular issue. The meaning of statutory language being in many cases ambiguous, the potential for legal action is considerable in the modern state. The upshot is that cases are often formulated in legal terms far removed from the underlying social or economic reality and might even be reformulated in the course of their progress. The area of company takeovers is illustrative: raiders and targets may be able to point to technical breaches of the Companies Code[37] and of numerous provisions in the Takeovers Code itself.[38] In addition, the development of procedural law opens further avenues to contested legal points. When the National Companies and Securities Commission sought to investigate the role of News Corporation Ltd in certain share purchases in Thomas Nationwide Transport in 1982, it probably had little suspicion that it would be taken to the High Court on the basis that it had not accorded natural justice.[39] The result may be what in the United States has been called the 'lawsuit before the lawsuit' (the second of which may never eventuate) or 'companion litigation'. Thus the investigation just mentioned was settled in early 1985 on the basis of undertakings given to the NCSC by News Corporation, but not before it had also gone to the full court of the Federal Court on two separate occasions, each involving the *Freedom of Information Act 1982*.[40]

Lawyers handling a case are clearly important in this transformation process. The focus might be narrowed to one legally relevant issue or widened from a private dispute into one involving issues of public importance. A significant development in the law might result from a strategy adopted in relation to a client's case. In rare cases, it might even emerge from a court's decision on an issue not raised by the person's lawyers. Is it any wonder that many clients do not understand why they succeed, or more importantly, fail in court, when the matter has been transformed beyond their recognition? Moreover, if the legal process is dealing with legal conceptualizations, it might not be addressing the underlying social issue. Neither point is necessarily objectionable: many individuals approach lawyers precisely so that the legal implications of their problems can be used to their advantage (or to the disadvantage of their opponents), and avoiding the underlying social issue may well be functional for society. In addition, the outcome of many cases is dictated, as will be seen, by non-legal considerations, as cases are disposed of in a routine way or are settled.

Attrition of cases

At the centre of thinking about civil courts is the model of formal adjudication—parties present their cases to a court, the adversary process operates and a matter is disposed of by formal adjudication. Despite this popular picture, relatively few of the cases which are begun in court are adjudicated. Instead, the great majority are discontinued, disposed of by default judgment or settled. For example, in the study of cases commenced in the three Australian State supreme courts mentioned above, in only about half did at least one defendant formally enter an appearance, fewer cases still entered a court list, and less than eight in 100 in New South Wales and about three in 100 in Victoria and the ACT were adjudicated by way of a full hearing.[41]

Overall, then, the passage of cases through the courts can be characterized as a continuation of the pyramidal structure already shown for grievances. Not all cases pass through each stage of the process, with many dropping out along the way and being dealt with other than by the intervention of judges. Much depends on the type of matter; whereas many personal-injury cases enter a court list, few debt or mortgage default matters reach this point.

III DECISION-MAKING

Formal adjudication of civil law cases is atypical. Australian civil courts dispose of the bulk of cases by routine administration or by providing a forum in which cases are settled. Characterized in this way, the civil courts parallel other organizations in society to a greater extent than if the focus were to be, as it often is, on adjudication alone. Whether handling cases by routine administration or by facilitating settlement is desirable is a separate issue from that of describing the manner in which courts actually work in practice. However, the normative question inevitably arises, just as it does in the criminal courts, where the counterparts of routine administration and settlement are the routine sentencing of those pleading guilty in lower courts on the one hand, and plea bargaining on the other.

Routine administration

Much of what the courts do in disposing of cases involves routine administration—approving outcomes agreed elsewhere or determined by structural factors. A court order might be desired to guarantee compliance with those outcomes or because it is a precondition to further action. One aspect of routine administration is the consent judgment, where parties have settled a case and simply enter judgment.[42] Another aspect is the default judgment.[43] With routine processing, court officials undertake a limited inquiry to ensure that an application fits established categories (often, this only involves checking that documents are correctly completed) and then give their imprimatur by entering judgment. There are no contested issues, as where both parties want a divorce and have agreed on custody and property. (Divorce is an example of a court order being a legal prerequisite to persons taking certain action, in the particular case, remarrying.) As with divorce, a court might order an individual's bankruptcy or the winding up of a company in a routine manner when there are no disputed matters. Nonetheless, such orders have profound consequences—a change in a person's status in the case of bankruptcy (similarly with divorce) and the end of a company's existence in the case of a winding up.

Debt collection and mortgage default are well recognized as areas where the civil courts frequently engage in routine processing of cases. As noted, such claims typically result from institutions such as business, banks and building societies taking action against individuals. While not legally necessary, a judgment might be valuable to a creditor or mortgagee taking further action such as seeking the insolvency of a debtor or writing off the debt to tax. Although individuals might have a defence or cross-claim in relation to debt and mortgage claims, these are not always raised because of the cost—the very fact of a debt or possession action indicates a lack of financial resources—or because of social factors such as ignorance. Of the commenced cases in the survey mentioned above, default judgments were entered in 14.9 per cent of the cases in the New South Wales Supreme Court, 23.1 per cent of cases in the Victorian Supreme Court and 25.4 per cent of cases in the Australian Capital Territory Supreme Court. A survey of the Victorian County Court found that default judgments occurred in over a quarter of cases commenced, and official figures from the Melbourne Magistrates' Court show that over 95 per cent of the summons issued annually are default summons. Much default work involves debt collection and mortgage default on family homes.[44]

Greater procedural safeguards ought to be introduced in the routine processing of cases, especially default work, since plaintiffs' cases are not always unassailable.[45] One approach would be to require a plaintiff to establish a prima facie case as a precondition to obtaining a default judgment. At present plaintiffs who obtain a default judgment are in a strong position, because of the difficulties of having it set aside. The costs of legal action can be added to the original claim, and if judgment is entered an order for costs can be obtained. Even if there is no defence to a claim for debt or for possession, it is desirable to have a procedure whereby the possibility of assisting individuals to repay by instalments and over a longer period is always properly explored.

Settlement

The conventional legal wisdom is that civil litigation is wasteful and disruptive, and that strong efforts ought to be made to settle cases out of court. The law facilitates settlement in various ways, such as the protection given to 'without prejudice' communications.[46] Clearly what courts do has an influence on settlements; as some writers put it, settlements occur in the 'shadow of law'.[47] Courts do this through their decisions, which are used in bargaining and which shape ideas as to what is acceptable and expectations as to what would occur if a matter went to a hearing. An obvious example is the amounts awarded in personal injury cases, which are taken into account in settling similar later claims. In addition, the cost of litigation, in particular the rule that costs follow the event, induces settlements. Settlements occur because most cases are relatively straightforward and do not involve major uncertainties about the law or the facts.

Do the civil courts facilitate settlement more directly through certain of their rules and procedures? For instance, does the date from which interest is calculated on judgments provide an incentive for plaintiffs to have a case disposed of quickly? The interest payable on judgments is probably not high enough to constitute any real incentive to settle, especially in the commercial area where it is often economically rational behaviour to postpone payment as long as possible. An example of court rules being designed to facilitate settlements are those for payment into court by defendants.[48] These supposedly induce settlements by providing for a cost penalty for plaintiffs who are awarded less than the amount a defendant pays in—they might have to bear the defendant's cost as from the date of payment in. While the practice is uncommon in some Australian jurisdictions, it is used frequently in Victoria because of the favourable attitude to it of the State Insurance Office. There is some statistical evidence that payment in is associated with settlement, although it may be that payment is made more frequently in cases where settlement is more likely.[49] Victorian practitioners representing defendants in personal-injury work generally believe strongly that payment in is a means of effecting settlements. 'Discovery' is a third instance where rules of court theoretically further settlement, by enabling parties to make a more accurate evaluation of the strengths and weaknesses of a case. (Discovery is the process whereby the parties to litigation must prepare lists of documents relevant to the litigation. An opposing party can then inspect any document relevant to its case.) There is little, if any, evidence to support the theory. If discovery encourages settlements it might be because it makes the cost of litigation unacceptably high for one or more of the parties, not because they are better informed as a result of it.

Settlement practices, and the potential for settlement, vary with a range of factors including the parties involved, the existing or future relationship between them, the type of case, legal costs, certainty of outcome,[50] and the attitude and reputation of the lawyers involved.[51] Some cases are more difficult to settle than normal because of the personal animosity of the parties, because they are test cases, or because of what is at stake. A continuing relationship between the parties, on the other hand, is conducive to settlement because a range of informal sanctions push in that direction. First offers by defendants in the personal injury area are generally regarded as far too low and plaintiff solicitors expect that two, three or possibly more will be necessary before the amount will be close to what they think a case is worth. On the basis of reputation and experience lawyers evaluate whether their opponents genuinely want settlement. Lawyers might not rush into settlement negotiations for fear of giving the impression that their case is shaky. Clients sometimes determine the pace of settlement negotiations; for example, financial necessity might make them interested in a quick settlement. Lawyers sometimes delay matters deliberately in the interests of clients, for example, if they are representing a defendant debtor, a person who wishes a particular custody arrangement to continue, or a target company in a takeover battle. In commercial litigation, where large sums of money are at stake, it is possible by excessive discovery, procedural manoeuvres and appeals to frustrate the other side and possibly to force it to a settlement. The practices of institutional litigants regarding settlements is also an important factor; for instance, certain third-party insurers favour an early settlement of claims in personal-injury litigation.

There is a high incidence of settlements at the door of the court. An undesirable aspect of this practice is that a litigant has to make within minutes a decision which might affect his or her whole life. However, lawyers defend late settlements as being necessary if they are to perform their duties to their clients. This view is put strongly by lawyers who believe that it is only at the door of the court that realistic offers are made. However, another explanation for settlements at the door of the court is that where late briefing occurs it is only on the eve of the hearing that the barristers can properly and realistically appraise a case. Yet another explanation, given by practitioners, is that settlements often eventuate at the door of the court because only then do the parties appreciate what a court hearing involves. Practitioners' perceptions of the particular judge allocated to hear a case might also affect whether or not they try to settle it.

Traditionally, Australian civil courts facilitated settlement indirectly, through the 'radiating' effects of their decisions and the existence of rules such as those relating to interest payable on judgments and payment into court. Following the introduction of pre-trial conferences in Australia, the civil courts now play a more active role in the settlement of cases. The way in which pre-trial conferences are conducted varies in practice between different jurisdictions and different courts in the same jurisdiction. While the rules might be designed ostensibly to formulate the issues to be tried, courts sometimes use the opportunity of the conferences to encourage negotiation and settlement. It seems that even if settlement conferences have not increased the rate of settlement, they have at least led to earlier settlements, as cases settle there rather than at the door of the court.

Adjudication

The attrition of cases means that it is relatively rare that the courts give authoritative rulings after a completed adjudication.[52] Even cases which obtain a date for hearing might have settled by the hearing, or at the door of the court. In addition, cases sometimes settle after the hearing has commenced, which might occur because the weaknesses of a party's case are exposed or because the partial hearing resolves important issues, with the result that the parties are able to agree on the others.

Cases where there is a completed adjudication do not always match the adversary model of the conventional wisdom. It might be that there is only an applicant, and no defendant, as where a party obtains an *ex parte* injunction, an executor seeks an authoritative construction of a will, a company applies for its winding up, or a liquidator wants a ruling on how he (or she) ought to proceed. Moreover, adjudications do not necessarily involve a judge. Masters now perform work which in the past was the responsibility of judges. In New South Wales, for example, the masters in the common-law division of the Supreme Court try claims for damages for personal injuries in running down cases in the non-jury list. The master in equity in New South Wales, and the master in Queensland, have not insignificant functions in company law and have delivered reported judgments in this area.

A further qualification is that where there is a jury trial, a completed adjudication will obviously not involve a final ruling on the case by the trial judge, although he or she rules on the evidence, instructs the jury on the relevant law and makes observations to them on the facts. Although jury trial for civil cases is uncommon or non-existent in other Australian jurisdictions, it is still firmly entrenched in New South Wales and Victoria. In New South Wales jury trial is confined mainly to personal-injury claims involving industrial accidents. Juries are common in Victoria in personal injury claims for both industrial and motor vehicle accidents. Jury trial in civil cases is said to have advantages such as enabling community participation in the administration of justice, providing a means by which community values are taken into account, acting as a check on judges and reducing appeals. By contrast it is said that juries in civil cases are costly, cause inconvenience and possibly monetary loss to jurors, require the retention of rigid, technical rules of evidence, and introduce irrationality into decision-making which cannot readily be appealed against.[53]

Even if these qualifications are taken into account, adjudication is still far removed from the world of most jurisprudents. Delays, expense, and tactics all distort the ideal model. Outcomes may reflect the nature, interests and representation of the parties, rather than the legal merits. Llewellyn described the position neatly in relation to the right to sue for damages for breach of contract:

[T]he right could rather more accurately be phrased somewhat as follows: if the other party does not perform as agreed, you can sue, and *if* you have a fair lawyer, and nothing goes wrong with your witnesses or the jury, *and* you give up four or five days of time and some ten to thirty percent of the proceeds, and wait two to twenty months, you will *probably* get judgment for a sum considerably less than what the performance would have been worth—which, if the other party is solvent, and has not secreted his assets, you can, in further due course, collect with six percent interest for delay.[54]

At the end of the process, after the parties present their positions, courts do give authoritative rulings on matters. But if there is an underlying dispute, adjudication will not necessarily lead to its resolution. Obvious examples are provided by the Family Court, whose decisions might exacerbate, rather than resolve, the underlying dispute between the parties. As will be seen, in all areas where an adjudication has occurred the parties might do nothing, might refuse to accept the outcome, or might pursue non-legal avenues for redress of the matter.

Rules are central to adjudication, although not determinative. They are supplemented by norms, such as those falling under the rubric of legal ethics, which influence the behaviour of lawyers and judges involved in the process. The basis of the rules and norms is to ensure that decisions accord with the relevant law and facts. But they also affect matters such as participation of the parties in the decision, public support for the courts, procedural fairness, rationality and finality.

Adjectival rules (procedural and evidentiary) must address matters such as the definition of issues, the identity of the adjudicator and whether he (or she) ought to be disqualified in the particular case, the hearing of the matter (for example, requiring the adjudicator to give all parties an opportunity to present their case, determining how matters are to be proved), the method of decision-making (for example, allocating responsibility for decisions between judge and jury, confining a decision to evidence and arguments presented by the parties at the hearing with all present), the nature of the decision (for example, whether it is to be announced in open court, whether reasons are needed in support), and the extent of any appeals (for example, time limits, whether confined to issues of law).[55]

Under the common-law adversary system, procedural rules confine adjudication, in the main, to the issues raised by the pleadings (the documents which commence the proceedings). Courts are reluctant to force a party not to pursue what they think are trivial or spurious issues, just as they do not interfere by calling witnesses without the consent of the parties. While courts are now under a duty to suggest amendments to pleadings to ensure justice there are cases where, through ignorance or incompetence, matters are not pleaded or raised on which a party might succeed or the court might come to a different conclusion. Evidentiary rules and norms are designed to elicit relevant evidence and to minimize distortions resulting from practices such as coaching witnesses and fraud.[56] There is still the problem that evidence might be inaccurate for reasons such as honest mistake and lapses of memory. However, under the common-law system courts make definitive findings of fact and use them as a basis for judgment, even though they have only been established on the preponderance of evidence.[57] Overall, the adversary system is based on the assumption that the judge should play a relatively passive role during the trial, relying on the parties to present their side of the matter to the best advantage. The stance is said to aid neutrality, since the judge need not make any premature decisions about a matter.

Substantive rules of law have a direct application to results. A variety of issues arise. Which rules of law are relevant? What do they mandate, if anything, in the particular case? How are they to be applied consistently with what has occurred in prior similar cases? What if they do not clearly cover the issue in dispute: is reference made, or should it be, to analogous rules, to underlying principles of law, to the public interest, to morality, to justice, or to yet other factors? Do the results the rules produce accord with community notions of morality and justice? To what extent do and should courts develop new rules?

What actually determines the judicial response to these issues does not necessarily coincide with what judges say are the relevant considerations. A judge's background and values, social needs, public policy, general legal values and specific legal doctrines blend in a complex mix. The issue has given rise to considerable jurisprudential discussion; it is beyond the scope of the present inquiry. The point to highlight is that there is a significant element of choice in judicial decision-making. The distinction between the literal and purposive interpretation of legislation—what the language says or what it was intended to accomplish when drafted—masks, rather than illuminates, this truth. Language is open-textured, and there is always some scope for discretion in its interpretation. What is said to be a literal interpretation is often heavy laden with policy choices, albeit downplayed or concealed. In any event, the literalist is making a choice to downgrade the policies underlying legislation in favour of its terms.

The facts of a case, previous decisions and, when relevant, legislation, are still the meat of Australian judicial decisions. As regards legislation, the Federal Parliament has indicated that the courts should prefer a construction which will promote the purpose or object underlying an Act, whether or not that purpose or object is expressly stated therein.[58] In any event, courts are giving some emphasis to the policy considerations in decisions.[59] Risk-spreading through insurance has featured in negligence cases; freedom of consultation in legal professional privilege cases; and access to justice in cases dealing with standing.[60]

Indeed most Australian judges now acknowledge that they have some role in making law, although they say that this is within the confines of extending established principles by means of inference, deduction and analogy. An account of this approach was given in a paper read to a conference of judges by Sir Frank Kitto, a justice of the High Court between 1950 and 1970:

I would certainly include in the proper function of the Judge the right and duty to give effect as existing law to such developments of the case law as principles already enunciated by the Courts imply or justify by reason of their inherent capacity for extension by logical processes, including in those processes not only inference and deduction but also analogy where analogy is sound. I am inclined to think that if you put it in some such way as that—limiting judicial development of the law to development by applied logic from *within* principles already established, and therefore excluding as impermissible purported developments (they really ought to be called alterations) fastened onto existing law by the Judge who thinks that his God-given understanding of justice tells him infallibly what the law ought to be and that he needs no other justification for asserting that that is what the law is—you may find a reconciliation between the old-fashioned, over-terse proposition that the Judge applies the law and does not make it and the proposition, nearer the truth but still not exact, that the Judge has a law-making function.[61]

Few Australian judges go as far as Mr Justice Kirby, President of the Court of Appeal of New South Wales, who has criticized the absence of judicial activism in Australia. His view seems to be that precedents ought to be examined carefully so that justice is achieved in particular cases and that the policy behind legislation ought to be wholeheartedly implemented.[62] Of course judges deny suggestions that wider political and economic factors influence their decisions.[63]

A consequence of the dominant view is the judicial belief that if the law is settled, judges ought to apply it even if the particular results are undesirable. Change in such circumstances must come from Parliament, possibly at the initiative of law reform bodies, but not from the courts. Mr Justice Mason has put the reasons for this as follows:

I do not doubt that there are some cases in which an ultimate court of appeal can and should vary or modify what has been thought to be a settled rule or principle of the common law on the ground that it is ill-adapted to modern circumstances. If it should emerge that a specific common law rule was based on the existence of particular conditions or circumstances, whether social or economic, and that they have undergone a radical change, then in a simple or clear case the court may be justified in moulding the rule to meet the new conditions and circumstances. But there are very powerful reasons why the court should be reluctant to engage in such an exercise. The court is neither a legislature nor a law reform agency. Its responsibility is to decide cases by applying the law to the facts as found. The court's facilities, techniques and procedures are adapted to that responsibility; they are not adapted to legislative functions or to law reform activities.[64]

This approach is consistent with those who believe in the supremacy of politics in our society. However, a view with wide appeal, especially in legal academic circles, is that judges ought to be more active in changing settled law. A justification for this is said to be that Parliament is increasingly paralysed by an institutional inability to cope with change.[65] The evidence for this is tenuous. In any event, advocates of judicial activism fail to specify in detail the respective spheres of judicial and parliamentary action in a democratic society.[66]

IV   OUTPUTS

That legal maxims hunt in pairs is neatly illustrated in relation to remedies: *ubi jus ibi remedium* (where there is a right, there is a remedy), as opposed to *ubi remedium ibi jus* (where there is a remedy, there is a right). Whatever the truth of the matter historically, it is certainly the case that the law relating to remedies has a profound influence on what the civil courts can do. Two issues are discussed here: first, the outcome of cases for the parties involved, and second, whether those outcomes have an impact on wider social behaviour.

Outcomes

Various outcomes of civil cases have already been alluded to— settlements, discontinuances, consent orders, default judgments, summary judgments and judgments after trial. The remedies granted by civil courts range from declarations as to what the law is, through money awards (liquidated and unliquidated damages), to specific orders such as injunctions, specific performance, company liquidation and custody orders. The grant of specific orders such as injunctions is hedged with limitations, however, and overall the range of court orders is more limited than that of legislation. Typically, Australian civil courts have only a limited concern with the parties before them, unlike, say, some children's courts or the courts in totalitarian societies, where a case provides an avenue for the examination of a person's larger personality and behaviour.

   Court orders typically decide that one party is legally right and the other legally wrong. Compromise is not acceptable, even though it might be in keeping with community views of doing justice, or conducive to resolving the social disputes underlying litigation. The issue arises in an acute form when two parties are adversely affected by the fraud of a third party, who disappears or is unable to pay compensation to the person suffering the loss. Both parties might be innocent or both might share some responsibility for the fraud having occurred. Yet the courts do not formally divide the loss according to the justice of the case but decide the issue in black and white terms. As Mr Justice Mahoney of the New South Wales Supreme Court has put it:

It has been said that a system of law must provide remedies against unjust enrichment or unjust benefit in the sense of preventing a person retaining money or benefits derived from another which it is against conscience that he should keep... This does not mean that the intuitions of the judicial conscience, or even those of the commentators, are to be treated as a Kantian end in themselves. "Justice and merits" do not (at least in the great number of cases coming before an appellate court) provide a principle the application of which will indicate who should succeed... Many of such cases involve, not a choice between parties having unequal merits, but a determination of which of innocent parties is to bear the injustice created by the fraud of a third. What is indicated by such formulations is that, in deciding cases, the court is to be guided by the substance of matters and not by nice distinctions.[67]

In a decision in 1978, the then Chief Justice of South Australia (Dr Bray) considered that any change in such matters was for the legislature: 'We cannot do that of our own motion without usurping legislative power.'[68] In fact legislation has provided for an apportionment of loss in some cases, most notably with contributory negligence.[69] Prior to the relevant legislation, a plaintiff who was negligent was barred completely from recovering against a negligent defendant, but now the courts need only reduce the damages recoverable to the extent thought just and equitable given the plaintiff's share in the responsibility for the accident. Similar adjustments may occur in some small claims courts, which are empowered to decide according to what is just and equitable in the circumstances.[70]

Australian civil courts might be characterized as plaintiffs' courts, in that the majority of parties instituting action are successful. In the survey of cases commenced between 1977–80 in the Supreme Courts of New South Wales, Victoria and the ACT, of the outcomes recorded, including settlements, the great majority favoured plaintiffs and the chances of a defendant prevailing appeared relatively slight—about 20 per cent in New South Wales and about 10 per cent in Victoria and the ACT. Perhaps this should not be surprising when so many matters proceed to default judgment. Moreover, it seems a reasonable assumption that most plaintiffs act rationally and have calculated that they are likely to succeed before they institute legal action. However, just because a plaintiff succeeds does not mean that the defendant has lost. Typically, for the purposes of settlement negotiations, plaintiffs claim for more than they know they will obtain, and defendants deny liability whatever their real views. The final result in which the plaintiff ostensibly succeeds might be closer to what the defendant, rather than the plaintiff, really wanted all along.

Because plaintiffs are very successful overall in obtaining relief, courts authorize the transfer of considerable sums of money. However, individual parties do not necessarily recover substantial amounts when money awards are obtained through settlement or judgment. In very few cases in the survey mentioned did recoveries exceed $100 000, and most of these were in New South Wales. Even then they represented no more than 10 per cent of the total number of cases where an outcome involving money was recorded. There were recoveries in the survey exceeding a million dollars, but these were rare. Moreover, significant numbers of these recoveries in the higher courts seem to fall below the upper jurisdictional limit of the lower courts. Cost penalties in the rules of court are supposed to deter parties from commencing actions in higher courts if the amount sought falls within the monetary limit of the lower court. But parties might think other factors more important, such as the form of relief, the need to impress the other side with the seriousness of a case, what they perceive to be the quality of the judges, and the nature of enforcement procedures. This is especially the case since most matters are settled, and the issue of costs does not loom as large when cases are settled as when they are tried. In any event, lawyers might obtain an indemnity from their clients to cover the cost of proceeding in the higher court.[71]

The binding quality of court decisions derives partly from the standing which courts have in society. Many parties obey the decision of a court, whether or not they agree with it, because it issues from an institution with such authority, and thus there is no need for enforcement action. However, the binding quality of court decisions might involve an element of coercion. In some cases parties might seek to have judgment executed by obtaining the appropriate order, for example, a writ of possession, a levy of property, an attachment of wages, or a charging order. Often, an order for execution is obtained *in terrorem* (as a warning), so that court officials need never implement it, since subsequently the property is transferred, the sum of money paid, or other appropriate action taken. Sometimes coercion is necessary, however, because of evasion or defiance of a court order. Well publicized is the family law area, where the extent of non-compliance with maintenance orders is high. Enforcing judgment generally requires a party to approach the court afresh and might even involve him/her in further litigation. This creates problems in areas such as domestic violence. A woman might obtain an injunction which supposedly restrains a man from assaulting her, but if he breaches it she must negotiate the hurdles of seeking an order against him for contempt of court. Legislation in some jurisdictions attempts to overcome this problem by providing that breach of such an order is an arrestable offence.[72] Even if a party succeeds in a particular case, that success might be undermined because of some other action by the other party.

Social impact

There are many conceptual problems in assessing the social impact of judicial decisions, as opposed to the outcomes for particular litigants. These parallel those already outlined in the previous chapter in relation to the impact of legislation.[73] What can be said is that, as a practical matter, a relatively small number of the cases decided in the civil courts have a significant impact on public policy. They touch important areas of the political process, determine major civil liberties issues, result in the delay or abandonment of major developments, or dispose of economic prizes or burdens. Constitutional decisions of the High Court provide some examples: the 1948 bank nationalization case[74] prevented the Chifley government nationalizing the private banks; the 1951 Communist Party case[75] held that it was unconstitutional for the Menzies government to ban that party; and the 1983 Tasmanian dam case[76] provided the constitutional basis for the Hawke government to halt the construction of the Franklin dam in south-west Tasmania. In addition, a series of cases in areas such as the excise power of the constitution have influenced the approach of Australian governments to important economic issues such as revenue raising. In the non-constitutional area, decisions of the High Court on tax legislation have a significant impact on public policy. For example, the interpretation of tax legislation by the court under Chief Justice Barwick favoured artificial tax avoidance schemes, thus undermining the equity, efficiency and simplicity of the tax system.[77]

In other areas of public law the influence of judicial decisions is usually less dramatic and pervasive. Judicial review of administrative action provides an example. There are relatively few applications for judicial review to begin with. Many of these are unsuccessful, thus upholding, possibly reinforcing, government policy. Even if successful, the particular applicants might not succeed when the matter is administratively redetermined, and other applicants in a similar position might be thwarted by changes in procedure.[78] Nonetheless, decisions sometimes have effects beyond their particular circumstances. In the public sector, the manner in which the Federal Court has interpreted the doctrine of natural justice (as incorporated in the *Administrative Decisions (Judicial Review) Act* 1977) has influenced the procedures followed in relation to promotions in the Australian public service.[79] The decisions of the Federal Court and more particularly, the Administrative Appeals Tribunal, have brought about specific changes in the administration of the *Social Security Act* 1947. For instance, AAT decisions relating to invalid pensions led to the establishment of a task force, which drew up new guidelines under which the role of social workers in assessment was upgraded. A simple example of public law affecting behaviour in the private sector is the response to decisions of the High Court on taxation. Once particular tax avoidance measures have been sanctioned, many taxpayers will structure their affairs to reap the advantage (if they have not done so previously).

It is difficult to identify a large number of single private law decisions which have had a significant impact on social behaviour. Despite the attention lavished on private law decisions by lawyers, they do not have the same dramatic social consequences as much legislation, even though the latter might be rarely, if ever, litigated.[80] For example, the establishment of small claims courts has been of far greater social importance than particular cases on contract, although it is the latter which feature in the contract books and law school teaching. Similarly, town planning legislation has been more influential than decisions on the law of nuisance, and consumer credit legislation than decisions on the sale of goods. Perhaps this limited impact is not surprising when the implications of particular private law cases are not obvious to most members of the community.[81] Moreover, case law is generally not a powerful factor in constituting economic and social relations when compared with other factors, notably community mores and the drive for profits. For example, in 1982 Alcoa of Australia Ltd faced an important challenge to the establishment of an aluminium smelter at Portland, Victoria.[82] But the key to whether the smelter went ahead was not the threat of an adverse decision—the Victorian government could always frustrate the litigation by legislation—but economic viability, in particular, the price of electricity.

This is not to deny that some particular private law cases have an effect on behaviour in the wider community. For instance, premiums for compulsory third-party motor vehicle insurance would probably have risen in New South Wales if the High Court decision in *Todorovic v. Waller*[83] had not been statutorily reversed. After decisions such as *O'Dea v. Allstates Leasing System (WA) Pty Ltd*,[84] finance companies are likely to redraft their standard form contracts so as to increase the chances of their remedies against customers being upheld (in that case, by ensuring that any sum payable on termination by the customer is not regarded as being payable on breach and therefore is not a penalty). In *Shaddock L & Associates Pty Ltd v. Parramatta City Council*,[85] the High Court held that the council was liable for the loss sustained by the plaintiffs when they relied on erroneous information it supplied about a road widening proposal. The upshot was that the Commonwealth Public Service Board advised departments and statutory authorities that it might be possible to avoid such liability by indicating that, while all care was taken in providing information or advice, no responsibility was accepted.[86]

A cluster of cases, or repeated litigation, in an area of private law might have greater social significance. The whole complex of contract law, say, has had an effect on the way contracts are negotiated and implemented. A series of tort cases 'opened the floodgates' to persons injured in motor vehicle and industrial accidents, allowing them to obtain compensation through litigation. As a result, what is effectively a social welfare function is performed by the courts, rather than a government agency, because of favourable doctrinal developments and the growth of private insurance. However, it is extremely doubtful whether liability rules have had any deterrent effect on the way people drive or work, compared with the influences of road traffic penalties and health and safety at work legislation.[87] On the other hand, the way damages are assessed in such cases—generously or otherwise—might affect the level of premiums payable by motorists and employers to insure against liability. Still in the area of tort law, it is said that Australian defamation law greatly inhibits investigative journalism.[88] The proposition is dubious when many areas ripe for investigative journalism, but in which defamation is irrelevant, go unexplored. And there are whole areas of economic and social life—education, transport, the arts, and so on—where private law is largely irrelevant.

As well as social factors, the courts' own institutional limitations might cause them to have little impact. For example, courts rely on the executive to enforce judgments and to punish those in contempt of its orders. They might also have a limited impact because their decisions are undermined, either directly or indirectly. There have been some blatant examples of administrative action of this character. Following the decision in 1977 in *Green v. Daniels*,[89] in which the High Court granted a declaration to the effect that a school-leaver was entitled to unemployment benefits from the time she had left school, the Director-General of Social Security held that she was ineligible on other grounds and also refused to re-open the cases of other school-leavers who had been rejected on the grounds ruled to be unlawful. Investigations by the Commonwealth Ombudsman, protracted by the Director-General's obduracy, and an adverse report by the former to the Prime Minister under the *Ombudsman Act* 1976, finally led to *ex gratia* payments being made to a few of the school-leavers affected.[90]

A more dramatic factor is legislation which reverses the decisions of courts. Where the financial consequences of their decisions are significant, for example in damages for personal-injury claims, the legislature might act relatively quickly to overturn them. For instance, in 1984 the New South Wales Government responded to the upward trend in damages awarded to those injured in motor vehicle accidents by legislating to limit the manner in which the courts assess certain heads of damages.[91] Underlying its action was the desire to cut the premiums payable by motorists for third-party insurance, a politically sensitive issue. Legislative reversal may be especially swift if government revenue is directly threatened. Federal Parliament quickly overturned the effect of the *Green v. Daniels* decision, mentioned above, on the future payment of unemployment benefit to school leavers.[92] The Government introduced amending legislation within three months of a High Court decision suggesting that, under the relevant Act, a veteran's pension could not be refused just because there was no evidence linking a claimed disability (or death) to eligible service.[93] The *National Health Act* 1953 was amended in 1983 to stem any increase in government expenditure as a result of a number of decisions regarding the determination of fees for nursing homes.[94]

Without such financial incentives spurring them to action, however, governments are usually more dilatory about introducing legislation to reverse the effect of judicial decisions. For example, in 1947 the House of Lords held that farmers cannot be liable in negligence if their animals stray onto a road and cause an accident.[95] Considerable criticism of the decision followed on the basis that it was inappropriate in societies with heavy, fast-moving traffic on the roads. Yet New South Wales was the first Australian State to abrogate the rule, in 1977, although possibly some States did not act because the rule was thought not to apply in Australia.[96] Much depends on whether the government or a relevant minister is sympathetic to changing the law. A New South Wales Labor Government was quick to abrogate a High Court decision which held that contributory negligence was a defence to an action for breach of statutory duty—an action often relied on by workers seeking compensation for industrial accidents.[97] New South Wales, South Australian and Tasmanian Labor governments eventually modified the effect of a House of Lords decision, *Lister v. Romford Ice & Cold Storage Co. Ltd.*[98] That case has the effect that if a person is injured as a result of the negligence of an employee, and successfully sues the employer on the basis of its vicarious liability, the latter (or its insurance company) can indemnify itself by suing the employee. The result is to render the insurance policy of no practical effect in such cases, with the employee having to pay any damages personally. The time which elapses before the effect of a decision, or body of decisions, is reversed may be compounded if a matter is referred to a law reform body for comment and recommendation. It may be that some governments have taken this course with a view to delaying controversial legislation.

A final point to make in this regard is that the courts might be able to limit legislative reversal of their decisions by their interpretation of the relevant legislation or the application of other common law doctrines. In other words, judicial decisions and legislation might be part of a continuing process, adjusted by the judges or by government as a response to each other.

V CONCLUSION

Concentrating on trouble or hard cases misses much of the process of Australian civil courts. In many respects, the courts are functioning as administrative agencies or as facilitators of compromises rather than directly resolving contested issues of law and fact. Even if the concern is hard or trouble cases, it would seem crucial to understand how they come before the relevant court for decision. The use of disputes as an organizing category for understanding courts overlooks important aspects such as their role in law-making, social control and the assertion of public values. In addition, there are the many occasions when parties approach courts to obtain the imprimatur of the state in relation to a matter, without any suggestion that there is a dispute, or even a potential dispute, involved therein. While civil courts are part of the political process, most litigation is oriented to the claims of individuals and organizations, far removed from what is ordinarily obtainable, under existing arrangements, through the political process. Courts are institutions of the state through which power can be asserted or confirmed: but so long as individuals continue to advance so many claims through the courts, in particular with accident litigation, it is difficult to argue that the courts are solely, or even predominantly, concerned with ratifying the legal claims of dominant groups in society. And given the limited impact of liability rules on behaviour, it seems beside the point to concentrate attention on the efficiency of those rules.

By contrast, the approach to courts adopted in this chapter provides a framework for understanding their internal operation, as well as their relationship with public policy. It lays a tentative basis for formulating theories about matters such as how legal procedures operate and the functions of law. Take just a few of the issues touched on above. First, there is the uneven use of Australian courts in terms of who brings cases and over what issues. How else are grievances dealt with in Australia, how is conflict channelled, and how are challenges to basic structures filtered so that the courts rarely deal with them? Second, there are many cases before Australian civil courts where commercial and property interests obtain judgment in default against individuals. How is it possible to talk about the latter having legal rights if those rights do not govern what actually happens? Third, the transformation of issues, and the identification of the legally relevant, raise questions about power, in particular about how the understanding and interpretation of events takes place in a legal context. Finally, there is the role of Australian courts in public policy. Compared with parliaments which can work through the executive arm of the state, it seems that Australian courts are generally marginal in this regard. An important exception is the role of the High Court in some constitutional matters. Otherwise, even if the outcomes in particular cases have ramifications for society, these can be reversed in many cases by legislation, as has occurred with certain of the High Court's interpretations of tax legislation.

CHAPTER THREE

GOVERNMENT

Law performs various roles in relation to government. First, it underpins a society's theory of government. That theory might not be given a complete expression in law, but the two should not be too sharply inconsistent, because otherwise the legitimacy of the system as a whole comes into question. Inasmuch as the theory is given legal expression, it might still not be justiciable. Nonetheless, that does not affect its legal character; justiciability might be a sufficient, but is not a necessary, condition for the existence of law. Second, law lays down, in specific terms, the structure of government. The latter involves matters such as the relations between different levels of government and between different institutions of government at the same level. The law relating to the structure of government might be set out in a written constitution, in legislation, in case law or in convention. Again, it might not always be justiciable. Third, law provides rules for the conduct of the political and governmental process. These rules perform the fundamental function of ensuring the continued legitimacy of the system of government.

The present chapter examines aspects of these three issues. At the outset, there is discussion of the theory of responsible and representative government. In particular, the issue of government accountability is examined. How do law and the legal system make those exercising government power theoretically accountable, and how effective are they in practice? Then the chapter turns to how law structures government power in the federal system. There is also a study of constitutional conventions and how these structured the relations between the Governor-General and the Government, and between the two houses of the Federal Parliament, in the events surrounding the dismissal of the Whitlam Government in 1975. Finally, we come to the function of law in guaranteeing the integrity of the political and governmental process. The main focus here is on the rules which attempt to minimize conflicts of interest on the part of the political and permanent officials of government.

I GOVERNMENT ACCOUNTABILITY

The theory of government in Australia is of governments being both responsible and representive—responsible, in that the executive government is accountable to the parliament, and representative, in that a sovereign parliament is elected by the people. Law says something about both principles, although they are not necessarily justiciable. While not mentioned directly in the Australian constitution,[1] the principle of responsible government is said by the High Court to permeate it.[2] As we shall see, the federal system means that the Australian Parliament is sovereign in some areas only, with the States being sovereign in others. Although there is nothing in the Australian constitution about it, the High Court has with general acceptance taken to itself the function of defining those areas. Moreover, the power of the Senate in relation to supply means that the executive government of the Commonwealth is answerable not only to the more representative of the two houses of Federal Parliament. The Australian constitution says more about representative government, at least for the national Parliament. The House of Representatives, says section 24, shall be composed of members directly chosen by the people, while the Senate, in accordance with section 7, is directly chosen by the people of a State voting (until Parliament otherwise provides) as one electorate.

In recent times, there has been considerable discussion of the degree of accountability implied by the theory of responsible and representative government. Growth in its size and powers are said to have led to unaccountable government. Law, it is continued, has a significant part to play in calling government to account through the courts and other forms of external review (especially in the guise of the new administrative law).[3] My personal view is that governments are as accountable as they have ever been, and probably more so than the other institutions and centres of power in society. But if the premise be accepted, how efficacious are the commonly espoused legal remedies? And, just as important, how consistent are they with the theory of responsible and representative government?

Political accountability

The lines of political accountability in a system of responsible and representative government run from the permanent officials of government, to ministers (these acting on behalf of the ministry), to the

Parliament, and finally to the electors.[4] Law plays some part in under-pinning these lines of accountability.

In terms of the accountability of Parliament to the people, legislation provides machinery for establishing electoral boundaries, defines the qualifications of voters and requirements for candidates, details how elections are to be conducted, and sets up courts of disputed returns in the event of disputed elections and other matters. There is a blemish on representative government, in that the principle of 'one vote, one value' is not well enshrined in all jurisdictions, although legislation in some goes a way to ensuring that the decisions of independent electoral com-missions on electoral boundaries are not overturned for immediate party political advantage.[5] In recent years both the Commonwealth and New South Wales have legislated for the public funding of elections, and for disclosure of campaign contributions, mainly because of the escalating costs of elections (notably, of television advertising) but also to minimize corrupting influences and to guarantee fairness between the major political parties.[6]

In the Federal sphere, the accountability of executive government to parliament is based on various sections of the constitution: ministers must sit in Parliament (s.64), there must be parliamentary authorization of spending (ss.81, 83), and taxation and appropriation legislation must originate in the House of Representatives (so that any ministry must have the support of that body—s.53).[7] In addition, the executive government is generally required by legislation to table delegated legislation made by it and often prepares annual reports on its specific activities. Parliamentary investigation of executive government, through the committee system, is supported by the contempt power and by statutory provisions. Ultimately, ministers and officials of the executive can be punished for not attending as witnesses, although as a practical matter little can be done if ministers decline to co-operate or officials refuse to answer on what they say are political matters.[8] Finally, the courts reinforce the accountability of the executive inasmuch as they require it to act in accordance with statutory law. A specific aspect of this principle arose in several Australian cases involving land and mining leases. These established that a minister cannot bind himself in advance regarding the disposal of such leases but must act in accordance with the relevant statutory steps.[9]

The law is less helpful regarding the accountability of the permanent officials of government to ministers and hence the ministry. Statute law is quite general: the Commonwealth *Public Service Act 1922* states that the secretary of a department 'shall under the minister be responsible for its general working, and for all the business thereof, and shall advise the minister on all matters relating to the department'.[10] Moreover, the responsibility of secretaries is exercised within the framework of the

Australian constitution, section 64 of which provides that ministers are appointed to administer departments. Consequently, and subject to statute, ministers may decide what work a department shall do, may authorize it to shed or reduce particular responsibilities, and can generally direct and control it in the performance of its functions.[11]

Recognizing administrative necessity, the courts have said that ministers can delegate power to officers of their department, although it is specifically entrusted to them under statute.[12] In exercising it the officers are bound by government policy and any directions of the minister. Ministerial direction cannot, of course, authorize a breach of the law.[13] It is sometimes said that a minister cannot revise or overturn the decision of a delegate unless statutorily authorized or in the case of irregularity.[14] But as a matter of principle, such action is purely an intra-governmental concern in which the courts have no business. The position may be different where the person affected by the decision has been informed, for then an estoppel may have occurred and the person may have acquired legal rights.

So far, reasonably good. But some seem to think that once an officer is entrusted with an independent discretion by statute or regulations, the ground rules change. While acknowledging that the officer can take government policy or a ministerial direction into account, they take the view that unless the officer decides the matter him- or herself, rather than merely acting on the policy or direction, the decision is 'infected' and subject to judicial review.[15] The contrary approach—that the vesting of discretion in an official does not give the official the power to ignore government policy or a ministerial direction,[16] just as under our theory of government the vesting of discretion in the Governor-General does not mean that the Governor-General acts without advice—is the only one consistent with both the history of government in Australia and the principles of responsible and representative government. As to the former: in Australia it has been a matter of political and administrative expediency, rather than of deliberate policy, whether discretions have been entrusted to ministers or officers.[17] As to the latter: if officials can act inconsistently with government policy or ministerial directions, to whom or what are they accountable? To say 'to the law', if this means the courts, begs the question, as we will see in the next section. Only if ministers, on behalf of the ministry, have the last word, and only if they are answerable politically, can the acts of government be brought to book in an orderly fashion.

Despite blemishes, the theory of responsible and representative government generally produces acceptable results in the Australian context. The lines of political accountability implied by the theory give governments adequate power to govern, while still making them answerable to Parliament and the public on a regular basis. That there are other avenues of accountability does not amount to an alternative theory of government. For example, the press has a part to play in furthering accountability, but as presently constituted cannot form the basis of a system of accountability. The press is unaccountable to other than itself, it is chameleon in character, sections of it encourage unduly the unlawful leaking of information, and important outlets discount any public interests in favour of the so-called 'right' to know whatever they want to publish.

Neither federalism, the absence of any strong tradition of individual ministerial responsibility, nor the reality of political parties, significantly blurs the lines of accountability. In practical terms, for example, an ordinary person might approach the local member of Parliament—of whatever political party—who raises the matter with the appropriate minister, who in turn passes it on to the department. If the response is unsatisfactory, the member can take the rarely used course of raising the matter in Parliament or with the media. Although there is no systematic research, local members of Parliament are probably quite effective.[18] Admittedly more powerful persons and groups usually have an advantage by approaching the minister or department directly, often with the assistance of lobbyists.

But it is not the purpose here to assess the health of responsible and representative government in Australia. Suffice is to say that the critics' assumptions are in many respects exaggerated. Latham CJ echoed a common view when he referred to 'the idea of substituting for law the administrative absolutism of officials'.[19] Senior officials do have great power, but to suggest that they always, or even mainly, exercise it absolutely ignores a number of factors including the political constraints, the scrutiny of the media, departmental rivalry, the forces of business, labour and other large interest groups, and any sense of obligation to respect the rights and opinions of the electorate.[20] None of this is to endorse the *status quo* in relation to political institutions or to suggest that problems, say, of the accountability of officials to ministers, especially those in statutory authorities and non-departmental agencies, do not exist. Parliamentary procedures, committees, and facilities can be improved and government administration made more accountable through internal mechanisms and restructuring.[21] Law has a role in this, to which we will return. First, however, it is appropriate to examine the role of the legal system as source of accountability.

Role of the courts

What is the role of the courts in the accountability of government? Historically, Australian courts have reviewed government and local government decisions on grounds such as the non-observance of natural justice, *ultra vires*, and jurisdictional error.[22] To do so they have often distorted, or ignored, the clearest parliamentary intention that they should not do so, as contained in a privative (exclusion) clause. The grounds of review have a deceptive universality, although their application varies with the administrative context.[23] Perhaps it would be more realistic to consider judicial review in different contexts, for example, regulation, benefit distribution and internal governmental management. The difficulty with this approach, however, is how to draw the boundaries of the particular contexts in any intellectually satisfying way. For example, it is likely that the principles in the area of benefit distribution will vary depending on whether industry subsidies or social welfare benefits are at stake, if only because the contexts are so different.

Judicial review of administrative action, as in England, is supposedly concerned with procedural matters, rather than the merits of particular decisions.[24] In practice, however, the courts inevitably began to touch on the latter once they developed grounds of review such as acting for an improper purpose; taking into account irrelevant considerations; failing to take into account relevant considerations; and unreasonableness. For determining proper purpose and relevant considerations in relation to legislation can come, says the present High Court, not only from enumerated provisions, but also 'from a construction of the Act read as a whole', 'by reason of the general character of the statute', or 'as a result of implications which may be drawn from the subject matter dealt with'.[25] The view of Latham CJ in 1945, that if no purposes are expressed, the courts cannot interfere on the basis of improper purpose, has long since been abandoned.[26] So, too, it seems has Sir Owen Dixon's caution, that where no limits are expressed in a statute, the legitimate considerations for its exercise must always be open to wide differences of opinion.[27] When we come to a doctrine like unreasonableness—that a decision can be upset if no reasonable person or body could have made it[28]—it becomes patent that judicial review of administrative action is much more than a branch of statutory interpretation, more a mode of intervention based on judge-made law.

What is the justification for the role which the courts have assumed in this area? To suggest, as is sometimes done, that the courts are simply ensuring compliance with the rule of law is too facile if intervention is based on doctrines which the courts themselves have created. There may be a case for saying that the courts can review on the basis of simple *ultra vires*—that the decision was not authorized by the legislation under which it was purportedly made. There may even be a case for saying that where the legislation explicitly lays down the considerations or purposes which should inform the exercise of a discretion, the courts should intervene on the basis of relevant considerations or improper purpose. In both situations the justification would be that the courts are simply giving effect to the legislation.

But giving effect to the legislation cannot adequately explain the course of much judicial review of administrative action. It is often more profitable to concentrate on what the courts do than what they say, since concepts are bent to fit the occasion.[29] In recent times the High Court has given as justification for wide review the need for a substitute for, or at least a supplement to, the system of ministerial responsibility which, it is asserted, is inadequate.[30] Even if the premise is accepted, there is still no automatic justification for judicial review of administrative action. First, there is the fundamental issue of the legitimacy of judicial power in a democratic society. Some would brush this aside by redefining democracy:

Democracy, whatever else it means, means that *no one person or body should have absolute power* in a society. To achieve this we need not adopt a rigid 'separation of powers'; it is enough that power be pragmatically distributed among a number of institutions, each able to check and cajole the others... This model of pragmatic interaction among different institutions, and not the model of a 'pyramid' with one institution or another 'on top', is the proper model for the relationship of parliament and courts.[31]

So much for the traditions of representative and responsible government, in which those elected by the people have sovereign power, subject to the Australian constitution. It is not to the point to invoke United States analogues: their complicated, Madisonian interplay between institutions of a majoritarian and non-majoritarian character are grounded in quite different historical and social foundations.[32]

Then there is the issue of institutional competence. One aspect is that of relative competence. Administrators can develop an expertise in, and detailed overview of, an area, which the courts cannot have. Yet rarely do the latter defer to these, or acknowledge the delicate balance between the need to protect individual interests on the one hand with the need for effective administration on the other.[33] Another aspect has to do with the courts themselves. Just how they are supposed to function as other than a very exceptional avenue for redress is difficult to fathom. Since judicial review can only be given by superior courts, there is the obvious barrier of cost. It is not surprising that the incidence of applications for judicial review of social security decisions has been low.[34] There is also the doctrinal barrier of standing, which restricts the categories of those who may seek redress. Moreover, historical accretions and technicalities give a lie to the aphorism that those with a right have a remedy. Legislation such as the Commonwealth *Administrative Decisions (Judicial Review) Act 1977* has been necessary to render obsolete the old learning associated with the remedies of *certiorari*, prohibition and mandamus.* Even so, compensation is rarely payable where persons have suffered loss as a result of government activity, although compensation is probably far more appropriate in most cases than simply negating a decision or ordering its reconsideration.[35]

Furthermore, there is the limited ambit in practice of judicial review. Taking a broad view, we might contend that judicial review has focused on the deployment of government force, rather than on the distribution of wealth through subsidies, pensions and government contracts.[36] As one author puts it (we need not endorse his conclusion):

The distribution of government largesse in the form of welfare payments, government contracts, or licences, has come to be regarded as the New Property. This challenges the assumption that administrative law is designed to protect rights in a traditional, purely private law sense. It produces a call for the extension of judicial review to such areas.[37]

The *Administrative Decisions (Judicial Review) Act* 1977, and the possibility of appeals on questions of law from the Administrative Appeals Tribunal, have meant greater scope for review of decisions in relation to government contracts and welfare payments respectively.[38] But clearly legislation was necessary to achieve this.

Finally, the issue of effectiveness arises. If courts overturn a decision, that might be all that the applicant desires. But if he or she wants a new decision, it is a matter of reapproaching the decision-maker, since the courts do not substitute their own for the original decision. Moreover, there is considerable scope for executive government to disregard the import of a judicial decision. For years after the High Court had held that Northern Territory regulations might be invalid because of their improper purpose of frustrating an Aboriginal land claim, the Northern Land Council was still seeking access to documents to prove its case.[39] In more general terms, judicial review is sporadic in terms of the total volume of decision-making, even in an area such as migration, which has been comparatively heavily litigated before the Federal Court and other courts.[40] Whether such litigation has had an impact on the quality of administration depends largely on anecdotal evidence. Since effective control over administration needs to be systematic and continuous, however, it would seem not to be great.

---

* *certiorari*—order quashing a decision of a person or body; prohibition—order prohibiting a person or body from doing, or continuing to do, something; mandamus—order commanding a body or person to perform a public duty

Furthering accountability

While the courts might not have a significant impact on government accountability, law in a more general sense has. Tribunals, ombudsmen and bureaucratic structuring can all contribute. There is no question of the legitimacy of these, for they derive from legislation or involve intra-governmental measures.

This is not the place for yet another outline of the 'new administrative law'. The major landmarks in the Commonwealth sphere are well known: the *Administrative Appeals Tribunal Act* 1975, the *Ombudsman Act* 1976, the *Administrative Decisions (Judicial Review) Act* 1977 and the *Freedom of Information Act* 1982. Perhaps a few remarks about the Administrative Appeals Tribunal (AAT) are in order. The AAT is a relatively high-level tribunal which hears appeals from decisions made by ministers, officials and statutory authorities under Commonwealth legislation. (Victoria has now followed suit by establishing an AAT.) Presided over by a Federal judge, it comprises judges, lawyers and other experts. Section 28(1) of the Act provides that a person affected by a decision may obtain reasons for it. Social security gives rise to the largest single volume of applications for review before the AAT, although a large number of these cases are settled before hearing.

By contrast with the courts, the AAT is empowered to reconsider the merits of a decision, and with a few exceptions, substitute its own for that originally made.[41] However, the Federal Court has held that in doing this the AAT is not bound to apply government policy if it determines that this does not produce the correct or preferable decision.[42] This approach misconceives the statutory mandate, which does not place the AAT at large, but puts it in the shoes of the original decision-maker. After all, under the Act the AAT can exercise 'all the powers and discretions' of the decision-maker only in the making of the decision. Now an analytical distinction can be drawn between formulating and applying policy. Therefore, in the making of a *decision* policy is simply applied; it cannot be questioned. But even if a wider view is taken on the statutory language, only if the original decision-maker can make policy can the AAT enter the policy area. As indicated earlier, as far as government policy determined at the political level is concerned, decision-makers are bound to implement it. It would only be if a decision were made by a minister, determined in accordance with policy he or she made, that the AAT could question the policy. At this point, however, prudence enters:[43] the AAT itself has appreciated the precarious position it would be in were it to adopt a cavalier approach to ministerial policy and generally has tended to regard itself bound by it.[44]

Conventional legal accounts eschew discussion of the impact of the 'new administrative law'. The various institutions function to redress the grievances of some individuals and groups, but how effective are they? In particular, to what extent are investigative and conciliatory procedures more effective than the adjudicative and adversary? Have the institutions had a preventive effect, improving the quality of primary decision-making? Hundreds of thousands of words have been spilt outlining the new administrative law, parsing this or that technicality or decision, but there is no systematic study of these fundamental questions.[45] There is some anecdotal evidence about the second. One welfare worker has claimed that the Department of Social Security has disregarded the reasoning of some decisions of the AAT.[46] Certainly it has sought legislative amendment to confirm its view on overpayments, as against that of the AAT. In some areas, however, the department has used AAT decisions as a basis for reformulating administrative guidelines, for example, for special benefits. Other departments have done likewise; for example, it seems that the AAT's review of criminal deportation appeals has led the government to reconsider and modify its policy and to reformulate it in clearer and more precise terms, which take greater account of the impact on individuals and their families.[47]

There are other ways that the law can further accountability. Legislation constitutes, and delineates, the functions of public service boards, auditors-general and inspectorates. Then there is the 'internal law' of administration, the manuals, procedures and norms which are primary determinants of decision-making. Accountability can be incorporated into them by intra-governmental measures so that it becomes part of the routine of administration. Limits are imposed by the subject-matter of administration and the nature of the clientele. Finally, there is the possibility of greater public participation in government administration.[48]

II THE STRUCTURE OF GOVERNMENT

The Australian constitution establishes the legal framework for government, indicating the respective powers of the Commonwealth and State governments, spelling out in varying degrees the nature and functions of the Federal Parliament, executive and judiciary, and providing a mechanism for constitutional change. Despite the constitution being in written form, attention must be given to a range of legislation, to judicial decisions, and to customary rules and practices to understand the full impact of the law in structuring Australian government. In its fullest sense, constitutional law involves the study of all these.

So, for example, English legislation such as the *Bill of Rights Act* 1689, which provides in one section that money cannot be levied for or to the use of government without parliamentary approval, forms part of Australia's constitutional heritage.[49] The High Court has constructed a body of constitutional jurisprudence, relating mainly to the Australian constitution, but also to matters such as the prerogative[50] and public interest immunity.[51] The Australian constitution says little about the system of government in the States; the latter requires a study of State legislation, case law and customary rules and practices.[52] The law governing the public sector is contained in legislation, from public service Acts to that constituting statutory authorities;[53] in case law, such as the law of negligence[54] and misconduct in public office;[55] in executive acts, such as the administrative arrangement orders which outline the responsibilities of departments of the Federal public service;[56] and in manuals, guidelines and codes, such as those setting down some of the conflict of interest rules referred to in part III of this chapter. A final example is the role of conventions, which are the unwritten rules of constitutional behaviour considered to be binding by and upon those who operate the constitution, although not legally enforceable.

This part contains a very limited sampling of topics, designed to show how law structures the operations of Australian government. To illustrate the part played by the Australian constitution, and its exegesis by the High Court, there is first, a section on federalism. The main theme of this section is that while law is the ultimate source of authority regarding the operation of the federal system, in important ways it has had only a marginal impact on how the federal system actually works. Then, secondly, there is a study of constitutional conventions, using as a case study the events surrounding the dismissal of the Whitlam government in 1975. Here we see the other side of the coin: in Australia, unless conventions are underwritten by law, they take a back seat to the exercise of political power and have little, if any, influence in times of constitutional crisis.

Federalism

By contrast with the United States, where individual rights are the focus of constitutional attention, in Australia federalism is central to the discussion of constitutional law. The nature and limits of, and prohibitions on, the Federal Government, and hence the interplay with State powers, are the meat of Australian constitutional decisions and literature. Their importance to the exercise of governmental power in Australia is obvious from a random selection of the issues raised before the High Court: the extent of Commonwealth power to protect the environment;[57] whether the Commonwealth can operate commercial enterprises and whether it can entrust these with a legal monopoly;[58] how far the Australian family courts can be empowered to deal with matters such as the custody of children;[59] the degree to which the Commonwealth can spend money on, and engage in activities relating to, areas which do not fall within its enumerated legislative power;[60] the validity of government-supported marketing schemes for primary products;[61] and the types of taxes which the States can exact.[62]

However important these issues might be, a study of constitutional law tells little about the dynamics of Australian government. Law sets boundaries to Federal government powers, yet their exercise has turned largely on other factors. Take the trends in constitutional adjudication whether, say, the High Court has favoured Federal over State power. The evidence is that these have not always, or even mainly, been matched by political, economic and administrative trends. Until the Engineers case[63] in 1920, the High Court pursued a policy of co-ordinate federalism, in which each level of government was regarded as co-ordinate and independent in its respective area.[64] Expression was given to this policy in the doctrine of the immunity of instrumentalities, in which neither the Commonwealth nor the States were treated as subordinate to each other when acting in their spheres of authority, except with concurrent legislation, when section 109 requires Commonwealth laws to prevail over State laws in cases of inconsistency; and in the doctrine of reserved powers, which was designed to ensure that the States had exclusive power over certain domestic affairs.[65] While the fiscal balance between Commonwealth and State governments in this area might have reflected the legal position, there was a considerable degree of co-operative federalism in the political and administrative spheres.[66] Typical was the River Murray Waters Agreement 1914, which settled a problem which seemed likely to lead to prolonged litigation between the relevant States.

Engineers in 1920 overturned the doctrines of implied immunities and reserved powers. Henceforth, said the High Court, the constitution should be read according to the ordinary rules of statutory construction without preconceptions about the type of federalism it envisages. With its notion that Commonwealth powers should be given a broad effect, irrespective of any impact on the States, *Engineers* permitted, as a matter of law, a form of coercive federalism, if this be defined as a system where decision-making powers are concentrated in the hands of the national government. The potential for coercive federalism was enhanced by another decision of the High Court, in 1926, regarding section 96 of the Australian constitution.[67] That section provides that the Commonwealth Parliament may grant financial assistance to any State on such terms and conditions as it thinks fit. In the 1926 decision, and subsequently, the High Court has held that the Commonwealth can require that financial assistance provided under the section be applied to a specific object, although the object is outside its powers; and can even circumvent express limitations on its powers.[68] Payments can be left to the discretion of a Commonwealth minister, a State can be obliged to contribute matching funds to receive assistance, and grants can be by way of repayable loan.

Financially, politically and administratively, however, the inter-war period was mainly one of co-operative federalism, illustrated by the co-operation between the Prime Minister and the State premiers during the 1930s in formulating budgetary and economic policies in response to the depression; and the establishment of bodies like the Agricultural Council, comprising Commonwealth and State representatives, to achieve uniform action, to co-ordinate policies and to exchange information.[69] There were exceptions. *Engineers* itself led to a powerful Federal body to deal with industrial matters, although this was largely independent of the Federal Government. The States had little choice but to concur with the Financial Agreement of 1927, and that led to the 'garnishee legislation' of the early 1930s. As a response to the depression, the New South Wales Labor Government under Lang deliberately defaulted on the payment of certain interest on its public debts. Commonwealth legislation, upheld by the High Court,[70] provided for seizure of State revenue along the lines of garnishee proceedings. While Lang was near the mark in his characterizing this as coercion,[71] it is difficult to uncover other incidents of coercive federalism in the inter-war period.

The Uniform Tax case[72] in 1942 meant that, in practice, the States were unable to levy income tax. Financially, it might be said that the decision ushered in an era of coercive federalism, in which the Commonwealth dominated the States by effectively excluding them from the most lucrative form of revenue raising, then determining their expenditure by making them specific-purpose grants. This interpretation recalls Latham CJ's remark in the Uniform Tax case, that the arrangements might be used to end the political independence of the States, but that such a result could not be prevented by legal decision.[73] Additional factors to be considered in Commonwealth financial supremacy in the post-war years are High Court decisions excluding the States from imposing many forms of indirect taxation, and the control which the Commonwealth was able to exercise over the Loan Council.

It is arguable whether the Uniform Tax case led to coercive federalism in the financial sphere. The uniform tax system enabled the Commonwealth Government to determine in large part the total amount the States would spend—would this ever have been significantly different from what the States themselves would have raised and spent?—but it did not mean that the Commonwealth determined how the money would be spent. After 1942, the Commonwealth made most of its payments to the States without attaching conditions under section 96.[74] Even at the height of what is alleged to be coercive federalism, the period of the Whitlam Government (1972–75), specific-purpose grants comprised only 51 per cent of payments to the States.[75] But even if it be conceded that the Uniform Tax case led, financially, to a period of coercive federalism, the post-war years seem to be better characterized in the political and administrative spheres as 'organic federalism'.[76] Inter-governmental co-operation was furthered by the establishment of bodies such as the Australian Forestry Council, the Australian Transport Advisory Council, the Australian Water Resources Council, the Fisheries Conference, the Australian Minerals Council and the Standing Commit-tee of Commonwealth and State Attorneys-General.[77] Governments enacted uniform legislation to achieve a common approach to problems of national significance; an example was the uniform companies legis-lation passed in 1961.[78] Complementary action attempted to achieve co-operatively what governments did not think they could do by themselves, the Offshore Petroleum Resources Agreement 1967 being a case in point.[79] Indeed, a co-operative approach followed despite the High Court, after it decided that the Commonwealth had exclusive power in Commonwealth places.[80]

The period of the Fraser government (1975–83) was initially characte-rized as one of co-operative federalism, in that the Commonwealth attempted to introduce joint planning, reduced conditions attached to financial grants to the States, and introduced tax-sharing arrangements. The substance of the 'new federalism', as it was called, need not detain us.[81] It can be argued that the crucial change produced by the 'new federalism' in financial relations was the limitation on payments to the States, in order to restrain public expenditure, rather than the changed form such relations took in the reduction of specific-purpose grants under section 96. From the point of view of the present discussion, the key issue is that the period of co-operative federalism was not paralleled by any shift in philosophy in the High Court. Indeed, co-operative federalism took a battering in *New South Wales v. Com-monwealth*,[82] where the High Court undermined the basis of the off-shore petroleum arrangements. Legislation was necessary, in the form of the *Coastal Waters (State Powers) Act* 1980, to restore the pre-existing arrangements.

The Tasmanian Dam case[83] in 1983 had the immediate and well-publicized effect of enabling the Commonwealth to prohibit, for en-vironmental reasons, the construction by the Tasmanian Hydro-Electric Commission of a dam in the south-western wilderness area of that state. The constitutional impact of the decision is considerable because of the wide view of Commonwealth powers taken by the majority of the High Court. The case expands, for instance, the interpretation of the cor-porations power and hence Commonwealth capacity to regulate areas of manufacture, mining and agriculture. Yet again there has been a considerable dissociation between constitutional law and the politics, finance and administration of Australian federalism. The credo of the Hawke Government (1983–) in this area is that organic is preferable to coercive federalism. Pragmatism and consensus govern many aspects of relations with the States as they do other aspects of government policy. Certainly Commonwealth power, conferred by the High Court in particular areas, is a backdrop to negotiations which the Commonwealth has with the States and might lead the latter to agree more readily to, say, measures such as the *Australia Act* 1986.[84] But when environmentalists advocated Commonwealth intervention in relation to road-building in the Daintree forest in north Queensland, the Federal Minister said: 'The Commonwealth cannot prevent all actions by State or local governments which result in damage to the environment. The situation in respect of South West Tasmania was special and unique'.[85]

Constitutional conventions

Conventions are a large part of British constitutional theory and practice. Conventions are said to explain the responsibilities of the major organs and officers of government and the relations between them—between the Cabinet and the Prime Minister, the Government as a whole and Parliament, the two houses of Parliament, and ministers and the civil service. Conventions, the argument goes, arise as a result of distinct agreement, a series of precedents, or possibly some acknowledged principle of government which provides a reason or justification. Conventions are obeyed, it is contended, because of the political difficulties which would follow if they were not, or because the disregard of conventions is likely to induce a change in the law or in the constitutional structure.[86]

Whatever their status in explaining the everyday working of the constitution in Britain, constitutional conventions in Australia have a more limited role. One reason is that many of what are conventions in Britain take a legal form in Australia. In addition, the existence and application of important conventions in the Australian context are uncertain. At a more fundamental level, it will be seen that the practice of politics in Australia is such that conventions do not determine behaviour precisely in those situations where they are supposed to be of greatest value. The lesson is, that if a constitutional convention is valued, it must be incorporated in law.

Many of what are regarded as constitutional conventions in Britain are either incorporated in the Australian constitution or are recognized in the decisions of the High Court. Take the role of the Crown. It is a fundamental principle that the Crown must act only on the advice of its ministers, except perhaps in limited circumstances. This is the basic principle that regulates the discretion of the Crown; it is inherent in day-to-day constitutional practice in both Australia and Britain. No longer does the Crown, as monarch or Governor-General, make policy; nor does it randomly select or dismiss its ministers. It must accept the policies of the Government, and indeed it must accept as the Government those members of Parliament who collectively can command a majority in the lower house. From the Crown's point of view 'responsible government' means government on the advice of a ministry that has parliamentary support.[87]

In Britain it is convention rather than law which fixes this principle. In Australia, however, the constitution expressly confers many executive powers upon the Governor-General-in-council, indicating that they can be exercised only on advice of the Federal Executive Council. As for other executive powers vested in the Governor-General, it is clear that the intention of the founders was that they should also be exercisable only on ministerial advice, except perhaps in the case of the reserve powers.[88] Nowadays, this is not simply a matter of convention, since members of the High Court have given recognition to the principle.[89]

The second and third points made in relation to conventions—their uncertainty and their subservience to politics—are illustrated by the events of 1975. A brief outline of the facts is in order.[90] In the weeks prior to 11 November 1975 a deadlock had developed between the two houses of the Australian Parliament. Various bills, including supply bills for implementing the Budget, had been passed in the House of Representatives where the Government had a majority but were blocked by the Senate, where the Opposition had control as a result of non-Labor States replacing with non-Labor senators a Labor senator who had resigned and another who had died. Both the Government and Opposition refused to give way, so that as the current supply came close to expiry, no solution to the deadlock was imminent. Finally on 11 November the Prime Minister, Mr Whitlam, met the Governor-General, Sir John Kerr, to advise an election for half the Senate in the hope that the Government would secure a majority. Without prior warning, the Governor-General dismissed the Prime Minister by withdrawing his commission. Almost immediately the leader of the Opposition, Mr Fraser, was commissioned to form a caretaker government on condition that he obtained supply and then advised an immediate double dissolution of Parliament. The Senate, at the initiative of the Opposition, passed supply; the House of Representatives retorted with a resolution of no confidence in the new government. Later in the afternoon the two houses were dissolved and the election on 13 December returned an overwhelming majority for Mr Fraser in both houses.

First, let us look at the filling of the casual Senate vacancies by the New South Wales and Queensland governments. Prior to these appointments, there was arguably a constitutional convention that States ought to fill casual vacancies by appointing the person chosen by the same political party as the senator who resigned or died. Until its amendment in 1977, the Australian constitution entrusted the decision to the relevant State

Parliament, but gave no indication of how the choice was to be made (section 15). However, in 1952, Western Australia having to fill a casual vacancy, its Premier, D.R. McLarty, wrote to the other premiers suggesting that 'a member of the same Party, nominated by the Executive of the Party, should be appointed when future vacancies arise through death or other causes'.[91] Most premiers agreed. All members of the Federal parliamentary Joint Committee on Constitutional Review in 1959 recommended that appointments to casual vacancies should be from the same political party. But it seemed not to recognize that there was an existing convention,[92] nor did Standing Committee D of the Australian Constitutional Convention in 1974.[93] However, in the great majority of the considerable number of cases between 1952 and 1975 casual vacancies were filled in the manner suggested in the McLarty letter.[94] On the whole, Sawer concludes, the practice went as close as one could reasonably ask to satisfying the various proposed tests for the existence of a convention.[95]

The second convention arguably breached was in deferral of supply by the Senate. There has been some argument about whether the Senate has the legal power to defer or reject supply.[96] The better view (the one most lawyers would endorse) is that it has,[97] but even if this is the case the question arises as to whether there was a convention that the Senate should not exercise any legal power it had to block supply. In October 1975, four professors at Australian law schools contended that there was such a convention. Their reasoning was that the convention was an essential part of responsible government in Australia—the House of Representatives is more representative of the people—and that otherwise there would be a gravely destabilizing factor in the parliamentary system. They continued that it was arguable that there would on occasions arise political circumstances of such an extraordinary kind as would conceivably justify the Senate's rejection of supply.[98] There was a similar assertion in a draft advice by the Solicitor-General of 4 November 1975. It appealed to precedent as the basis of the convention, in that the power had not before been exercised.[99] In fact, lack of use is probably insufficient to establish the convention, without evidence that there were occasions when the power could have been used to political advantage but was not by reason of a belief in the convention.[100]

As against these views in favour of the existence of a convention, Sir Garfield Barwick has said first, that there was no resolution or positive act of the Senate embodying the convention, and second, that such a convention could not exist because it would mean senators forgoing a power which 'should be available for the satisfaction of the electorate's requirements...a power held on behalf of the electorate as part of the democratic control of the executive government through the Parliament'.[101] Of the first point it need simply be said that the constitutional writing on the recognition of conventions would not require a resolution or positive act by the Senate. In relation to the second, it is inconsistent with the notion that the Senate is less representative than the House of Representatives, both because of the way it is chosen (States have equal representation) and the longer terms served by senators. It might also be noted that Barwick went on to say that it would be very rare that the Senate would exercise its power, which should be regarded as a power held in reserve to be used only on some very special occasions.[102] It is significant that, at the time, the Opposition did not deny the existence of a 'political practice' (they did not call it a convention) but said that extraordinary circumstances existed.[103]

Finally, there are the conventions said to have applied to the Governor-General himself. Under the Australian constitution, the Governor-General appoints ministers, who hold office at his pleasure (section 64). All sides concede that the power of dismissal exercisable under the latter section, a so called 'reserve power', is to be used only in exceptional circumstances.[104] The Governor-General justified his action on the principle that a government denied supply must resign or go to an election, since parliamentary control of appropriation and expenditure is fundamental. The principle applied, he argued, even though supply was being denied by the Senate, since the Senate is given the power by the constitution.[105] Even if these propositions be valid, it can be strongly argued that the Governor-General's action was premature.[106] In the present case, supply had not actually expired at the time of the dismissal and there might well have been some political resolution in the very near future.[107] Large amounts of appropriations are voted outside the appropriation and supply Acts, so that the Government could rely upon existing legislative authorization to carry on many of the functions of government. In addition, before his dismissal Mr Whitlam was also making arrangements so that the banks could provide facilities to public servants and government contractors until the crisis was resolved. In his statement the Governor-General was careful not to brand the possible arrangements as illegal; rather he considered that they 'did not amount to a satisfactory alternative to supply'.[108]

The present issue, however, is the ambit of the reserve power to dismiss. Prior to 1975, those constitutional writers who had discussed the power to dismiss confined its use to situations of clear illegality, fraud or duress at the poll, or exceptional cases where the fundamental principles of the constitution were being subverted.[109] Moreover, some regarded a request for the Prime Minister's resignation as a precondition to the exercise of the power. Precedents in the field were of doubtful assistance, for these had occurred either before the development of modern democratic government or were different in material circumstances or open to such criticism as to be of doubtful prescriptive value.

The only Australian precedent, the dismissal in 1932 by the New South Wales Governor of the Lang Government, was arguably an example of illegality. In other words, there is a case for saying that by convention the Governor-General should not have acted until supply had been exhausted and unless alternative financial arrangements were clearly illegal.[101] On the whole, it can be argued that he should have warned Mr Whitlam of the course he intended to pursue.[111]

The dismissal of the Whitlam Government in 1975 exposed the uncertainty and fragility of Australian constitutional conventions. This is one more area where theories stemming from British constitutional law and practice are found not to fit in the Australian context. Conventions may provide useful points of debate, they may be rules of political prudence, they may even explain behaviour in some instances, but they wither in the inhospitable environment of Australian politics.[112] As one commentator has neatly put it: 'There is no real place for conventions in a political atmosphere where the prevailing mood was summed up by Deputy Prime Minister Doug Anthony as: "In politics if you see a head, you kick it".'[113]

III THE POLITICAL AND GOVERNMENTAL PROCESS

Much of the conduct of politics is untouched by law. Australians can join political parties and be elected to positions within them without having any great concern with the law, unless it be the law of defamation. There is even some doubt about whether Australian courts will enforce the rules of political parties against their members, or require that natural justice be accorded to those threatened with disciplinary action or expulsion.[114] Law (in the form of electoral legislation) impinges to a greater extent when persons stand for public office.[115] Once persons are elected to public office, law such as that relating to parliamentary privilege and contempt of Parliament becomes relevant. Its purpose is protective—to ensure that members can carry out their functions and to deter conduct which lessens public esteem for this institution.[116]

One of the most important functions law can perform is in contributing to the integrity of the political and governmental process. But in Australia, whether there is equality in voting is a matter of politics rather than law.[117] Advertising during elections is subject to criminal controls on its truthfulness, although there is no simple procedure in the majority of Australian jurisdictions for obtaining an injunction against misleading advertisements.[118] There are no specific legal restrictions on lobbying, as in some other countries,[119] although the Commonwealth Government has introduced registration requirements—a general register for lobbyists and a special register for lobbyists whose clients include foreign governments or their agencies. Both registers are confidential. Access to ministers and officials is conditional on registering—a powerful, albeit non-legal, incentive to do so, if ministers and officials police the requirement by demanding evidence of registration.[120]

Important guarantees of the integrity of the political and governmental process are those relating to conflict of interest. The remainder of this part of the chapter focuses on legal and non-legal provisions in Australia which seek to obviate conflicts between private interest and public duty.[121] The points made in Chapter 1 relating to legislative technique and efficacy are pertinent to the discussion.

At the outset, it must be emphasized that law is only one influence on the standard of behaviour in public life, along with social, economic and political factors. For example, one would look to the latter to explain the rarity in modern Australia of flagrant forms of corruption such as bribery. Thus it is unprofitable to bribe voters on a large scale when the results in individual electorates turn on trends determined by State or national campaigning.[122] Moreover, elections have taken on a relatively ideological complexion since the rise of the Labor Party. In addition, the public services became relatively rational and internally responsible bureaucracies after reforms beginning from the 1880s. Australian public servants are also paid sufficiently to avoid the need for much of the petty corruption which exists in many Third World countries.

While flagrant forms of corruption are unusual in Australia, conflicts between the private interests and the public duties of government officials have developed. The expansion of government activities has produced many situations in which discretionary authority can be misused, induced by the expectation of private gain.[123] Perhaps the most significant difference between the legal control of flagrant forms of corruption and other conflicts of interest is that the latter often relates to action which *might* further private interests at the expense of public duty.[124] A conflict of interest does not necessarily involve actions which actually favour private interests; but the appearance that a private interest may be favoured undermines public confidence and justifies control.

Conflict of interest: the legal heritage

The laws regulating conflict of interest derive from a concern about flagrant forms of corruption and the dominance of Parliament by the Crown. Existing provisions are frequently inadequate or irrelevant and require revision in order to provide a firm basis for more expansive conflict-of-interest measures.

First, the criminal law. Australian courts have held that bribery of a member of Parliament is a common law misdemeanour punishable by fine or imprisonment.[125] In the case of *R. v. Boston*,[126] the High Court of

Australia accepted that a member could be charged with conspiracy for making an agreement to use his influence exclusively outside Parliament, and not by vote or speech inside, to put pressure on a minister on a particular matter, even though it was beneficial to the public interest. The court assumed that this decision was consistent with the English common law but failed to consider the question of parliamentary privilege. Because the decision involved a State Parliament, the question remained whether the *Boston* decision was applicable to the national Parliament. Section 49 of the Australian constitution provides that it should have the privileges of the House of Commons, unless other provision is made. Bribery involving members of the latter is a matter of privilege, and the courts have no jurisdiction.[127]

The matter was clarified by amendment to the Federal Crimes Act in 1982: it is now an offence, punishable by a court, for a member of the Australian Parliament to seek or receive a bribe on the understanding that the exercise of any duty or authority as a member will be affected.[128] Certainly the courts seem a more appropriate forum for dealing with bribery of members of Parliament than the parliaments themselves.[129] They have the expertise to ensure a fair trial, while in a parliament political considerations might prevail. The fear which originally gave rise to the exclusion of the courts on privilege matters—that the executive would use criminal prosecutions to harass legislators—is now unwarranted. However, the real point is that there are far more important problems in this area than the corruption of members of Parliament, in light of the fact that as such members have little influence over governmental decisions.

What, then, of the executive—ministers, public servants and statutory office-holders? At common law it is illegal either to offer or accept a bribe for the purpose of influencing the performance of duty by a public officer.[130] Statutory law confirms this and extends bribery to cover receipt of bribes by someone other than the public official.[131] Bribery not only involves the payment of money directly to public officials, but may take the form of gifts, sponsored travel, or contributions to campaign, party or party-related funds. While these would fall within the statutory provisions, they may be given in general terms to create a 'favourable climate' for decision-making. The absence of any nexus between them and specific action by the public official may make it difficult to secure a conviction. Adequate control of them requires other approaches. For example, gifts and sponsored travel might be better discouraged by disclosure and regulation.

Compared with other countries, Australian government seems to be remarkably free of bribes. There are a few well-documented cases. For example, in 1956 a royal commission in Queensland found corrupt conduct on the part of the Minister for Public Lands, in that he solicited a donation to party funds in return for favourable consideration in the grant of a Crown leasehold.[132] In 1986 a former Minister for Corrective Services in New South Wales was prosecuted for being part of a conspiracy in which money was corruptly given to him to induce him to release certain prisoners on licence.[133] While few cases of corruption come to light, however, the underlying reality might not be as favourable as it sometimes appears. It was only after his death—at which point defamation law no longer operates—that allegations became public about a former Premier of New South Wales corruptly receiving money so as to influence his control of the police.[134] There have been allegations about ministers in the Queensland Government.[135] No doubt there is a not inconsiderable number of instances of corruption at local government level, because of its control over land use and development.

In addition to the criminal law, there have been some other long-established provisions governing conflict of interest. Derived from an early nineteenth-century ruling in the House of Commons, Standing Order 196 of the House of Representatives prohibits voting by members with a direct pecuniary interest. But successive Speakers of the House have emasculated it by excluding from its ambit questions of public policy, so there is little left of the prohibition.[136] There is now a resolution requiring a declaration of pecuniary interest or other benefit by a member speaking in the House or a committee.[137]

Perhaps the oldest provision of relevance to conflict of interest is the concept that those holding an 'office of profit' under the Crown cannot sit in Parliament. The concept was adopted in Australia at both the national and State level. For instance section 44 of the Australian constitution provides that 'Any person who . . . (iv) Holds any office of profit under the Crown, shall be incapable of being chosen or of sitting as a senator or a member of the House of Representatives'. The section excludes ministerial appointments. Section 45 declares that if a senator or member of the House of Representatives becomes subject to section 44, his seat thereupon becomes vacant. Monetary penalties for breach of the section have been reduced, and are limited to $200 unless a person continues to sit after having been served with the papers initiating a prosecution.[138]

The 'office of profit' concept is over-inclusive in its operation. From the time of the Restoration in 1660 its aim was to exclude from Parliament those who might be servile to the Crown, which was attempting to use the considerable patronage at its disposal to win support for its policies.[139] Later the concept was supported to insulate certain offices, for example, those of judges, civil servants, members of public authorities, from being held by members of Parliament engaged in political controversy; to maintain the principle of ministerial responsibility by preventing civil servants, for whose decisions a minister is responsible, from becoming members of Parliament themselves; to eliminate the opportunity for members of Parliament to pursue self-interest; and to ensure that parliamentarians devote their time to their parliamentary duties.[140] However, Australia has witnessed several cases involving office of profit, where parliamentarians assuming even relatively minor and innocuous positions have been disqualified.[141] Substantial barriers exist to amending the Australian constitution,[142] although nothing in section 47 prevents the national Parliament from excluding the courts and dealing with possible disqualifications internally.

A 1782 Act regulating government contractors in Britain was based upon a rationale similar to that of the legislation disqualifying individuals holding an office of profit, namely, to ensure that the independence of members of Parliament would not be undermined by the Crown's allocation of government business.[143] The idea was incorporated in the Australian constitution, which provides that a person

shall be incapable of being chosen or of sitting as a senator or a member of the House of Representatives [if he has] any direct or indirect pecuniary interest in any agreement with the Public Service of the Commonwealth other than as a member and in common with the other members of an incorporated company consisting of more than twenty-five persons.[144]

The section was not invoked until 1975, when the case of a senator whose family company had certain contracts with the Australian public service was referred to the court of disputed returns. Barwick CJ effectively emasculated the provision as it relates to conflict of interest situations, holding that it does not apply to casual and transient contracts. To be covered, a contract must be one in which the Government could influence the contractor in his parliamentary duties.[145]

The long-standing provisions about office of profit and government contractors are of limited application in present conditions. They have some value in ensuring that members of Parliament, and to an extent other public officials, do not seek improper benefits. However, older office of profit law yields a harvest of general principles which should govern the duties of public officials such as the duty to act according to judgment and conscience, uninfluenced by pecuniary considerations; the duty to act honestly; the duty not to put oneself in a position of temptation; the duty not to pursue private advantage; and the duty to refrain from activities which interfere with the proper discharge of one's functions.[146] The problem is how are these general principles to be adequately applied.

Conflict of interest: current developments

Three broad approaches have been used in recent years to deal with conflict-of-interest problems: disclosure, regulation, divestiture. Under the first approach, legislators and public officers are required to disclose their interests to allow a judgment on whether their public duty and private interests conflict. Under the second approach, the behaviour of public officials is regulated so that conflicts or the appearance of such are obviated. Under the last approach, the public official is required to dispose of those interests which could conceivably conflict with his or her public duty. Supporting each approach is a variety of mechanisms including voluntary codes of conduct, internal discipline and criminal sanctions.

Conflict-of-interest measures have been taken in Australia partly on the ground of protecting public confidence. Well-publicized examples in recent times of conflicts of interest have led to criticism of some ministers and public officials.[147] In some jurisdictions, notably Queensland, these have been ignored. But where measures have been taken, the question remains whether they are restoring public confidence. Requiring legislators to disclose their private pecuniary interests may simply convince some members of the public that their worst fears are justified. Moreover, there is the question of effectiveness: have these particular measures ensured that public duty is paramount over the pursuit of private interests?

1 Disclosure

Disclosure on the part of legislators and public servants of their interests is a major facet of modern conflict-of-interest regulation in Australia. It takes the form either of a declaration in specific circumstances or of a general register (which may be public). It is preferred to divestiture, since it is thought that many persons would avoid public office if it meant abandonment of business involvements and personal investments. Disclosure is said to increase public confidence in government, to demonstrate the high level of integrity of the vast majority of officials, to deter conflicts of interest because officials realize that their actions will be scrutinized, to deter persons who should not be entering public service from doing so, and finally, to make more readily ascertainable the performance of public officials.[148]

As against this, it is argued that greater disclosure has significant drawbacks. For example, it is arguably unfair to impose heavy reporting burdens on the honest majority because of the behaviour of a minority. It has also been suggested that many conflict-of-interest situations are a grey area and thus intrusion into an individual's privacy and the threat of criminal sanctions cannot be justified. A further argument questions whether certain public officials should be subject to such requirements when similar disclosure requirements do not exist for other public officials or those working in the private sector. The ease of evasion and the failure to highlight crucial interests are other objections to disclosure.

With public disclosure, there is the possibility of fostering idle news-mongering.

Privacy remains the strongest argument against disclosure, especially if officials must also register the interests of their spouses and young children. Legislators may implicitly consent to disclose by virtue of seeking public office, but the same can hardly be said for members of their immediate family. There is also the very practical issue of what punishment can be imposed if a spouse refuses to divulge the necessary information. Powerful arguments exist, however, in favour of requiring disclosure of the interests of the immediate family. First, family assets are frequently intermingled so that it is unrealistic to treat them separately. Second, a person could circumvent disclosure requirements by conveying interests or directing income or gifts to a family member. Finally, a person can be influenced by family interests as well as personal interests.

Disclosure can be *ad hoc* or systematic. The first has the advantage of relevance to the immediate situation, although it requires the individual to recognize the conflict and to declare that fact. Systematic disclosure, usually in the form of a register, has become the more popular in the Australian context. Public registers have been introduced for several Australian parliaments.[149] Enforcement of the requirement to register lies either in the penal jurisdiction of a parliament to deal with contempt, or in statutory provisions for a fine and ultimately exclusion from Parliament for wilful contravention.

By contrast with parliamentary disclosure, disclosure by members of executive government is generally private and generally unenforceable as a matter of law. For example, recent prime ministers have required ministers to make full statements of their private interests and of those of their immediate families inasmuch as they are aware of them. A short form of the statement is now tabled in Parliament, while more detailed information, including the monetary values of interests, is provided privately to the Prime Minister.[150] Guidelines on official conduct of Commonwealth public servants mandate a declaration of actual or potential conflicting interests, which are then entered on a central record of interest declarations.[151] The possibility of formal disciplinary action for misconduct, under the *Public Service Act* 1922, ultimately underlies observance of the guidelines. For a few statutory authorities, there are legislative provisions obliging a declaration of interests.[152]

2 Regulation

Regulation was the traditional approach to controlling conflict of interest, but it has had a more limited role in recent times. Gifts and sponsored travel, however, have given rise to guidelines for the Commonwealth public service.[153] So, too, has the 'revolving door', the movement between public and private sectors. The guidelines for post-separation employment say that officers are expected to obtain assent on resignation or retirement, which may be conditional and may be withheld for up to two years.[154] Their aim is to avoid the suspicion that officers will bestow favours in the hope of future benefits, and that the organizations into which they move will gain an unfair advantage through the information and contacts the officer has previously acquired.[155] The only way these provisions can be enforced is to deny access to government departments and agencies to those who have not obtained the requisite assent. Apparently a significant number of separations are not being handled through the procedures, and some officers are choosing to breach them rather than risk formal refusal.[156]

3   Divestiture

Limited divestiture operates as a tool of conflict-of-interest policy in Australia. Commonwealth ministers accept that they must divest themselves of shares or similar interests in any company or business involved in the area of their portfolio.[157] Similarly, under guidelines for conduct, Commonwealth public servants might be required to divest themselves. Transfer from the position in which the conflict arises would be the consequence of a refusal to dispose of the interests in question.[158] For the purposes of compliance, transfer to a trustee or to a member of the officer's family is not sufficient divestment.

Codes of conduct have some attraction as a method of implementing conflict-of-interest rules, whether they rely on disclosure, regulation or divestiture. There are few in Australia: legislation establishes one for members of the Victorian Parliament, and guidelines contain one for Commonwealth public servants.[159] Codes are more flexible than criminal provisions; they clarify new or complex situations where basic moral principles are uncertain and it is too early to draft or apply law; they enhance the influence of progressive elements in an institution and thus tend to raise standards of the whole; and they furnish a basis for instructing new members of the group of their obligations.[160] The difficulty inherent in many codes is that they are vague and difficult to implement. They often contain ineffective and inadequate sanctions and enforcement machinery. While compliance with the Victorian parliamentary code is enforceable by the contempt power and by statutory provisions for fining and exclusion, the Commonwealth public service code is backed only by the general power to punish misconduct. The establishment of a committee or body charged with interpreting codes and vigorously applying their provisions would be a step toward ensuring adequate enforcement.

IV CONCLUSION

Three aspects of the role of law in government have been examined. There are links between them. For example, the accountability of government is affected by its structure. It can be argued, for instance, that the federal system is one of the most significant causes of lack of political accountability in Australia. Agreement is reached between the representatives of Commonwealth and State governments for, say, uniform legislation, and it becomes impossible as a practical matter for these arrangements to be changed by the various parliaments. Similarly, the lines of political accountability are distorted by the intrusion of lobbyists, which tend to represent the organized the powerful. Again, the structure of government has a bearing on conflicts of interest. New opportunities for impropriety have arisen with the growth of executive government, its fragmentation, and its extensive links with industry.

There are also links between these matters and what has been said in previous chapters. Regarding legislative technique, discussed in Chapter 1, for example, we have seen that certain laws, such as those relating to office of profit, are largely irrelevant to modern problems or contain penalties disproportionate to the wrongdoing. Other conflict-of-interest laws lack the backing of adequate sanctions, such as empowering the cancellation of government contracts in the event of undisclosed conflicts of interest. Chapter 1 touched on the issue of the capture of regulatory agencies; in this chapter we have seen how conflicts of interest can occur because of the close relationship between government departments and agencies and those with which they deal. Again, some substance has been given to the argument advanced in Chapter 2 about the limited impact which the courts have through their decisions.

It may be appropriate here to draw some threads together about the deep roots which our system of governmental law has in society. Australian society has a low opinion of politics and politicians. Lawyers reflect this attitude in their almost cavalier readiness to write off the lines of political accountability and to substitute mechanisms of legal accountability, however inconsistent this might be with the theory of responsible and representative government. Certainly politics and politicians can disappoint; so political conventions might be observed for reasons of self-interest, but Australian politics being as unruly as they are, they are often breached if it is expedient for this to be done. But at the end of the day, contempt for politics and politicians is contempt for ourselves.

Ours is also a society which exalts production and wealth. Possibly this is why lawyers expend great energy on government accountability, but do not address the problems of devising a viable system of redress for individual grievances against many of the activities of private organizations. Certainly it should not be surprising that conflicts of interest occur and that public measures to control them should be relatively weak. Queensland stands out in this regard; there ministerial conflicts of interest are almost a virtue as demonstrating a commitment to development of the State. Nor should it be surprising that public measures to control conflicts of interest concentrate on government, although the temptations and opportunities for abuse in the business community must exceed anything in government.

CHAPTER FOUR

THE ECONOMY

Law and economics interact in a variety of ways. First, government is a substantial economic actor in its own right. Through its powers to spend, tax and borrow, it allocates resources directly, as well as influencing the calculations of private economic actors. Just how those powers are exercised turns on economic theories, notably the exact mix of Keynesian and monetarist ideas, but their constitutional basis and legal form remain relatively constant. Second, government engages directly in economic production as monopolist (as with defence), but mainly in competition with private economic actors (as with communications and health). Government involvement in productive activity can be through government departments, through authorities constituted by statute, or through companies incorporated in the ordinary way. In each case, however, their activities are functions of government.

Moreover, government attempts to control the behaviour of private economic actors through regulation. Sometimes this is to facilitate private economic activity, as with legislation directed against restrictive trade practices, legislation permitting the formation of companies, or legislation strengthening the security interest of lenders. Sometimes it is to further economic goals for the economy as a whole, as with the regulation of economic institutions like banks. But mainly it is to advance non-economic goals. In almost all cases regulation takes legislative form, rather than (as is often the case in Britain) operating informally through agreement or codes of conduct. Legislation lays down the rules to be observed by private economic actors and often constitutes an agency to be responsible for implementation. Regulation might be institutionally focused or directed at types of economic activities (for example, particular product or factor markets). It might involve direct controls over matters such as output or price, or indirect measures such as consumer protection or environmental standards.

Finally, law provides the backdrop for private economic activity through its rules in areas such as contracts, private property rights and trusts. Their relatively fixed nature facilitates rational calculations by entrepreneurs. The legal system can be invoked to adjudicate disputes, a threat which gives the rules an enforceable character.

I PUBLIC FINANCE

Government has an enormous economic impact on the allocation of resources in the market through its powers to spend, tax and borrow. These powers are used for both economic ends (fiscal and monetary policy) and social ends (government transfer payments include pensions, other forms of social security and subsidies to industry and farmers). For each power, I will discuss the constitutional base before moving to its legislative form and impact. For reasons of space, the discussion is confined to the Commonwealth Government.

Government spending

Law provides the constitutional foundations for government spending, establishes mechanisms for protecting the public collectively against its misuse, but in only a limited number of categories of spending confers rights on individuals to make claims for its payment to them or to object to its particular disbursement. These three aspects are considered in turn.

Parliamentary approval of spending is fundamental to the system of responsible government, in which the executive is accountable to parliament. With the Commonwealth Government this principle is enshrined in the Australian constitution. First, all revenues or moneys raised or received by the executive government of the Commonwealth must form one Consolidated Revenue Fund, to be appropriated for the purposes of the Commonwealth in the manner imposed by the constitution (section 81); and second, no money shall be drawn from the Treasury of the Commonwealth except under appropriation by law (section 83). As Mason J has put it:

Section 83 gives expression to the established principle of English constitutional law enunciated by Viscount Haldane in *Auckland Harbour Board v. R.* [1924] A.C. 318, at p. 326: "No money can be taken out of the Consolidated Fund into which the revenues of the State have been paid, excepting under a distinct authorisation from Parliament itself". An *Appropriation Act* has a twofold purpose. It has a negative as well as a positive effect. Not only does it authorise the Crown to withdraw money from the Treasury, it "restrict(s) the expenditure to the particular purpose" as *Isaacs and Rich JJ*. observed in *Commonwealth v. Colonial Ammunition Co. Ltd* (1924) 34 CLR 198, at p. 224.[1]

The principle of the financial initiative of the Crown—that it is up to the Government to initiate financial measures—is also partly recognized in the constitution (section 56). No more will be said of that here.[2] Mention has already been made of the continuing legal doubts as to whether section 81 permits the Commonwealth to spend money in pursuit of a policy for which it cannot legislate directly because it is within State power.[3] Notwithstanding the doubts, millions of dollars are appropriated in this way every year. From the point of view of responsible government this is unobjectionable: Parliament must still approve a measure, which it does by approving the appropriation for it. In addition, other legislation might be necessary if activities associated with the policy are to be engaged in (for example, of a regulatory character). Moreover, parliamentary disapproval of appropriation bills has been traditionally regarded as a vote of no confidence in the Government, although the only example in the Australian Parliament appears to be that which precipitated the resignation of the Fadden Government in 1941.

The Australian constitution also moulds the form taken by Commonwealth parliamentary approval of spending. Section 54 says that a proposed law which appropriates revenue or moneys for the ordinary annual services of the Government shall deal only with such appropriation. The significance is that under section 53, the Senate cannot amend such bills. Without section 54, a government might be tempted to tack on to an appropriation bill a measure which the Senate could otherwise amend. To comply with section 54, Commonwealth appropriation from the Consolidated Revenue Fund must be divided. There are different interpretations as to what is required. Whatever this is, it is not legally enforceable because the courts regard it as relating to the internal affairs of Parliament, which are not subject to review.[4] As the result of a political compromise in 1965, however, the division now runs as follows: Appropriation Bill (No. 1) appropriates money for salaries of government employees, administrative expenses and other aspects of the ordinary annual services of government; Appropriation Bill (No. 2) covers capital expenditure generally and grants to the States; and the Appropriation (Parliamentary Departments) Bill is for the running of the parliament.[5] From what has been said, it is clear that the Senate cannot amend Bill No. 1, although the events of 1975 made clear that it can reject or defer. The 'Budget' is the term used for the Treasurer's annual financial statement, the appropriation bills, documents relating to the bills, and other specific legislation to give effect to the budget. Appropriation Bills Nos 3 and 4 parallel the division in Bills Nos 1 and 2. They are introduced near the end of the financial year, since government departments almost invariably exhaust some of the funds provided in the main bills, and appropriate funds for the remainder of that year. Conversely, supply bills make interim provision for the financial year until Bills Nos 1 and 2 are enacted.

Specific, as well as general, appropriations can be made under section 83. For example, authority for appropriation from the Trust Fund—which holds moneys of a trustee nature and moneys of trust accounts in the nature of working accounts (for example, for defence factories)—is provided under the *Audit Act* 1901 or legislation establishing the particular trust account.[6] It has long been accepted that loan moneys are not covered by section 81. They need not go into the Consolidated Revenue Fund; instead they are paid into the Loan Fund, although section 83 demands parliamentary authorization for their expenditure or repayment.[7] Neither is section 81 addressed to the funds generated by statutory corporations.[8] Moreover, parliamentary authority is not essential to the validity of a contract which involves the expenditure of funds. However, it is necessary if the Government is to fulfil its obligations under it, although authorization can take the form of a grant covering the class of service to which the contract relates (for example, in an appropriation Act) or of establishing a fund from which payments may lawfully be made.[9] The justification for the rule that validity does not turn on prior parliamentary approval is that otherwise contractors with government would be in a gravely disadvantageous position.

In fact some 70 per cent of Commonwealth government spending is authorized not by the annual appropriation bills but by what have been called special or standing appropriations of the Consolidated Revenue Fund or the Loan Fund under specific-purpose legislation, or are met from the Trust Fund.[10] Such appropriations do not involve annual authorizations and need not be for a specific amount or period. The term 'special appropriation' is used where a specified amount is provided, spelt out in separate legislation establishing the particular programme. 'Standing appropriations' refer to open-ended appropriations of the Consolidated Revenue Fund made by passing enabling legislation for the programme. The amounts appropriated by standing appropriations depend on the demand for payments by claimants satisfying eligibility criteria specified in the legislation. There is a trend away from standing appropriations, partly to ensure tighter control of government spending, and partly because an expansive interpretation of the phrase 'the ordinary annual services of government' by the Attorney-General's Department means that what have hitherto been standing appropriations must go into the general appropriation legislation. It has been said that legislation would probably not be construed as an appropriation if, while authorizing expenditure for particular purposes, it did not specify a maximum amount, or establish criteria for ascertaining what sums may be spent.[11]

Apart from the constitutional foundations, there are mechanisms designed to prevent unauthorized and improvident spending. Internal to Parliament are the parliamentary committees, which in recent times have expanded in number and the range of matters investigated. Long established is the Joint Committee of Public Accounts.[12] The committee is concerned with reviewing the efficiency of public administration but is hampered by a lack of staff and resources.[13] Legislation also establishes the Parliamentary Standing Committee on Public Works which, in reporting on a public work, takes account of suitability, advisability and efficiency.[14] Other parliamentary committees, such as the Senate Standing Committee on Finance and Government Operations, and the House Standing Committee on Expenditure, have no statutory basis. No parliamentary committee, however constituted, has final power to secure compliance with its recommendations but must rely on criticism and public report. A recent assessment is that the recommendations of particular committees have proved influential for decisions taken at both government level and within the public service.[15]

The Auditor-General, appointed by the Governor-General under the *Audit Act* 1901, is responsible for audits of Commonwealth departments, Territories, authorities, companies and other instrumentalities. Reports on these audits are presented to Parliament; in fact, the Auditor-General has a special relationship with Parliament and independence from ministerial control.[16] In addition to whatever compliance can be secured by criticism and public report, there is the sanction of section 32 of the Audit Act: no money can be drawn by the Minister for Finance from the Commonwealth public account (i.e., the Consolidated Revenue Fund, the Trust Fund and the Loan Fund) unless the Auditor-General is satisfied, and so certifies, that it does not exceed the amount available for expenditure in respect of the services or purposes in accordance with the appropriation.[17] Where the Auditor-General has given the certificate, the Minister for Finance then obtains a warrant from the Governor-General authorizing the drawing. Possibly the Auditor-General would have standing to seek an injunction against unauthorized spending.[18]

A further control operates at the level of government departments and agencies. Under the Audit Act, those responsible within government departments and agencies for public moneys ('accounting officers') cannot obtain access to them unless payment has been authorized by appointees of the Minister for Finance as being lawfully available and properly made.[19] For the purposes of the section, moneys are not lawfully available for payment unless there are sufficient moneys from the relevant appropriation (or, in the case of the Trust Fund, standing to its credit) after taking previous payments into account.[20] Any person guilty of any wilful act of commission or omission contrary to these provisions commits an offence and is liable to a penalty.[21] These statutory provisions are reinforced by the more detailed Finance Regulations, which provide as well for matters such as quotations and tenders in the case of contracts for supplies.[22] The Minister for Finance can impose minor penalties for non-compliance with the Finance Regulations.[23]

The third aspect of government spending about which something should be said relates to individual rights. An appropriation Act, it has been said, 'does not speak the language of regulation, it neither confers rights or privileges nor imposes duties or obligations. It only permits of moneys held in the Treasury being paid out. . . '.[24] Five of the judges in the case from which this passage is taken held that an appropriation Act is not justiciable, although the reasoning is not uniform. The reasoning of three of the five is that appropriation legislation is intra-governmental in character.[25] Of course appropriation legislation which 'neither confers rights or privileges. . .', is akin to much legislation in the modern state, which confers wide discretionary power, the exercise of which cannot be challenged in a court. So if appropriation legislation authorizes expenditure on a particular item, the courts will not compel the government to spend the money for that purpose or take steps to ensure that it is enforced.[26]

In addition to simply authorizing expenditure, however, Parliament might set out specific statutory provisions imposing expenditure duties on executive government which are legally enforceable. Much depends on the discretion conferred by the statute establishing the scheme of bounties, grants, subsidies, pensions, and so on. At one end of the spectrum there may be an absence of legislative standards or the legislation might actually confer wide discretion on the administering authority. Take, as an example, the *Automotive Industry Authority Act* 1984, enacted as part of government strategy to make the automotive industry more economically efficient. Among the functions of the Authority listed are 'to provide, or to support by way of financial or other assistance, services that could contribute to the improvement in management efficiency in the automotive industry'.[27] In the absence of any statutory indications as to how the power is to be exercised, no one could seek judicial review of a decision of the Authority not to grant financial assistance, or to grant a lesser amount than requested, so long as there was no bad faith and the Authority genuinely exercised its discretion.[28] By contrast, judicial review is possible if legislation sets out in relatively objective terms the criteria to be satisfied. So, for example, section 10 of the *Bounty (Computers) Act* 1984 provides that bounty payable to a manufacturer of bountiable equipment in respect of the equipment is an amount equal to 25 per cent of the value added to the equipment by the manufacturer. While there might be disagreements in interpretation, 'manufacturer', 'bountiable equipment', and 'value added' are all defined at length in the Act.[29] A decision to refuse bounty could be challenged if, for example, in the interpretation of those terms irrelevant factors were taken into account or departmental policy as to their application were inconsistent with their meaning.[30]

Individual rights to government spending have been furthered by the establishment of bodies other than courts to provide external review. Most significant in this regard are the social security appeals tribunals and the Veterans' Review Board in relation to pensions. In addition, the Administrative Appeals Tribunal has been given jurisdiction to reconsider particular spending decisions, and from its decisions appeals on points of law are possible to the Federal Court and thence to the High Court.[31] Appeals about bounties, export development grants and pensions have consequently been considered by the AAT and the courts.[32]

Taxation

There are some fundamental constitutional principles on which taxation legislation is built. However, the bulk of legal activity in relation to taxation is directed to defining the obligations of individuals under the relevant legislation. The courts are important here, for their decisions partly determine the efficacy of legislation. Not to put too fine a point on it, in the 1960s and 1970s the High Court of Australia sanctioned massive tax avoidance, seriously undermining the equity and efficiency of the existing system, at the same time damaging its own standing in the community.

The cardinal constitutional principle in this area is that taxation cannot be imposed by the executive government, but requires parliamentary authorization.[33] Qualifications on the principle are that the Government can exact payment for services without parliamentary approval, and that it may demand and collect new taxes, or increases in existing taxes, in anticipation of legislation (which will therefore be partly retrospective).[34] Coupled with this principle, that parliamentary authorization is essential to taxation, is the principle of the financial initiative of the Crown, mentioned above in the context of appropriation. Consequently, only the Government should be able to make proposals for an increase, or alleviation, of a tax or duty, or for the alteration of the incidence of these. This principle is preserved in the standing orders of the House of Representatives.[35]

Superimposed on this principle of parliamentary authorization are the considerations deriving from the Australian constitution. The Commonwealth Parliament has a concurrent power with the States to tax, but not so as to discriminate between States or parts of States. This is spelt out in section 51(ii). Tax legislation cannot originate in the Senate, nor can the Senate amend it, although it can reject, defer, or request amendments (section 53). To safeguard the general power of the Senate to amend bills, other than money bills, the first paragraph of section 55 prevents 'tacking' in relation to tax bills, by providing that laws imposing taxation must deal only with that subject and that a provision dealing with any other matter shall be of no effect. Moreover, to permit the Senate to discriminate amongst the tax measures over which it will exercise its powers to reject, defer or request amendments, paragraph 2 of section 55 says that laws imposing taxation shall deal with one subject of taxation only, and that laws imposing customs duties shall deal with duties of customs only (and similarly, with laws imposing duties of excise). Indeed, section 90 gives the Commonwealth Parliament exclusive power to impose duties of customs and excise, as well as to grant bounties on the production or export of goods. Finally, section 114 forbids both the Commonwealth and the States imposing taxes on each others' property.

What impact have these provisions had? The prohibition against the Commonwealth Parliament discriminating in its tax laws has had little effect, even when coupled with the wider prohibition in section 99 against preferences in revenue law. The High Court has held, quite sensibly, that only if discrimination is on the face of tax legislation, rather than because of the factual context, can it offend section 51(ii).[36] Otherwise tax legislation concerning particular producers would be discriminatory just because they happened to be concentrated in one or a few States. While doubts have been expressed about the legality of the zonal allowance system, benefiting taxpayers in isolated areas, it has never been effectively challenged.[37] Section 53, and what Dixon J once called 'the hitherto ineffectual menaces of s.55',[38] can also be quickly disposed of. They go to form rather than substance so that, for example, in deference to the first paragraph of section 55, the regularly enacted income tax Acts, which impose taxes at particular rates,[39] are separate from the *Income Tax Assessment Act* 1936, which deals with complex definitional matters and the machinery of collection such as returns, penalties and collection.[40]

By contrast, section 51(ii) has had an impact. Its interpretation by the High Court enables it to be used for economic management and to effect structural changes and other public policies. Consequential effects and substance are ignored by the High Court in characterizing legislation as taxation legislation, in favour of its direct legal effect. Thus varying rates, exemptions, credits, allowances, accelerated depreciation and other favourable treatment have been used to reduce large land holdings,[41] to channel investment into governmental and semi-governmental securities[42] and for many other purposes, such as promoting the mining industry and Australian films.[43] The notion of tax expenditures—that tax allowances are equivalent to subsidies—reflects the extent to which tax law might serve such purposes.[44]

In addition, sections 51(ii) and 90, or at least their interpretation by the High Court, have affected the federal balance. The story of uniform taxation has already been outlined. As indicated, the Uniform Tax case[45] in 1942 strengthened the position of the Commonwealth, although it hardly led to coercive federalism. Less well known has been the impact on federalism of section 90, dealing with duties of customs and excise, possibly because the relevant High Court cases are very rarely State versus Commonwealth cases, but rather involve individuals challenging the constitutionality of legislation. But the upshot is that the High Court has interpreted excise so that, generally speaking, the States are precluded from imposing taxes related in some way to goods. From the viewpoint of the economist the decisions cannot be justified. Excise duties, imposed on producers, are distinct from sales taxes, imposed on subsequent sellers, and consumption taxes, imposed on final users. After a morass of litigation over eighty years, however, it is now clear that a tax on the sale of goods, at any point in the chain of distribution, is generally an excise for the purposes of section 90, even though it might be presented as a licence fee, a receipt duty or an operating fee.[46] Coupled with the exclusion of the States, in practice, from the field of income tax, these decisions mean that the States have a narrow tax base. Consequently, they are confined to payroll tax, which adversely affects employment or to the taxes which are inequitable or inefficient.[47] It has been said that all this has led to a situation which minimizes electoral accountability and financial responsibility.[48] But even if this is accepted, there are many advantages to Commonwealth domination: there is effective control for the purposes of macro-economic policy; uniformity eliminates a source of tax avoidance and undesirable interstate competition; and a national tax system makes it easier to achieve equity.

Parliament and the courts have always been solicitous of the rights of individual taxpayers. First, there has long been an appellate structure —long before, say, that for social security—so that taxpayers can challenge assessments made of them. Speaking in the context of incontestable taxes, determined by administrative discretion, Dixon CJ opined in one case that it had

been generally assumed that under the Constitution liability for tax cannot be imposed upon the subject without leaving open to him some judicial process by which he may show that in truth he was not taxable or not taxable in the sum assessed . . .[49]

Whatever the constitutional correctness of these remarks, the *Income Tax Assessment Act* 1936 enables taxpayers to contest assessments. The first stage is the statutory duty on the Commissioner of Taxation to consider a written objection to assessment.[50] If still not satisfied, the taxpayer may have the matter referred to a board of review or dealt with in a State supreme court.[51] The three-member boards of review date from 1921 and have the advantage over a court of proceeding *in camera*. Moreover, they are able to substitute their view for that of the Commissioner, which makes them the most sensible avenue for appeal if the Commissioner has exercised a discretion, although not if a question of law is involved.[52] Appeals can be taken and referrals made on questions of law from a board of review to a State supreme court.[53] From a State supreme court, a taxpayer can proceed to the Federal Court and then to the High Court of Australia.[54] The wide use of this machinery was noted above.[55]

Second, Parliament has been reluctant to take retrospective action against blatant tax avoidance.[56] Against retrospective legislation it is said that it adversely affects commercial and personal freedom.[57] Appeals to freedom in this area are little more than rhetoric without more specific argument. Not only is personal liberty unlikely to be affected, given the nature of the penalties set, sought and imposed, but invoking the notion of commercial freedom in this way would condemn the great bulk of business regulation. It is then said that the imposition of liability ought never to be by reference to completed acts which did not at the time attract liability.[58] Now some of the recent retrospective legislation might simply have made certain liability which was probable. But even if this is not conceded, retrospectivity, while generally undesirable, is sometimes necessary to protect the revenue from highly artificial and contrived schemes. Then the cardinal factor is whether legitimate expectations are unreasonably affected by retrospective legislation. To be 'legitimate', expectations must be objective in character; they cannot turn on the idiosyncratic beliefs of individuals. Moreover, they must be *unreasonably* affected, since it is very difficult to think of a change in taxation law which does not adversely affect in some way expectations about earning prospects, potential savings and consumption, and so on.[59] Where tax avoidance schemes constitute blatant tax avoidance, there should be no objections to retrospectivity on this score. The absence of any real commercial purpose in such schemes, the secrecy surrounding them, and the attempt to take advantage of legal provisions which could not conceivably have been intended in the particular way, all militate against it.[60]

Thirdly, the courts have said explicitly that there needs to be clear and unambiguous language before concluding that a person is taxable.[61] Consequently, if the language of the statute has not precisely expressed its underlying policies, the courts have insisted that it is not their function to give effect to those policies. Moreover, they have gone a step further by concentrating on form rather than substance. If documentation or transactions are found to be genuine, they will not go beyond these to uncover the tax avoidance achieved.[62] Tax avoidance in this view is quite legitimate, distinct from evasion, since taxpayers are under no moral or other obligation to arrange their affairs so that tax is payable.

In fact statutory language is to varying degrees open-textured, especially in complex areas like taxation. To demand clear and unambiguous language is to deny the complexity of human action and the difficulties of capturing the future in language. By refusing to work in partnership with Parliament, to give effect to underlying legislative policies, the courts have compounded the density and length of tax legislation, since the only plausible legislative response is to lay down provisions in great detail. They also forfeit the respect of Parliament and the community. Historically this has led to the establishment of alternative tribunals which, it is hoped, will be more understanding of the difficulties facing governments. The obvious drawback to the courts' concentrating on form rather than substance is the protection given to shams. Although still maintainable at the analytical level, the line between avoidance and evasion then becomes very blurred, and in some cases disappears.

The doctrines described in the last paragraph but one were applied *in extremis* by the High Court when Sir Garfield Barwick was Chief Justice. While the conventional wisdom is that this was a period of legal literalism, in fact the decisions involved policy choices, albeit unarticulated. The judgments of Barwick CJ are illustrative: he ignored previous decisions, sometimes his own, created new rules, and reached results which contradicted fundamental principles of tax law and accountancy.[63] All was cast, however, in densely reasoned legalisms, which made difficult legal criticism by other than expert tax lawyers.[64] Since the departure of Barwick CJ, the High Court has expressed a different view, more sympathetic to underlying legislative policy.[65] No doubt this was stimulated in part by the public reaction against the Court as a result of its tax decisions.[66]

The upshot of High Court decisions in the 1970s was to encourage widespread tax avoidance. As the government draft White Paper put it in 1985:

The 'loss of innocence' occasioned by (among other things) a string of High Court rulings from the mid-1960s to the early 1980s has been such that closing off one loophole has served, in the main, to divert taxpayers' attention to another.[67]

Highly artificial and contrived tax avoidance schemes, generated by accountants, lawyers and other professionals, went well beyond hitherto accepted forms of tax avoidance such as income splitting, tax shelters and capitalizing income in multiple trusts.[68] The High Court gave its imprimatur to such schemes in a series of decisions, of which *Curran*, *Patcorp*, *Slutzkin*, and *Westraders* are among the best known.[69] In 1979–80, when these schemes were at their peak, the amount of tax at stake has been estimated as being about $500 million.[70] The revenue loss occasioned had serious repercussions for government budget strategy. Moreover, there were important implications for the equity of the tax system, since wage and salary earners were bearing an increasing share of the tax burden. These factors led to legislative action, of varying degrees of efficacy.[71]

Government borrowing

As part of its executive power, the Commonwealth can enter contracts, including contracts of loan. Neither parliamentary approval nor appropriation is necessary prior to the loan, although, as has been mentioned, appropriation is a prerequisite to its expenditure and repayment because of section 83 of the constitution.[72] The constitutional provision is underpinned by the *Audit Act* 1901. All moneys raised by way of loan, except bank overdraft, must be paid into the Loan Fund, and the Minister for Finance cannot expend any moneys standing to its credit except under the authority of legislation.[73] Legislation authorizing the raising of loans invariably contains authority to spend the moneys on the particular purposes for which they were raised and on the expenses of raising them.[74] As regards repayments, that legislation might also appropriate the Consolidated Revenue Fund to the extent necessary to repay interest, capital and other charges.[75] However, where the money is to be raised by the issue of government securities to the public, resort may be had to the specific legislation relating to government securities, the *Commonwealth Inscribed Stock Act* 1911 and the *Loan Securities Act* 1919, which automatically appropriate the Consolidated Revenue Fund.[76]

The federal system imposes additional requirements on Commonwealth borrowing. Commonwealth power to borrow is not, it seems, confined to purposes falling within Federal legislative power, but the limits of the appropriation power (whatever they be) are relevant.[77] More important is the Financial Agreement of 1927, to which the Commonwealth and States are parties.[78] The Agreement constituted the Australian Loan Council, comprising Commonwealth and State representatives. Commonwealth and State borrowing proposals must be submitted to the Council. If it decides that the total amount can be borrowed at reasonable rates and conditions, the relevant party may go ahead. If not, the Council decides the reduced amount to be borrowed (cl. 3(8)–(9)). These decisions are by majority, although the Commonwealth has two votes and a casting vote (cl. 3(14)(b)). In making them the Council is not concerned with evaluating the reasons for loan expenditure, and the governments may spend amounts raised as they wish. Allocation of the reduced amount, however, is by unanimous agreement or, failing that, by the formula in the Agreement (cl. 3(9)–(10)). The Commonwealth arranges borrowings for itself and the States, subject to decisions of the Council. A State may borrow outside Australia in its own name by unanimous decision of the Council (cl. 4(2)).

Legally, the Financial Agreement is a contract between the parties, but protected by section 105A of the Australian constitution against other provisions of the national constitution, the constitutions of the States and Commonwealth and State laws.[79] Like any contract, it can be varied or rescinded by unanimous agreement of the parties.[80] All government borrowings by way of loan must be submitted to the Council (cl. 4(4)). The exceptions are borrowing for converting, renewing or redeeming existing loans; for temporary purposes; for defence purposes authorized by Commonwealth legislation; and borrowing by the Commonwealth and States within their own jurisdictions, from bodies constituted under Commonwealth or State law or from the public by counter sales of securities (subject in both cases to maximum rates for interest set by the Council).[81] A borrowing for temporary purposes implies one to satisfy a transient financial need; a term loan for twenty years would not fall within this category.[82] In addition to borrowing on behalf of State governments, the Commonwealth borrows for macro-economic policy reasons and to finance its budget deficits. Apart from the previously mentioned exceptions, the Commonwealth's borrowings are subject to the decisions of the Loan Council.

The financial ascendancy of the Commonwealth after World War II, deriving largely from the uniform tax system, meant Commonwealth domination of the Loan Council. The Commonwealth began funding borrowing by the Commonwealth on behalf of the States from revenue, first by means of loans but later by capital grants.[83] Nothing in the Financial Agreement prevents this, since the partners are specifically empowered to use their own public moneys for any purpose (cl. 5(1)(b), 6(1)(b)). The upshot was that the Commonwealth began to see borrowing by the Commonwealth on behalf of the States as having important implications for its own budget, in particular the deficit. There was therefore every incentive to control this. In the view of some, the result has been to give private-sector borrowing priority over public-sector borrowing, with the latter being too low relative to the country's needs.[84]

Like any contract, the Financial Agreement does not bind non-parties. Consequently, local and semi-governmental bodies, which are legal entities separate from the States, are not covered by the Agreement, although from 1936 their proposed borrowings were considered by the Council under the so-called 'gentlemen's agreement'. Various forms of borrowing developed during the mid-1970s which were, however, outside the 'gentlemen's agreement'. This culminated in the replacement of the 'gentlemen's agreement' by the 'global approach' in 1984 (described shortly). These developments largely arose because the 'gentlemen's agreement' was expressed in terms of loan borrowings, and therefore did not cover other methods of financing such as leveraged and non-leveraged leases,[85] sale and leaseback, trade credits, and security deposit arrangements whereby mining companies (say) were obliged to finance infrastructure like railways. The States began using these to avoid the Loan Council and Commonwealth restraints on public investment expenditure. Between 1980–81 and 1983–84, various forms of borrowing outside the Council rose from one-tenth to two-thirds of total State, local and semi-governmental borrowing.[86] As a result the Council had increasingly less influence on the totality of public demand on the capital market, which posed particular difficulties for the Commonwealth in overall economic management. Now under the 'global approach', initially agreed at the Loan Council in 1984, there are voluntary global limits for all forms of conventional and non-conventional borrowings by government authorities, government-owned companies and trusts (but not statutory marketing authorities and government-owned financial institutions).[87]

The Commonwealth could borrow money both by term loan and by the issue of securities. Term loans are used relatively infrequently; they have been entered with institutions such as the Export Import Bank and the International Bank for Reconstruction and Development, in some cases to be on-lent to government enterprises. Generally speaking, the relevant law for term loans is the private law which would apply to a loan to a commercial borrower. To assure the lender that Australian law is consistent with the loan and how it is to be used, and to confirm its legally binding quality, term loans have sometimes been endorsed by specific legislation.[88]

The Commonwealth raises money mainly by the issue of securities. In general, lower interest rates are payable, and longer periods obtainable, than with term loans, although a disadvantage is that there may be important administrative costs such as those associated with printing prospectuses. There is special legislation governing forms of indebtedness represented by the issue of securities. The *Commonwealth Inscribed Stock Act* 1911, and the *Loans Securities Act* 1918, are referred to shortly.[89] In addition, there is ancillary legislation. The *Loans Redemption and Conversion Act* 1921, as its title suggests, allows the Treasurer to be authorized to pay off, repurchase or redeem any loan by way of securities, or to convert any such loan into any other Commonwealth loan. The *Loan Consolidation and Investment Reserve Act* 1955 establishes a reserve, the purpose of which is to repurchase or redeem securities which represent a portion of the public debt. The receipts of the reserve are derived mainly from appropriations of the Consolidated Revenue Fund and from interest on investments.

Treasury bonds, Treasury indexed bonds, Treasury notes and Australian savings bonds are the Commonwealth securities used to raise money from the Australian public.[90] All are issued under the *Commonwealth Inscribed Stock Act* 1911, although authority to borrow must be granted by other legislation or be for the purpose of carrying out an obligation under the Financial Agreement 1927.[91] In practice, when bulk authorization for the creation of domestic stock is sought, the borrowing authority which may be drawn upon when stock is issued is cited; determination of the actual authority used takes place subsequently. Treasury bonds have fixed maturity dates and pay interest semi-annually at a fixed rate; they may be issued at a discount or premium on the par value. Indexed Treasury bonds are indexed to the rate of inflation as measured by the Consumer Price Index either as to capital or interest. Treasury notes are short-term; they are sold at a discount on the par value. Australian savings bonds have fixed maturity dates and pay interest semi-annually at a fixed rate; they are issued at par. Prior redemption at par is possible, but subject to conditions. With all three securities, the 1911 Act provides that principal and interest rank equally and are a charge on the Consolidated Revenue Fund.[92] After the expiration of the notice for the redemption of any loan, interest ceases.[93] All moneys raised must be placed to the credit of the Loan Fund.[94] The securities issued are personal property.[95]

Since amendments to the Act in 1984, Treasury bonds, Treasury indexed bonds, Treasury notes and Australian savings bonds cannot be issued as bearer securities. (Inscribed stock issued prior to July 1984 may still be exchanged for bearer securities—s.51E(1).) The amendments were prompted by the administrative costs associated with bearer securities, and the concern that some investors chose to hold bearer securities as a means of evading income tax and the upper limit of $200 000 on a holding by any one investor in Australian savings bonds. Consequently, securities are now issued as inscribed stock. The name, address and description of the owner, and the amount held, is entered into registers administered by the Reserve Bank.[96] Certificates of proprietorship must be issued when requested, and are prima facie evidence of title, but are neither transferable nor negotiable.[97] Rather, the person whose name is inscribed is deemed to be the owner and has power to dispose and transfer.[98] There are detailed provisions for the transfer of inscribed stock.[99] The Act also contains criminal provisions against forgery, false personation, and falsification of books or documents in relation to issuing stock.[100]

New issues of Treasury bonds, Treasury indexed bonds and Treasury notes are by tender. Registered tenderers lodge bids with the Reserve Bank. Tenders are facilitated by the provisions in the Act for delegations and authorizations.[101] Following the tenders, there are tap series for Treasury bonds and Treasury indexed bonds, designed for the household sector. There is an active secondary market in Treasury bonds, in which the Reserve Bank participates to effect its monetary and liquidity management objectives.[102] Participants in the market must comply with legal regulation, notably that in the *Securities Industry Act* 1980 because the definition of securities in that Act includes government securities. The Reserve Bank discounts Treasury notes, undertakes open-market purchases and sells from its portfolio. A secondary market exists in these also, although it is conducted largely among authorized dealers and the trading and savings banks.[103] There is no formal market in Australian savings bonds.

Treasury bonds, Treasury indexed bonds, Treasury notes and Australian savings bonds are issued to the public. Although capable of a wider distribution, Treasury bills, also issued under the *Commonwealth Inscribed Stock Act* 1911, are not available to the public. Internal Treasury bills are issued to cover investments of Commonwealth trust funds, and public Treasury bills are issued only to the Reserve Bank as instruments used in residual financing or for some funding for the States.

Overseas borrowing by way of the issue of securities is under the *Loans Securities Act* 1919, which allows moneys to be borrowed in foreign currencies. Prerequisites are that the Treasurer has authority 'under an Act' to borrow the moneys and that the Governor-General authorizes the borrowing. The phrase 'under an Act' seems to have been taken to require that, where Executive Council approval is being sought for an issue, it is necessary to specify the particular Act from which the authority is said to derive. (This contrasts with the procedure for domestic borrowing, although the contrast is not a particularly important one in practice.) The Loans Securities Act and the *Loans (Taxation Exemption) Act* 1978 make provision for exempting securities issued overseas from withholding tax. The types of securities issued depend on the market from which the moneys are being sought. Local legal requirements are one aspect in whether, say, bearer bonds are issued as opposed to inscribed stock. In foreign financial markets, and with private placements overseas, the Commonwealth competes for funds with the governments of other countries and commercial borrowers.

The principles of public finance prevailing in the first part of this century required governments to set aside sinking funds for the repayment of moneys borrowed.[104] The National Debt Commission was constituted by the *National Debt Sinking Fund Act* 1923 for the redemption of the Commonwealth debt. Under the present legislation, the *National Debt Sinking Fund Act* 1966, the Commission consists of the Treasurer, the Chief Justice of the High Court, the Governor of the Reserve Bank, the Secretary to the Treasury and the Secretary to the Attorney-General's Department, and a States representative. Under the present Act, the National Debt Sinking Fund is maintained within the Trust Fund. The Treasurer must pay into the Fund certain amounts, in particular a proportion of the net Commonwealth debt created annually. The Commission is authorized to apply moneys standing to the credit of the Fund in reduction of the public debt by repurchase or redemption of Commonwealth securities. Securities repurchased or redeemed are deemed to be cancelled and cannot be issued.

The Financial Agreement places State sinking funds established in respect of State debts under the control of the Commission. Amendments to the Agreement in 1976 resulted in the absorption of the States' sinking funds into the National Debt Sinking Fund. Separate accounts are maintained for the Commonwealth and each State. Contributions by the Commonwealth and the States in respect of State debts are regulated by this Agreement.[105] As a matter of law, the amounts are debts payable to the Commission and could be recovered in the ordinary way by legal process.

II GOVERNMENT AS ENTREPRENEUR

Australian governments have long engaged directly in economic activity. Economic necessity, rather than political ideology, were at the back of the 'colonial socialism' of the nineteenth century. The distances to be covered, and the absence of large local capitalists, placed the onus on government to develop the railways and communications. Early this century Labor politicians saw government enterprise and nationalization as the means of combating monopoly and achieving social justice.[106] Non-Labor governments recognized the inevitability of economic activity by government but sought to give it form in the independent statutory authority run on business lines.[107] Labor justified nationalization of airline services—held to be unconstitutional—on the ground of compensating for underinvestment.[108] Once nationalization fell out of favour for both ideological and political (including legal) reasons,[109] the idea of government enterprises was championed by those such as Gough Whitlam as one of the ways of achieving economic and social goals such as greater efficiency and a curb on monopoly power.[110] Even non-Labor governments accepted competing public enterprise in some areas, such as with the two-airline agreement which was justified partly on economic grounds.[111] Present non-Labor policy, however, favours privatization.

The focus of this part is on government bodies which perform business activities which could be performed, or are being performed, by the private sector. For convenience, reference is made mainly to Commonwealth, rather than State, enterprises. Characteristics which such bodies usually have in common 'are that they are incorporated, at least partly self-financing, staffed outside the Public Service Act and autonomously managed with ministerial power of direction'.[112]

Legal form

The statutory corporation has been the usual form for government enterprises. Examples include the Australian Broadcasting Corporation, the Australian Film Commission, the Australian Industry Development Corporation, the Australian National Airlines Commission, the Australian Postal Commission, the Australian Telecommunications Commission and the Commonwealth Banking Corporation. Typically, legislation incorporates the body, gives it the capacity to sue and be sued and enables it to acquire, hold and dispose of real and personal property. These attributes of corporate personality place statutory corporations in a position similar to that of the private enterprise company incorporated under the Companies Act. Without more, however, government enterprises would be poorly placed to engage in commercial activities. Normal procedures and controls operating in a government department are not always appropriate in the commercial environment where decisions might have to be made quickly and exceptional skills hired for a specified task or a short period.[113] Consequently, some government enterprises can appoint their own officers, who are not public servants, and employ persons on short-term contracts. Some are also financially autonomous, except that they might rely on a parliamentary subvention. Income and other taxes might be payable in the ordinary way, some pay dividends to the Government on capital advanced, and some borrow commercially (although possibly with a government guarantee).[114]

These factors bear on whether government enterprises have any unjustifiable advantage over private enterprises with which they compete. The boot is on the other foot if a government enterprise is obliged to engage in uneconomic activities. The 'recoup principle' applies to a limited extent with some government enterprises in this position: where they are formally directed to undertake an uneconomic activity,[115] they can recoup their losses from the government.[116] But uneconomic activities might be undertaken as a result of indirect pressures rather than a formal direction, and even if a formal direction is given, compensation might not be sought or given pursuant to the recoup principle.

Even in the absence of a formal ministerial power to direct, it can be argued that members of a statutory corporation must give effect to government policy subject, of course, to the legislation which might explicitly, or by clear implication, exclude that possibility.[117] As a matter of general principle this follows because statutory authorities are an arm of the executive government.[118] To assume that the creation of a statutory corporation implies an intention that it should enjoy freedom from government policy is to ignore the very pragmatic manner in which choices are made about using the departmental structure, or creating a statutory corporation, or incorporating a company under the companies legislation.[119] Nor is complete autonomy essential for business efficiency and flexibility, so long as interference is not on a day-to-day basis. In practice the desire for the statutory corporation to be successful will restrict interference. In some instances social and political pressures will give added weight to a policy of minimum government interference.

Moreover, there is no ground for applying private law notions in an area of public law. The rule in company law is that the primary duty of directors is to the company of which they are directors, not to any party that nominated them.[120] In fact the courts have recognized commercial reality and given some leeway to nominee directors to safeguard the interests of their nominators.[121] It would be quite inappropriate to invoke the strict rule for statutory corporations. That rule derives from the need for accountability to the shareholders.[122] Statutory corporations have no shareholders: if members/directors are to be accountable, it must be to the government which has appointed them, through the relevant minister, subject of course to their statutory obligations.

Apart from the control exercisable formally over an enterprise which is a statutory corporation, government might influence its behaviour indirectly through those it chooses to appoint as members.[123] The formal position, generally speaking, is that members are appointed by the Governor-General, acting on advice. Appointments are for fixed terms, although members can be reappointed. Members must make declarations of pecuniary interest and avoid conflicts of interest.[124] Usually the Governor-General may terminate an appointment, or an office is deemed to be vacated, if a member becomes permanently incapable of performing his or her duties, becomes bankrupt or is absent without leave from a series of meetings.

Rather than invoking the form of a statutory corporation, government sometimes utilizes the legal form of an ordinary company for commercial enterprises. QANTAS Airways Ltd and AUSSAT Pty Ltd[125] are well-known examples, but there are or have been others—Aboriginal Hostels Pty Ltd, Amalgamated Wireless (Australasia) Ltd, Applied Ecology Pty Ltd, British Commonwealth Pacific Airlines Ltd (in which British and Canada also had shares), Commonwealth Oil Refineries Ltd, Commonwealth Hostels Ltd, Commonwealth Brickworks Ltd and Commonwealth Accommodation and Catering Services Ltd. Usually all or the majority of shares will be held by the Government. Generally speaking, there are no legal objections to the Government acting in this way. However, if the Commonwealth lacked legislative power to establish a statutory corporation, it would probably lack the executive power to incorporate a company with comparable objects.[126]

There has been an increasing tendency for statutory corporations to incorporate subsidiaries under the companies legislation. To advance Aboriginal business interests, the Aboriginal Development Commission has shareholdings in a range of companies. To compete with its private-enterprise rival, the Australian National Airlines Commission has, as its fully owned subsidiaries, companies which provide holiday and travel services. Like some other banks, the Commonwealth Banking Corporation has incorporated a range of subsidiary finance companies. And so on. Legally, statutory corporations can incorporate subsidiaries or buy shares in companies already incorporated if it is not *ultra vires* their statutory powers. In *Kathleen Investments (Australia) Ltd v. Australian Atomic Energy Commission*,[127] the High Court held that the Commission could have had power to purchase shares in Mary Kathleen Uranium Ltd. (The issue was not finally determined since the Court said that the case had been incorrectly pleaded.) Its Act enabled it to acquire and hold personal property (shares are personal property); one of its functions was to encourage others to undertake exploration for, and mining and treatment of, uranium; and it was empowered to do what was necessary or convenient for or in connection with the performance of its functions. It is clear from the judgments that although some of the objects of the company went beyond those of the Commission, that by itself was not fatal.[128]

The ordinary company form offers several advantages for government enterprises. First, there is no need for special legislation to create such an entity, although there will need to be a parliamentary appropriation to subscribe for or purchase the shares. Second, it allows for participation by private interests. Third, government enterprises in the form of a company are more flexible than statutory corporations, in that there is no need for legislation to change their memoranda and articles. They may also be in a more competitive position, and are less likely to attract opposition, by acquiring the appearance of being in a favoured position with respect to such matters as government financial assistance.[129] Ministerial control can be exercised by suitably drafted articles and by means of a contract with the company.[130]

Accountability

Some lawyers work under the illusion that the courts can ensure the accountability of government, including government enterprises. There is the very occasional case where a government enterprise has been held to have acted *ultra vires* its statutory powers.[131] Even if such instances were multiplied many times, judicial review would be too unsystematic and too specific in its operation to ensure accountability. To ensure parity with private enterprise, certain statutory corporations are excluded from having to provide reasons for their decisions, as required by the *Administrative Decisions (Judicial Review) Act* 1977, in respect of their commercial activities.[132] For the same reason, it would seem that jurisdiction over government enterprises has not been conferred on the Administrative Appeals Tribunal.[133]

Limited accountability comes from parliamentary scrutiny. Most statutory authorities are obliged under their legislation to prepare annual reports, which are tabled in Parliament, and the Auditor-General's reports are also an opportunity for debate on their activities. Details of the exercise of a ministerial power of direction may have to be furnished to Parliament.[134] Ministers also refer questions asked by members about statutory authorities to the authorities involved, even on matters of detailed administration.[135] Parliamentary committees, such as the Senate Standing Committee on Finance and Government Operations, ensure further parliamentary accountability. Ultimately Parliament can change the constating legislation of statutory authorities if they are regarded as being too autonomous. No doubt these various mechanisms could work more effectively. But laments about the weaknesses of parliamentary accountability are frequently misdirected because they fail to address an issue which is just as important, namely, whether statutory authorities are performing their role effectively. Moreover, they are often simple-minded, for they fail to take account of the varying nature of statutory authorities. While close parliamentary scrutiny might be appropriate for some, it is not necessarily desirable in the case of others such as universities or government enterprises competing with the private sector.[136]

Financial scrutiny is perhaps the most effective form of accountability for government enterprises.[137] The Budget papers contain information on the estimates of expenditure for some government enterprises, either as part of those for the relevant department or in the information given for certain 'one-line' Budget-dependent agencies.[138] The Auditor-General examines the accounts of statutory authorities and some companies of which the government is shareholder.[139] However, auditing requirements for a statutory authority have not necessarily applied to its subsidiaries.[140] There is no legal reason for this: so long as a statutory authority has a majority of shares in a company, it can impose suitable reporting and auditing requirements through its power to appoint and remove directors[141] and auditors.[142]

III REGULATION, LAW AND THE ECONOMY

So far we have been concerned with the law relating to direct participation by government in the economy—government spending and borrowing, taxation and entrepreneurial activity. Law also provides the framework for economic activity by the non-government sector, both through regulatory legislation and through judge-made law. Some regulatory legislation is directly concerned with achieving economic ends. For convenience this is called economic regulation and is the first subject of this part of the chapter. But regulatory legislation in general has economic implications, as does judge-made law, and each of these is examined in turn.

Economic regulation is justified on prudential grounds, that is, to protect depositors and investors and to ensure economic stability; and as a means of achieving economic objectives, especially monetary and external policy and social objectives. In general terms, prudential regulation can be effected through controls on entry, official liquidity and solvency support arrangements, the disclosure and vetting of financial information, and so on. Monetary aims are pursued through controls on interest rates, lending policies, asset ratios and deposits. External policy is effected largely through exchange control. Typically, economic regulation is characterized by the conferment of a much wider discretion than in regulatory legislation in general. Moreover, economic regulation tends to be institutionally focused: in other words, there is discrete legislation for banking, insurance, building societies, credit unions and so on, instead of regulation of particular economic activities such as lending. For reasons of space, the discussion below is confined to the regulation of banks.

Regulatory legislation has already been examined at some length in the first chapter. The particular concern here, however, is the economic dimension of regulatory legislation. This is fairly obvious with some regulation. For over a century, companies legislation has provided the framework for a great deal of economic activity, because it creates a structure of rights and obligations which survive individuals and because of the advantages afforded by limited liability. Regulation of the stock market, of company takeovers and of foreign investment clearly channel economic activity. And so on. Rather than simply describing some of this legislation, however, we take up the themes used early in the book to ask: to what extent is regulatory legislation motivated by economic concerns? Are economic concepts given direct expression in the legislation? Do economic factors bear on its implementation? And what of its economic impact?

Finally, we turn to the courts. Two issues are addressed—the influence of economic ideas on judges deciding cases, and the economic impact of judicial decisions. The first issue is relatively straightforward, the second less so, since the issue is sharply contested and empirical evidence bearing on the matter is lacking. While it is easy enough to say that the law of contract as a whole facilitates private economic activity, it is very difficult to say the same about particular contract doctrines or whether alternative doctrines would make a scrap of difference.

Economic regulation

Any government must have legal control over its currency, not only to ensure a stable medium of exchange but also as an instrument of public credit (the power to print money).[143] Under section 51(xii) of the Australian constitution, the Commonwealth Government is empowered to do this. Consequently, the *Coinage Act* 1909 replaced English coins, made and issued under the prerogative, with Australian coins.[144] Since 1910 private banks and the States have been prohibited from issuing notes as legal tender.[145] Until 1976, gold was subject to tight control, even though no longer regarded as the anchor of public credit.[146] Various criminal provisions protect the currency against counterfeiting and forgery.[147]

Institutionally, control is exercised through the licensing of banks and the registration of non–bank financial intermediaries. The *Banking Act* 1959 imposes a daily penalty for those carrying on any banking business in Australia without approval.[148] In accordance with fairly orthodox principles, the High Court has held that contracts made by a body carrying on business in breach of the section are still enforceable civilly.[149] There are no criteria laid down in the Act as to how approval is to be granted. In practice prudential considerations, ensuring a range of banking services, and promoting competition in banking, are taken into account.[150] There is no definition of banking business in the Act. The High Court has given the concept of banking a wide definition, extending well beyond providing current account and cheque facilities to cover receiving deposits and lending the money so obtained.[151] Consequently, non–bank financial intermediaries, which fall within the extended definition, must seek exemption under the Banking Act from compliance with its terms (s.11).

As a prudential safeguard for depositors, the *Banks (Shareholdings) Act* 1972 limits any one shareholder or group of related shareholders to a holding of less than 15 per cent of the voting shares of a bank (s.10). Increases beyond 10 per cent, but less than 15 per cent, need the approval of the Treasurer. Exemption from the 15 per cent limit can be granted by the Governor-General if in the national interest—a term undefined in the legislation. Since 1985, exemptions have been granted to facilitate the establishment of a number of new banks. Shareholders have had to demonstrate an extensive record of foreign strength and stability, and the financial strength to maintain the viability of the bank; and have had to give an unqualified commitment to the prudential development of the bank.[152]

Under the *Banking Act* 1959 licensed banks obtain certain protection for their depositors, but are obliged to keep statutory reserve deposit accounts with the Reserve Bank; may have their policy on advances and interest rates determined by the Reserve Bank; if a savings bank, will have their investment policy determined;[153] and must furnish financial information on a regular basis and other information as the Reserve Bank directs. The *Financial Corporations Act* 1974 applies to a foreign, trading or financial corporation (the phraseology of section 51(xx) of the constitution), with assets in excess of one million dollars, if its sole or principal business activities in Australia are the borrowing of money and the provision of finance; if its assets resulting from the provision of finance exceed 50 per cent of total assets in Australia; or (in the case of a retailer), if it has instalment credit finances for terms over three months exceeding five million dollars (s. 8(1)). Such corporations must register under the Act—unlike licensing, registration cannot be refused—and furnish financial information to the government.[154] Over 800 corporations were registered under the Act in 1986. Under Part IV, controls are possible over asset ratios, lending policies and interest rates, but this part of the Act has never been proclaimed. While regulated to a greater degree than non-bank financial intermediaries, banks can offer a wider range of financial services and have appeal to some depositors for prudential reasons.

Exchange control is an area characterized legally by wide discretion. Traditionally this form of regulation has been used as an instrument of economic management (to conserve foreign exchange, to prevent destabilizing capital flows), for nationalistic reasons (to support foreign investment policy), and for subsidiary purposes.[155] Since the formal floating of the exchange rate in 1983, and further changes in 1984, the subsidiary purposes have become dominant and exchange control is concerned mainly with ensuring payment of Australian tax and underpinning foreign investment policy.[156] Perusal of the legislation, however, does not make this immediately apparent.

The Banking (Foreign Exchange) Regulations, made under section 39 of the Banking Act, restrict the transfer and ownership of money, assets and rights in and out of Australia, within Australia on non-resident account and outside Australia on Australian account.[157] Regulation 42(1) creates the offences of contravening, attempting to contravene or failing to comply with any of the regulations—a provision held to be *intra vires* the Banking Act.[158] The constitutional validity of the regulations derives from a variety of provisions of the Australian constitution.[159] The prohibitions in the regulations are worded to apply except with the authority of the Reserve Bank and so that the Bank can authorize agents to do things otherwise prohibited. Agents must comply with any instructions, directions or requirements of the Bank (reg. 44). Moreover, the regulations give the Bank express power to exempt from the application of the whole or any of the provisions (unconditionally or otherwise, and subject to the directions of the Treasurer), and to issue a general authority authorizing a person or class to do acts or things otherwise prohibited (reg. 38, 38A). Subject to the directions of the Treasurer, the grant of any authority by the Bank is in its absolute discretion and may be granted unconditionally or subject to such conditions as the Bank thinks fit (reg. 39). It is on the basis of those wide discretions that exemptions have been given from controls on certain investments and payments and for exports.[160] As a matter of law, it is not correct to say that these discretions can be exercised 'in a fully arbitrary and discriminatory fashion';[161] their exercise must be *intra vires*, take relevant considerations into account; and so on.[162] Nonetheless, it must be said that it is impossible to determine exchange rate policy by reference to the legislation—a matter to be deplored.

Informal controls are as important in some aspects of economic regulation as those given legal form. A good example is the LGS (liquids and government securities) convention, established in 1956, to ensure that trading banks can cope with increases in the demand for loans or the withdrawal of deposits, differences in the maturity patterns of assets and liabilities, and unanticipated shortfalls in cash flows.[163] By agreement with the Reserve Bank, the banks agree to hold currency and deposits with the Reserve Bank and Commonwealth government securities equivalent to a certain percentage of their deposit liabilities in Australia. For savings banks, a liquidity ratio is embedded in regulations.[164] Another example of informal control occurs with interest rates. As indicated, these can be controlled under the Banking Act, but in practice the Reserve Bank has avoided formal control and set maximum interest rates through informal processes.[165]

Regulatory legislation and economic activity

Regulation of business activity has sometimes been justified in economic terms.[166] Market failures have been identified and regulation prescribed as a means of promoting competition, controlling for externalities, correcting for inadequate information, dealing with excessive competition, correcting for underinvestment, controlling for moral hazard and rationalizing inefficient industry. These economic justifications can be illustrated by brief reference to the first three. Promoting competition lay behind the Trade Practices Acts of 1965 and 1974. As well as achieving productive efficiency and higher output, it was said, the legislation would also produce macro-economic results such as more growth and less inflation.[167] The best example of externalities is the polluting factory which, in the absence of regulation, does not have to pay the full cost of disposing of its wastes. Instead of that 'cost' being reflected in the price of the product, it is borne either by those living in the area (air pollution) or by recreational users and fishermen (water pollution).[168] Consequently, legal control of pollution actually reduces the misallocation of resources which results because it compels a business to take into account more fully the social costs of its operation. Externalities also exist with hazardous industrial processes (workers bear costs through ill-health, which is inadequately compensated) and unsafe consumer products (even if the law provides a remedy, consumers frequently fail to pursue it).[169]

Regulation prompted by the inadequate provision of information is designed to enable consumers and others to make more rational decisions.[170] One reason for this kind of regulation is that advertising is not really concerned with giving the consumer detailed information, while intermediaries who provide information, such as doctors, retailers or consumers' associations, often know too little about products or are not in a position to make information available, at least on a regular, usable basis. It may be that with inexpensive, one-off purchases, a lack of information is not necessarily disastrous, for consumers will learn from 'their' mistakes (although of course, those below the poverty line may be so hard pressed that they are not in a position to waste even a few dollars). But the ill effects of a product, even a relatively inexpensive one, may be quite catastrophic, as with an unsafe drug. With more complex and expensive products individual customers are not in a good position to make an evaluation or to draw on experience. Similarly, workers may not know enough about the health and safety problems associated with their work, such as the long-term hazards associated with certain manufacturing processes. Better information in these areas might result in harm being avoided and lead to a reduction in costs.

But typically regulation has been justified for a range of non-economic reasons: a reduction in fraud, misrepresentation and unfair practices in the market place; better-quality goods, services and housing; lower prices; State preference; national emergency; the preservation of wilderness areas; a reduction in pollution and the siting of industry so that it is compatible with residential living; an improvement in health and safety at work; and so on. There are also nationalist objectives such as retaining substantial control over economic activity in local hands through restricting foreign investment.[171] In addition, some regulation has also partly resulted from objections to undesirable attitudes and behaviour associated with the unregulated market—acquisitiveness, and the exploitation of and disregard for others. Instead of people being at the mercy of market forces, it has been said, regulation will advance values such as fairness, equality and control by people over their own activities.[172] Another objection to the unregulated market has been that the economic power it allows can be used to subvert political democracy both directly, through influencing law-makers, and indirectly, through corrupting the values of society.

Given the presence of non-economic considerations behind much of the regulation of economic activity, it should not be surprising that economic terms and concepts are often not close to the surface in the resultant legislation.[173] This is clear in legislation which directly prohibits an activity, such as the consumer protection part of the *Trade Practices Act* 1974 or the *Export Control Act* 1982 (which permits controls on exports). Even if legislation contains some discretion, while being generally prohibitory, economic factors might not appear on its face. Thus foreign control and national interest are the grounds which the Treasurer must weigh up, under the *Foreign Takeovers Act* 1975.[174] In practice economic factors seem to be taken into account as one aspect of national interest.[175]

Economic considerations might be mixed with other considerations in legislation which confers a significant discretion to recommend, to approve or to decide. The Industries Assistance Commission must have regard to the following 'general policy guidelines' when it holds inquiries and makes reports: it must attempt

(a) to encourage the development and growth of efficient Australian industries that are internationally competitive, export-oriented and capable of operating over a long period of time with minimum levels of assistance;

(b) to facilitate adjustment to structural changes in the economy by industries and persons affected by those changes, and to minimize social and economic hardships arising from those changes; and

(c) to recognize the interests of other industries, and of consumers, likely to be affected by measures proposed by the Commission.[176]

Take another example: in exercising its power and performing its functions, the Prices Surveillance Authority must have particular regard to the need to maintain investment and employment, taking into account the influence of profitability on these; it must discourage those in a position to influence substantially a market for goods or services from taking advantage of that power in setting prices; and discourage cost increases (arising from increases in wages and changes in conditions of employment) that are inconsistent with principles established by relevant industrial tribunals.[177] A final example which might be mentioned is the enormously wide power of the National Companies and Securities Commission to exempt companies and transactions from the Takeovers Code or to modify its operation.[178] In exercising these powers the legislation obliges the Commission to 'take account of the desirability of ensuring that the acquisition of shares in companies takes place in an efficient, competitive and informed market', but then goes on to specify additional, non-economic factors, having to do with ensuring that all shareholders of a target company can participate equitably in a takeover bid.[179]

Decisions under such legislation must take the economic considerations specified into account. That is the legislative mandate. But the legislation contains such wide discretion that it can hardly be said to require particular decisions. There is a series of English cases where courts overturned the decisions of local authorities on the ground that the decisions were not based on the economic considerations required.[180] The cases represent a gross intrusion by the courts into the political process. In each case the legislation either did not mention economic factors or was equivocal as to what was required. Moreover, underlying the outcome was the peculiarly English notion of the fiduciary duty of local authorities to ratepayers. These cases provide no authority for Australian courts to grant judicial review on the basis that economic factors have not been given sufficient, or conclusive, weight, if legislation confers a wide discretion to consider a range of economic and non-economic factors.

In any event, judicial deference would seem to be demanded by the comparative advantage which bodies like those mentioned in the last paragraph but one possess in economic matters. Australia's first anti-monopoly legislation came to grief partly because the High Court, and then the Privy Council (but not the trial judge, Isaacs J), failed to come to grips with basic economic arguments.[181] Even today one can question the contribution of the courts to competition policy because of the way they handle economic subject-matter. The legal system is concerned with clear-cut answers, it limits the available evidence and it focuses on matters like intent, good faith and consent, all of which are not necessarily consistent with economic analysis.[182] Although the evidence is slim, it may be that the present High Court recognizes its limitations in the field of economics. In 1984 it held that there was no tort of unfair competition in Australia, since its existence would be inconsistent with existing common law and statutory claims which businesses might have against competitors (passing off, copyright, trade marks, etc.). The main characteristics of such a tort, it said, would be 'the scope it allows, under high-sounding generalizations, for judicial indulgence of idiosyncratic notions of what is fair in the market place'.[183]

An exceptional case, where economic factors are dominant in legislation, is the restrictive trade practices part of the *Trade Practices Act* 1974.[184] If a provision will have the effect of 'substantially' lessening competition, its inclusion is prohibited in any contract, arrangement or undertaking, and corporations must not give effect to it.[185] The same test is used in defining whether exclusive dealing is in breach of the Act, except for product forcing, which is prohibited outright.[186] Similarly, with price discrimination, where suppliers give certain customers more favourable terms.[187] The test is deceptively simple; Deane J has said that the 'word "substantial" is not only susceptible to ambiguity; it is a word calculated to conceal a lack of precision'.[188] Moreover, general agreements affecting competition might be authorized, and exclusive dealing protected, where the public benefit outweighs the anti-competitive effect.[189] Public benefit, however, includes the economic goals of efficiency and progress.[190]

Monopolization and mergers also fall within Part IV of the Act. In the case of monopolization, the issue is whether a corporation in a position substantially to control the market uses its position adversely against competitors.[191] Mergers are prohibited if they result in, or strengthen, the power of the acquirer to control or dominate the market.[192] In both cases, although economic factors are not on the face of the legislation, they are implicit.[193]

Economic factors are rarely introduced formally into law enforcement. The closest is if legislation obliges steps to be taken which are reasonably practicable in the circumstances.[194] In the absence of a provision like this, it might not even be possible to consider economic factors. *Phosphate Co-operative Co. of Australia Ltd v. Environmental Protection Authority*,[195] was a case that arose in Victoria. Under the Act establishing the Authority, licenses could be granted for environmental discharge, subject to such conditions as the EPA thought fit. The High Court held that the statutory language indicated that the only concern should be the protection of the environment, unqualified by any consideration of an economic or other kind. Aickin J dissented, taking the view that the statutory authorities 'would be bound to consider at least some other matters of general public interest, including the economic interests of the community, which may outweigh the prevention or elimination of some particular example of pollution'.[196] In practice, however, enforcement authorities sometimes make a rough cost-benefit calculation on an informal basis, in deciding whether to institute legal proceedings against a regulatory breach.

There can be no doubt that regulation can have an economic impact, whether it be the annual gross subsidy equivalent of tariffs, the salary costs of government employees engaged in regulation, a decision of the Australian Conciliation and Arbitration Commission to increase the national wage, or the indirect financial assistance provided by regulation.[197] What of its impact, however, on economic goals such as greater competition, efficiency and growth? Some regulation is designed to promote, and is generally accepted as having furthered, such goals. An example is Part IV of the Trade Practices Act; another is legislation such as the *Automotive Industry Act* 1984, designed to restructure Australian manufacturing by use of protection policy.[198] It seems generally accepted that there are clear examples of the Trade Practices Act producing immediate benefit to the consumer, as in striking at collusive price fixing and resale price maintenance, although the main benefit is said to be longer-term—in promoting a climate for competition and efficiency, in encouraging efficient industry structure, and so on.[199] The latter is difficult to evaluate, and systematic studies are needed. For example, it might be that while restrictive practices have been abandoned, competition has been eroded by takeovers and mergers within an industry.[200] This is not to deny the difficulties in identifying the influence of the Trade Practices Act from all the other influences on competition.[201]

Much has been said, on the basis of economic theory, about the deleterious effects of most regulation on income-generating capacity. For example, it is said that there is little to support the economic argument that the two-airline agreement prevents wasteful competition (there is no basis for saying excess capacity will occur), provides a better network (there will always be small operators prepared to operate 'less profitable' routes), or avoids natural monopoly (there is virtually no empirical evidence that there are significant economies of scale in airline services). Nor do social considerations add much weight (safety, defence, natural development and fuel conservation objectives can be achieved in other ways).[202] While the intrusion of regulation into economic affairs may be appropriate in particular cases, such as this, a great deal of the criticism is based on dubious theory, without empirical evidence to support it.[203]

Courts, economics and economic activity

While judges do not decide cases with economic reasoning, there is no doubt that economic ideas influence the development of judge-made law. Until comparatively recently, judges were affected in their decisions on contract law by *laissez-faire* ideology.[204] So too with some aspects of tort law. In the nineteenth and first part of the twentieth century, workers might fail completely in a claim for damages for personal injuries, even if their employer was clearly at fault, because of the wide defences the judges evolved—*volenti* (that employees had voluntarily assumed the risk), common employment (that the injuries arose from the negligence of a fellow worker), and contributory negligence. These defences to a damages claim were given a wide scope 'in order to ease the employer's financial burden...'.[205] Later courts and parliaments gradually whittled them down in response to the growth of the political power of trade unions. Workers' compensation which is awarded irrespective of fault was also introduced.

Economic ideas have permeated the interpretation by some High Court judges of the Australian constitution. Section 92 provides the clearest example. In the 1950s the High Court firmly accepted that the section gave a right to individuals to engage in trade and to be subject to limited regulation only. This formulation gave scope to the judges to introduce their economic predilections under the guise of legal principle. For a while, under the influence of Dixon CJ, the High Court largely avoided the appearance of doing this by using an analytical approach, but that has since broken down and the judges now tend to look to the practical effects of legislation on interstate trade.[206] Barwick CJ, who was largely instrumental in overthrowing the Dixon formulation, introduced free-market ideas through section 92 to strike at legislation on consumer protection, food manufacture and the marketing of primary products.[207] Barwick CJ would have limited the reach of legislation to the control of deceitful, fraudulent, restrictive or monopolistic practices —a concession to regulatory legislation consistent with the ideas of Adam Smith. The middle, and majority, position on the High Court is occupied by judges whose decisions are more sympathetic to government regulation than the free-market views of Barwick CJ. Their decisions have been responsible for validating the type of legislation mentioned. In their view a law which regulates trade practices, even a law which prohibits undesirable trade practices, may be compatible with section 92, although to constitute permissible regulation there must appear to be an undesirable trade practice and the law must constitute reasonable regulation in the light of that practice. Their economic philosophy is consistent with the existence of a mixed economy, although they fall along different parts of a mixed-economy spectrum. As Mason J put it in one decision:

The freedom guaranteed by s.92 is not a concept of freedom to be ascertained by reference to the doctrines of political economy which prevailed in 1900; it is a concept of freedom which should be related to a developing society and to its needs as they evolve from time to time.[208]

In a later decision, Gibbs and Wilson JJ recognized, with regret, the strengthening of regulation in Australia's mixed economy:

Absolute freedom of interstate trade commerce and intercourse requires that the citizens of this Commonwealth shall within the framework of a civilised society be free to engage in these things. The difficulty is that the trend of political theory and practice is to develop and strengthen that framework more and more and often at the cost of individual liberty; but however conservative or reactionary it may seem to some, this court cannot write s.92 out of the Constitution. It must therefore do its best to preserve a balance between competing interests, a balance which favours freedom for the individual citizen in the absence of compelling considerations to the contrary.[209]

Economic ideas are less apparent, but none the less present, in other aspects of constitutional interpretation. For example, section 51(xxxi) provides that the Australian Parliament can make laws for the acquisition of property on just terms from any person for any purpose in respect of which it can make laws. The High Court has given the section a broad interpretation as to its reach and the amount of compensation payable.

Such an interpretation, while not necessarily directly motivated by free-market economics, is certainly in keeping with it because it acts as an inhibition on Federal government interference with private property rights.[210] Indeed, in one decision, Barwick CJ and Aickin J (both dissenting) described the section as a 'constitutional safeguard'.[211]

Economic ideas have had an influence on the judges of the Commonwealth Court of Conciliation and Arbitration, and (after 1956) members of the Australian Conciliation and Arbitration Commission, in balance with considerations like industrial relations and social justice. Since the Depression the Court/Commission has taken into account the likely economic effects of its wage-fixing decisions.[212] This has been done in various ways. Ought capacity to pay be the dominant factor, or achieving an acceptable growth in real wages? Should capacity to pay be measured by an increase in the level of prices, or a wider range of factors?[213] Whether articulated or not, economic ideas have been at the base of the varying answers given to such questions. Not surprisingly, doubts have been expressed over the years about the capacity of the Court or Commission to assess the economic evidence and the relation between economic and other factors.[214]

So far the discussion has been about the influence of economic ideas on the courts. What of the economic implications of what they do? Doctrines such as freedom of contract, the protection given to private property rights and the constraint of government activity have certainly been hallmarks of judicial activity. It can therefore be said that the common law has provided an underpinning to the operation of markets. Enforcing promises (as in contracts) facilitates transactions (and so promotes trade and hence wealth) by reducing the costs of policing markets. Private property rights contribute to economic efficiency since people who own property have an incentive to maximize the income stream generated by its use. In addition, it should not be forgotten that the courts play a role when economic adventures turn sour, perhaps because of government economic policy. Under insolvency law, they adjudicate on rights when this occurs (as between different types of creditors and as between creditors and the insolvent), thereby enabling entrepreneurial activity to begin afresh.[215]

But none of this takes us very far. Judges do not always favour the values mentioned. In any particular case the accretion of previous decisions might virtually decide a matter (the doctrine of precedent). Market considerations might take the back seat because in particular situations their application is uncertain or because other factors are present (the simplest example is contrary legislation). Moreover, there might be a conflict in values, for example, between freedom of contract and freedom of competition and entry. On this basis restraint of trade doctrines might take precedence over freedom of contract.[216]

Nonetheless, some writers have argued that the common law as a whole has furthered economic efficiency. The argument is not so much that the common law duplicates the results of free markets, but that it brings the economic system closer to producing the results that effective competition would produce.[217] The difficulty with this interpretation is that its proponents never explain adequately why it is that common law rules are efficient and how it is that they are efficient. One argument is that the common law is efficient irrespective of the motivations of judges because inefficient rules are litigated and eventually overturned.[218] The argument is not convincing to anyone with a passing acquaintance with the vagaries of litigation. Is it that judges have economic insight akin to that of the professional economist to choose the efficient outcome? It can hardly be said that judges have access to great quantities of economic data or are *au fait* with sophisticated economic analysis. The proponents of this view retort that many businessmen are ignorant of economic analyses yet still maximize efficiency—but this will hardly do. While the yardstick of profit is easily understood, it is much more difficult to say what is the most efficient outcome in many of the cases coming before the courts.

What of particular legal doctrines? Negligence has given rise to some discussion in Australia. That negligence has economic implications is illustrated by a decision of the High Court in 1979. In *Commissioner of Railways v. Ruprecht*[219] a railway shunter was severely injured when struck by a wagon during shunting operations due to the negligence of another employee (which in law is sheeted home to the employer). The issue was whether the worker should have his damages reduced because of contributory negligence in not looking to avoid the wagon. By majority the High Court said no. In his decision, Murphy J lays bare the economic dimensions of the case:

Sophisticated warning systems are now, and were then, readily available; for years, two-way radios, beepers and remote-control devices have been children's toys, but Mr Ruprecht and his fellow workers had no devices to warn of vehicle movements which might endanger them. . . . Those familiar with Australian industry know that safety precautions are habitually disregarded in factories and workplaces. Employers close their eyes because safety precautions slow down production and are expensive. Employees also often consciously disregard safety.[220]

The import of his decision is that it is unjust for employers who fail to adopt safety measures, perhaps because of the cost, to then use contributory negligence to cut into the damages payable for any resulting injury.

However, some writers have gone further in elucidating the economic impact of negligence. In negligence decisions doctrine demands that risk be balanced against the measures necessary to eliminate it.[221] On this basis, it has been said that in applying the doctrine of negligence the courts minimize social costs by pitching the standard of care at the efficient level. This creates an incentive on the part of enterprises or motorists to avoid accidents up to that point where the cost of doing this is less than the expected cost of paying claims. A simple example concerns the notion that courts should reduce the damages of those injured in motor car accidents who fail to wear seat belts. This would be regarded as efficient in inducing people to take cheap danger-avoiding action.[222] Negligence is contrasted with strict liability, which is said to be inefficient because it makes workers and motorists become careless (since they know that if they are injured they can still obtain damages regardless of fault).

None of this is very satisfactory. Strict liability might be more efficient in some areas because it places responsibility in advance on those who as a general proposition are the cheapest cost avoiders of accidents.[223] But even if it can be established that the 'law in the books' is efficient, the 'law in action' is something quite different. Many negligence claims are settled out of court with smaller damages than the courts would award and so presumably are at an 'inefficient' level. It is not always easy to know accident prevention costs or the probability of an accident occurring and thus pick the cheapest cost-avoider, or for the party so designated to know what is the efficient safety level. Just what 'incentives' common law doctrines signal is questionable; for example, the damages payable on death are much less than those obtainable for serious injury.[224] People are locked into particular situations by realities which are far removed from the fictions of free-market theory. The migrant worker undertakes low-paid and dangerous work not through choice but through necessity. Not even businesses react rationally to incentives to minimize hazards, and there are organizational factors which impede the introduction of safety standards throughout a company even if they are adopted as company policy. Quite apart from perceptual errors, it is clear that many of those with a legal claim do not pursue it at all. Most importantly, there are and must be other factors in the common law besides efficiency. The cheapest cost avoider is not necessarily the person most capable of bearing the loss. In fact tort doctrines in this area have been increasingly motivated by considerations of compensation and imposing the losses on those who can bear them (loss-spreading). If there is an economic rationale to modern tort developments, it is that the cost of accidents is a social cost.

IV   CONCLUSION

Few lawyers have taken an interest in the law relating to the economy except when it trespasses on private contractual or property rights. Yet we have seen that it is bulky, complex, and at times legally obscure. However indirectly, it influences the everyday lives of all Australians. Quite apart from the problems with which lawyers are typically pre-occupied, such as constitutional validity and statutory construction, the law relating to economic activity throws light on some of the larger problems in the relationship of law and public policy. For example, while the form of legislation governing government borrowing has remained fairly constant (notably, the *Commonwealth Inscribed Stock Act* 1911), the use to which it has been put has varied considerably in the light of shifts in economic theory. This recalls Renner's point that law can adapt to changing circumstances without necessary changing its form or structure.[225] Conversely, it can be argued that the same economic ends can be achieved through different legal forms. For example, the concept of tax expenditures was developed to reflect the equivalence of tax allowances to government subsidies. Economic law is an area where legislation is relatively open-textured or contains wide discretions to exempt from the ordinary provisions. Appropriation is one example, where legislation is at its vaguest, with the one-line appropriation for all activities of an agency. Foreign exchange law is another, for there is an almost complete dissociation between the words of the legislation and regulations on the one hand, and public policy on the other. Clearly there is a tension between, on the one hand, ensuring that public policy is lawful and falling within what Parliament has approved, and on the other hand providing the flexibility and initiative needed for its implementation. It would be wrong to conclude that accountability can only be furthered by more detailed legislation, for there are other mechanisms by which information about public policy can be distributed and debated.[226]

CHAPTER FIVE

THE ENVIRONMENT

From the time of white settlement, Australians engaged in an unrestrained exploitation, destruction and waste of the country's natural resources. Little thought was given to the adverse consequences for the environment of clearing land, extracting minerals, establishing industries and building towns in the rush for personal gain and societal development.[1] The results have included land degradation, pollution and urban blight. Only in recent decades has the environment become a matter of widespread public concern.[2] It is still far from being a dominant consideration in decision-making, either in the private or public sector compared, say, with economic considerations. Nonetheless, it is now a matter which decision-makers must increasingly have regard to if they are to avoid public criticism and, in many cases, to comply with the law.

In responding to public concern, albeit in some instances in only a limited way, Australian governments have legislated so that environmental considerations are in better balance with exploitation. At one level the legislation reflects a belief that without the intervention of the state, individuals and institutions will not have the inclination or incentive to subordinate economic to environmental concerns. The legislation does not mean that the balance between economic and environmental concerns is anywhere near even. (For example, to foster mining development, State governments have enacted statutes giving force to agreements with mining companies, designed specifically to override environmental legislation.[3]) The legislation is superimposed on private law doctrines, some of which have ramifications for environmental protection. Most of these are property-based, having evolved to accommodate conflicting uses of land and other resources. For this and other reasons they have not acted as other than a marginal control on exploitation of the environment.

The present chapter outlines the law relating to the environment. It is far from being an exhaustive exposition; rather, it is an attempt to provide a framework for understanding the role of law in this and other areas of public policy. Most of the chapter focuses on legislation. First, there is a study of aspects of legislation designed to set out, in a non-justiciable manner, governmental goals and intra-governmental machinery. Then some of the themes discussed in Chapter 1 are pursued, in this context of the form and implementation of environmental protection legislation. The third section details how legislation might be enforceable by individuals on ordinary principles of judicial review, or because it creates public rights which they can implement or confers private rights. Part IV discusses the relevant private law. Finally, there is mention of how law is otherwise relevant to attempts by individuals and groups to pursue environmental protection.

I LEGISLATION AND NON-JUSTICIABILITY

The bases, and variety, of environmental protection legislation, can be used to illustrate a number of points about legislation in general. First, there is the plurality of legal regimes, caused by the constitutional division of legislative power in this area between the Commonwealth and State governments.[4] The Tasmanian Dam case[5] is the latest instalment in this regard. Then there is the fragmentation of legal authority caused by the enactment of different statutes, all related in some way to environmental protection, but emerging in different historical periods, and in many cases being directed to inconsistent ends.[6] So, in Australian jurisdictions, legislation relating to conservation and resource exploitation, to planning and environmental protection, and to different aspects of the environment (land, air, water, dangerous substances and so on) may operate in discrete spheres with few linkages between them.[7] The legal fragmentation is probably also reflected in an institutional fragmentation, so that a range of authorities have functions in matters of environmental concern.

These issues will not be pursued here. Rather, this part of the chapter is directed at the issue of non-justiciable legislation. For legislation does not always create specifically enforceable rights or obligations. It may be aspirational in character or confer a policy-making discretion on government. That does not mean that the legislation is pointless. Legislation gives legitimacy to aspirations, constitutes institutions to pursue them, and can provide a backdrop against which specific decisions with legal consequences can be made. In such cases public policy is being pursued without specific legal restraints, in particular the restraint of possible court proceedings, although within a framework of law. One consequence is that decision-making need not second-guess what the courts might do, but can proceed unimpeded on the basis of political goals, technical considerations or economic calculations.

Statutory goals

Any particular statute or set of regulations might contain a provision of an aspirational nature, non-justiciable in character. Drafters have sometimes set out the aims of legislation in the title or preamble of Acts. 'An Act to conserve the environmental heritage of the State', runs the long title of the New South Wales *Heritage Act* 1977. The preamble to the Victorian *National Parks Act* 1975 reads, in part, 'Whereas it is in the public interest that certain Crown land characterized by its predominantly unspoilt landscape, and its flora, fauna or other features, should be reserved and preserved and protected permanently for the benefit of the public...'. While the long title and preamble may be used as an aid to interpreting other sections of the relevant Act if they are ambiguous, it is clear that they can have no independent legal effect.

Moreover, legislation may set out its objects. An oft-quoted example is section 5(1) of the Commonwealth *Environment Protection (Impact of Proposals) Act* 1974:

The object of this Act is to ensure, to the greatest extent that is practicable, that matters affecting the environment to a significant extent are fully examined and taken into account in and in relation to—
(a) the formulation of proposals;
(b) the carrying out of works and other projects;
(c) the negotiation, operation and enforcement of agreements and arrangements (including agreements and arrangements with, and with authorities of, the States);
(d) the making of, or the participation in the making of, decisions and recommendations; and
(e) the incurring of expenditure,
by, or on behalf of, the Australian Government and authorities of Australia, either alone or in association with any other government, authority, body or person.

There can be no suggestion that sections like this create any legal rights or impose any legal duties.[8] This remains the case even if an Act lays down as one of its objects a role for public participation, as with section 5 of the New South Wales *Environmental Planning and Assessment Act* 1979: 'The objects of this Act are...(c) to provide increased opportunity for public involvement and participation in environmental planning and assessment.' Only if the objects are incorporated by reference in justiciable sections of the Act do they have legal force.[9]

As well as aiding interpretation, these provisions have a wider aim, or at least function, to educate both governmental officials and the public about the desirability of the goals set out. Although this aspect of the legislation is not enforceable in the courts, the fact that there is a statement of goals may raise public consciousness about their desirability and may even lead to their adoption in practice.[10] That they are contained in legislation represents a clear statement of government policy, and provides support for those arguing that action consistent with them is desirable. In summary, the behaviour of officials and individuals may change, even though the legislation does not create legally enforceable rights and duties.

Intra-governmental arrangements

Many intra-governmental arrangements have no legal basis. As a matter of internal management, structures and procedures are instituted within government departments and authorities to achieve particular objectives including environmental protection. The courts have no role here. As Stephen J put it in one decision:

I imagine that no court would, even at the suit of the Attorney-General, entertain proceedings which complain of breach of, for example, some rule made by a departmental head concerning procedures to be followed within his department.[11]

Similarly, arrangements between departments have no necessary legal import. An example would be the memoranda of understanding between the Commonwealth Department of Arts, Heritage and Environment and other Federal departments as to the procedures to be followed to give effect to the *Environment Protection (Impact of Proposals) Act* 1974.[12] Agreements between governments at different levels might not be justiciable because they are too indefinite in their terms or are of a political nature not intended to create legal relations.[13]

Legislative underpinning for intra-governmental arrangements will not necessarily make a difference. A matter might still not be justiciable because it is directed at the structures and internal procedures of government. So a statute might establish a body designed to advise government or to educate the public, but neither its advice nor its educational efforts would be capable of challenge in a court. For example, the Australian Heritage Commission, established under the *Australian Heritage Commission Act* 1975, has the functions of identifying the national estate, advising government what to do with it and educating the public about it.[14] In practical terms the Commission prepares a register of the national estate. This is the only justiciable power the Commission has.[15] Its advisory and educational functions cannot be challenged, quite apart from the issue of standing. Traditional administrative law remedies do not lie, because decisions about advice and education do not affect the rights or legitimate expectations of persons,[16] and because the legislative provisions are too wide to enable anyone to say that there has been a breach.[17] Under the *Administrative Decisions (Judicial Review) Act* 1977, decisions can be reviewed although they are not finally determinative of rights or obligations, or do not have an ultimate and operative effect.[18] But they must be in some way conclusive for immediate purposes, which would exclude the performance of advisory and educational functions.[19]

Another type of legislation lays down statutory provisions for the production of policy statements, administrative procedures or guidelines. The latter might be non-justiciable, although decisions made in the light of them have legal consequences. For example, since 1968 it has been possible for statements of planning policy to be issued under the Victorian *Town and Country Planning Act* 1961. To use the statutory language, these are 'directed primarily towards broad general planning to facilitate the co-ordination of planning throughout the state by all responsible authorities'.[20] Approved statements are laid before both houses of Parliament.[21] Responsible authorities have to have regard to them in preparing planning schemes, making interim development orders or granting permits under them, and departments and public authorities must periodically submit their proposals for developments for comparison with the statements.[22] But the statements are designed to inform decision-making by public bodies, and of themselves have no legal force.

More recently, the *Environment Protection (Impact of Proposals) Act* 1974 empowered the Governor-General to make orders approving administrative procedures providing, *inter alia*, for the preparation of environmental impact statements.[23] The orders must be laid before each house of Parliament to be effective.[24] Ministers must give directions and take actions to ensure that the procedures are given effect and to ensure that any final environmental impact statement prepared is taken into account in decision-making.[25] But it is clear from the legislation as a whole that the procedures are not intended to produce a justiciable issue. That they do not have legal force is indicated, in particular, in that they must be procedures 'that are consistent with relevant laws, as affected by regulations under this Act', and ministerial action pursuant to them must be consistent 'with any relevant laws as affected by regulations under this Act'.[26] In other words, the courts have no role because the legislative intention is that the procedures are to be purely intra-governmental in character. If they are to have any force, it will be indirectly, as a result of subsequent administrative action such as decisions made in the light of them to license or approve, not because they themselves create legally enforceable rights and obligations.[27]

High-level policy-making

Where, say, legislation defines the powers or functions of a body, albeit unclearly, the courts will be slow to conclude that review for *ultra vires* is excluded.[28] Again, even if a minister or other authority is entrusted with power to act 'if satisfied' as to certain matters, or if in their opinion certain matters exist, the courts will still review if the minister or authority has acted without obtaining the requisite degree of satisfaction or without genuinely forming the opinion because, say, he or it can be said to have taken irrelevant considerations into account.[29]

But beyond a certain point legislation confers discretion of such a character that its exercise cannot be reviewed. Take the Federal *World Heritage Properties Conservation Act* 1983, which operates in relation to 'identified property'. This is defined as property forming part of the cultural or natural heritage, being property that the Commonwealth has submitted as suitable for inclusion in the World Heritage List or which has been declared by the regulations to form part of the cultural or national heritage.[30] Clearly the courts could not compel the Government to submit property for inclusion or compel it to make regulations. Take another example, section 26 of the *Archaeological and Aboriginal Relics Preservation Act* 1972 (Victoria).

The Minister may for the purpose of preserving relics—
(a) purchase or otherwise acquire a relic on behalf of the Crown;
(b) purchase land upon which immovable relics may be present; and
(c) erect screens, shelters or other structures or take such other action as is reasonably necessary.

There is no statutory duty to exercise these powers and a court could not compel their exercise.

In neither example is judicial review excluded because the focus is on a failure to act rather than on action. As in other areas of public law, the dichotomy between nonfeasance and misfeasance, or between acts of omission and commission, is not especially helpful.[31] A public authority may be under a public duty, enforceable in the courts, to give proper consideration to the question of whether it should exercise a power.[32] Rather, judicial review is excluded in the examples mentioned, because the powers are of a high-level, policy-making character. Such powers are not justiciable because it is for a minister or public authority, and ultimately the Government, to decide on political or financial grounds whether to submit property for inclusion on the World Heritage List or to purchase an Aboriginal relic. Were any court to treat the matter as justiciable, it would be exercising what are essentially functions of government.

An example of how the courts refuse to review powers of a high-level, policy-making character arose in *Cudgen Rutile (No. 2) Pty Ltd v. Chalk*.[33] Various companies held authorities to prospect for minerals in the Cooloola sands area in Queensland. Under the relevant Queensland legislation, they were therefore entitled to apply for mining leases and have them granted in priority to others. When the companies applied for mining leases, however, the Government refused to grant them, on environmental grounds. Along with other arguments, the companies contended that a court could hear evidence and then could fix the remaining elements necessary to give them effective mining leases. The court rejected the argument:

> But, apart from the fact that other discretions would still remain to be exercised by the Minister, their Lordships cannot accept that the matters referred to could be established by evidence, or could be matters justiciable by the courts. To hold that they were would be to require the court to exercise what are essentially functions of Government. The only standard which the court could apply, in fixing these undetermined matters, would be the standard of what appears reasonable, that is to the court. But it is the Minister, or the Governor in Council, whose judgment as to what is reasonable is required by statute. The judgment of the court is not and cannot be a substitute for the latter.[34]

In their implementation, however, such powers might give rise to legal challenge, for example, on the grounds of *ultra vires* or irrelevant considerations. To continue with one of the examples given above, it might be successfully contended before a court that the minister is preparing to purchase something not a relic within the meaning of the Act. In other words, once a public authority gives effect to such powers, it goes beyond the realm of policy and enters the operational realm of government. By so doing, it may place itself in a position where judicial review is possible and, in addition, where breach of its duty may give rise to an action in tort.[35]

II LEGISLATION—FORM AND IMPLEMENTATION

The framework for analysing legislation developed in Chapter 1 involved consideration of its emergence, form, implementation and impact. The emergence of environmental protection legislation need not detain us. Suffice it to make two points. First, modern environmental protection legislation derives from various sources, for example, public health legislation of the nineteenth century,[36] planning legislation enacted in the 1920s,[37] and pollution and environmental legislation of the 1950s, 1960s and 1970s.[38] While some of the relevant legislation has been incorporated into more general statutes, the underlying policies are far from being fully integrated. Second, by its nature environmental protection legislation is often a direct threat to property and commercial interests. Ambiguities, lacunae and lack of bite may be attributable to this. However, the conflicts underlying environmental protection legislation have sometimes been concealed by devices such as placing decision-making in the hands of experts, tribunals or courts.

As will be recalled, in Chapter 1 legislative form was divided into three categories—broad statutory standards, administrative regulation and prior approval (specifically, licensing). Each of these is examined below. In addition, there is some discussion of implementation in the light of the limited information available. Since there is a dearth of information about the impact of environmental protection legislation, that aspect is not pursued here.[39]

Broad statutory standards

It is not uncommon for environmental protection legislation to adopt a broad standard, coupled with a penalty. Some derives from older, public health law; some has been in place for a quarter of a century; and some is quite recent.

An example of the first type is that part of the *Health Act* 1911 of Western Australia, which instituted control over the establishment of offensive trades (specified in a schedule to the Act or declared to be offensive by proclamation).[40] It became an offence for persons to establish or to carry on an offensive trade without prior approval. These sections continue in force today.[41]

It was in the early 1960s that Australian governments legislated to implement the International Convention for the Prevention of Pollution of the Sea by Oil, 1954.[42] The main effect of the State Acts is to impose strict liability on certain persons where oil or an oily mixture is discharged into waters within the jurisdiction. Where the discharge is from any ship, both the master and the owner are liable. As well, the operators of equipment for the transfer of oil between ship and shore, and occupiers of land, might be liable for spills during a transfer operation. Breach of the provisions can result in the imposition of substantial fines.[43] Certain defences are recognized by the Acts. In relation to ships, it is a defence if the discharge was necessary to secure the safety of the ship, to prevent damage to the ship or cargo, or to save life and it was a reasonable step to take in the circumstances. Alternatively, the escape must have resulted from damage to the ship or from unavoidable and unforeseeable circumstances, and all reasonable steps must have been taken on discovery of the escape to prevent or reduce it.[44]

A recent example of a broad statutory standard, coupled with a penalty, is contained in Victoria's *Environment Protection (Unleaded Petrol) Act* 1984. That provides that a petrol retailer who fails or refuses to comply with a request from a person to be sold unleaded petrol shall be guilty of an offence.[45] Unleaded petrol is defined in regulations. The Environment Protection Authority can exempt petrol retailers when it is satisfied that at their site there is only one suitable underground tank for storing petrol or only one suitable pump, and less than 240 kilolitres have been or will be sold per annum.[46] Defences include an interruption of supplies (industrial dispute, vehicle breakdown, non-delivery by supplier, pump or storage malfunction) and circumstances beyond the defendant's control.[47] Other offences created by the Act include non-supply by a supplier and supply as unleaded petrol of a substance which is not.[48]

Environmental offences in this type of legislation are generally strict liability, so there is no need to establish *mens rea* (intention, recklessness or criminal negligence) on the part of the defendant.[49] However, the prosecution must still prove all elements of the offence, such as causation.[50] The Victorian *Environment Protection Act* 1970 attempts to lessen the burden of establishing causation by placing the onus on an occupier to disprove causation where pollution occurs from the premises of a commercial or industrial undertaking.[51] The legislation might incorporate defences such as unforeseeability, coupled with reasonable precautions. Offences in some cases are continuing offences (so long as pollution occurs), and on-the-spot fines can be imposed for some.[52]

Along with pecuniary penalties, this type of legislation sometimes contains other mechanisms for enforcement. There is the system of pollution abatement notices, which call on a person to comply with the relevant standards.[53] Failure to comply with a notice will be an offence and the person is liable to the imposition of pecuniary penalties.[54] In addition, there are statutory provisions which assist in the prosecution of offences. Under the Victorian Environment Protection Act, for example, a person is deemed to have caused water pollution if 'that person causes or permits to be placed...in a place where it may gain access to any waters' any prohibited or prescribed matter.[55] In a prosecution under that Act for non-compliance with noise standards for motor cars, evidence that a motor car was found to be in breach not more than six weeks after the date of the alleged offence is prima facie evidence that it was capable of being in breach at the date of the alleged offence.[56]

Administrative regulation

Administrative regulation in the field of environmental protection has taken various forms. Planning schemes, as will be seen, involve specifying uses for different areas of land. A similar approach is used in jurisdictions where legislation provides for the preparation of environmental protection policies. For example, the Victorian Environment Protection Act provides for environment protection policies, which when made (as orders in council) have regulatory functions akin to a planning scheme.[57] Such policies identify areas, specify the uses to be protected there, detail the methods for measuring whether the environment is being damaged or not, and if possible set a programme by which their objectives are to be achieved.[58] As with administrative regulation in general, a major difficulty of planning schemes and environmental protection policies is striking a balance between certainty and flexibility.

Another aspect of administrative regulation is the design standard. Some of the Australian design rules for motor vehicles concern pollution. State legislation adapts these standards and makes compliance with them a precondition of motor vehicle registration.[59] Compliance is relatively easily monitored, although it must always be a fine judgment as to whether it is appropriate to freeze a standard in law despite the possibility of a more efficient or less costly technology being evolved.

A final example are the prescribed standards for air, water and noise pollution.[60] An advantage of these is that the administering authority need not be concerned about the variety of ways in which pollution is produced, since the responsibility is on the polluter to adopt whatever technology it thinks appropriate to meet the standard. But there are obvious enforcement problems with scientifically based standards, in detecting breaches and then gathering evidence to prove them in court.[61]

Administrative regulation is underpinned by penalty or other provisions. An interesting example concerns tree preservation orders, made under the New South Wales *Environmental Planning and Assessment Act* 1979.[62] Since tree preservation orders are environmental planning instruments under the Act, the breach of any prohibition in them is an offence, and the courts can impose a pecuniary penalty. In addition, when a person is guilty of an offence involving the destruction of or damage to trees, the court may direct the person

(a) to plant new trees and vegetation and maintain those trees and vegetation to a mature growth;
(b) to provide security for the performance of any obligation imposed under paragraph (a).[63]

Prior approval and licensing

Prior approval as a legislative technique in this area of law is said to have the advantages of preventing environmental problems before they arise. By contrast, broad statutory standards and administrative regulation are said to be either uncertain in their application or haphazard in their enforcement.[64] Prior approval has a relatively long history in legislation relating to land, in particular building regulations. In the form of licensing, prior approval has been used for a variety of purposes such as controlling air and water pollution. Whether prior approval works in practice turns on the nature of the criteria used to grant approval and on the manner in which applications for approval are matched against the criteria.

According to the common law, owners of freehold land could do what they wanted with the land, short of committing nuisance by interfering with neighbours, or acting inconsistently with restrictive covenants and easements. Hence they could not be guilty of waste, and could cut down timber, remove vegetation and dig up the ground.[65] With time, however, legislation has limited the way land can be used. For example, building regulations lay down requirements as to the structure, size and shape of buildings, and prior approval must be sought for building to ensure compliance with them.[66] Building regulations can be used as a means of economic segregation, by maintaining minimum sizes for floor areas or building lots in some areas. The inflexible application of the regulations has given rise to public comment, in particular, inasmuch as they prevent the use of alternative building materials and methods.

Another level of control over land use is zoning, even though that term might not be used in the relevant legislation. Zoning schemes are formulated under planning legislation, which may require attention to be given to environmental considerations. Zoning schemes include a map, dividing an area into different zones. Particular types of use, defined in detail, are contemplated for each zone.[67] Use of land in a particular way, pre-dating planning control, can continue as a lawful non-conforming use, although inconsistent with the current zoning for that area.[68] Lawful non-conforming uses are an obvious blight on a system of planning, for many non-conforming uses are slow to change or to be discontinued. Consequently, the problems from the past cannot be remedied, unless by compulsory acquisition, which is impracticable in most cases because of financial restraints.[69] There will be power to rezone at any time, a decision not generally subject to independent review. Spot zoning, as it is called, is undesirable because it negates the notion of a general plan for an area. On the other hand, if spot zoning were not possible, the prohibitive nature of zoning would block developments which might well be acceptable.[70]

Prior approval enters because, although in particular zones certain uses will be permitted or prohibited absolutely, yet others will be permitted if consent is obtained. The consent may be subject to conditions.[71] Litigation has arisen in this area, on matters such as whether an activity needs prior approval or is permitted absolutely, and the nature of the factors which a planning authority can take into account in making its decision to approve or refuse.[72] Prior approval also features in relation to the sub-division of land. In determining an application for approval, a planning authority may take into account a range of factors, for example environmental impact, the social and economic effects, the character of the land and the development, traffic and transport, and landscaping.[73] Consent may be subject to conditions relating to such matters. A planning authority may also be empowered to impose conditions requiring the developer to dedicate land to the public and to contribute to the cost of public services. The courts have said that conditions must be fairly and reasonably related to the development for which permission is sought.[74]

With time the techniques of, and matters covered by, planning have widened. Since it is impossible to foresee exactly to what use particular land might be put, there needs to be some flexibility in the system. Requiring prior approval introduces that flexibility, especially if approval can be subject to conditions. It also avoids the problem of persons having to interpret standards and then finding that they have done this incorrectly and are therefore in breach of the law. When prior approval has been sought but wrongly granted, an authority might be precluded from taking any action.[75] Whether prior approval ought to be required in all cases where land is to be used, as in Britain, has been the subject of some debate in Australia.

Licensing features in a range of environmental legislation. Controls in the interests of scenic beauty tend to be by way of broad statutory standards, such as those in anti-litter legislation, but licences may be required in some jurisdictions for matters such as display advertising.[76] Legislation usually divides fauna into three categories—unprotected, protected and completely protected.[77] Unprotected fauna can be taken at any time, completely protected fauna can never be taken, while protected fauna can be taken in open season and/or by those with a licence. Where it can be shown that protected fauna are causing damage to property such as crops, special licences may be granted for its destruction. Common criticisms have included inadequate enforcement and penalties in the case of fully protected fauna, that certain species ought to be fully protected, and that in any event licences have been too readily granted and the conditions attached not sufficiently stringent or enforced.[78]

Statutory controls of air and water pollution involve licensing. The history of the Victorian legislation is instructive. In 1970 the Environment Protection Act attempted to license all who discharged, emitted or deposited wastes into the environment.[79] The definition of waste was extremely wide—any prescribed matter or any matter which was discharged in the environment in such volume, constitution or manner as to cause an alteration in the latter.[80] This very universality was self-defeating, and a wide range of activities were consequently exempted in 1981.[81] Notwithstanding this, the licensing system remained cumbersome, inflexible and largely ineffective as a tool of pollution control. Amendments to the Act in 1984 mean that only the occupiers of certain scheduled premises need to obtain licences to discharge wastes into the atmosphere, on land or into water.[82] The criteria for granting licences are set out in State environmental protection plans. In addition a system of control over the design and operation of plants has been effected: prior approval is necessary if persons propose to convert premises into scheduled premises, or to construct or alter scheduled premises or their mode of operation.[83] There is also a works notification scheme for noise pollution.[84] As a result of these changes, the Victorian legislation approaches, in general terms, the controls over pollution in other States.[85]

Implementation

A study of the Victorian Environment Protection Authority in the 1970s found inadequate training of investigation officers, internal conflicts, inefficiencies and low morale.[86] External factors were identified as being important contributories to this state of affairs—the often unenforceable or inadequate statutory provisions, lack of funding, and the restraining influence of the State government. The inadequacies were manifested in various ways. For example, under the guidelines then in force, prosecutions were to be exceptional. An unlicensed discharger was not normally to be prosecuted, despite oral and written requests to obtain a licence, if the discharge had no visible or readily detectable effect on the environment. Action was only to be taken if a breach of licence conditions was important. In any event, 'action' upon the first two breaches by a discharger was to be a request for an explanation. Only the third breach was to lead to preparation of a brief for consideration by the solicitor to the Authority.[87] Exceptionally, a single breach could lead to preparation of a brief in the case of a particularly flagrant breach or obvious pollution.

A decade later, the Victorian Environment Protection Authority apparently had a strategy of moderately strict enforcement, in which prosecution, adverse publicity on conviction, and revocation and suspension of licences were seen as important deterrents.[88] One factor was that the Cain Labor government, elected in 1982, promised more prosecutions for environmental offences before winning office. Although the State Pollution Control Commission in New South Wales instigates more prosecutions than the Victorian Environment Protection Authority, it sees prosecution as a last resort.[89] By contrast with the Victorian and New South Wales bodies, however, environmental protection regulation in other jurisdictions is non-adversarial and tolerant. Advancing development, and taking economic difficulties into account, are often the hallmarks of law enforcement in these States.[90]

Prior approval as a technique of legislative control does not eliminate the problem of implementation. Not only might conditions, say, in planning permits or licences be ambiguous, so that it is unclear whether they have been breached, but some individuals and institutions might deliberately flout them. The nature of the statutory provisions, and the resources available to an administering authority, are factors in whether it will take action, and if so whether it will prosecute, institute proceedings for an injunction, or undertake remedial work to ensure compliance.[91]

There are several aspects to the role of the courts in the implementation of environmental protection legislation. First, the courts interpret the legislation in both civil or criminal proceedings. The higher courts have not always been sympathetic to environmental protection legislation, preferring to construe it against a common law background and to protect property rights.[92] Where legislation is clear and unambiguous, however, the courts have to give effect to it, even if private property rights are adversely affected or they consider the consequences unjust.[93] Second, the courts impose penalties on those in breach of the legislation. Since environmental protection agencies institute prosecutions only when the chances of success are high, most defendants plead guilty. The courts are therefore confined to imposing fines or other penalties. On the whole Australian courts impose low fines for environmental protection offences.[94]

III LEGISLATION AND INDIVIDUAL ACTION

A recurrent theme of this book is that lawyers have failed to give adequate attention to legislation. This is so even in the area of the right of a private person or body to enforce legislation. Important issues such as justiciability and how public rights are identified are often subsumed in the issue of standing. What follows is an attempt to make sense of the issues, drawing on examples from environmental protection law.

Substantive law

There are three ways in which a private person or body might be able to enforce environmental protection legislation in the courts. First, it might be possible to establish that an official or authority, in administering the legislation, is in breach of some administrative law doctrine, for example, has acted *ultra vires* the legislation, taken irrelevant considerations into account in performing functions under it, or failed to exercise the discretionary power conferred by it.[95] Second, an individual might be able to enforce the public rights or obligations created by legislation where these are being breached, be it by a private individual or institution or a public body or official. Third, the legislation might be held to confer private rights on a person or group, who can enforce them as a matter of private law.

1 Administrative law doctrines
Administrative law doctrines have been mentioned already at various points, and it is sufficient here to give a few examples.

Relevant to simple *ultra vires* are the various decisions where a planning authority has failed to comply with procedural steps set out in the legislation, requiring it to give notice of a planning proposal. Because of the practical problems which would flow if a court held that a planning proposal was completely invalid as a result of non-compliance,[96] the courts have divided procedural steps into those which are mandatory and those which are only directory. Non-compliance with the former leads to complete invalidity, but as long as there is substantial compliance with the latter, a court will regard the legislative steps as being satisfied.[97]

Courts give judicial review on a variety of grounds such as irrelevant considerations, improper purpose and a failure to exercise discretion. For example, irrelevant considerations were used as a ground of attack on the decision of the Federal Government to consider environmental factors in whether permission ought to be given for the export of minerals extracted from the sands of Fraser Island. The High Court held that environmental factors were not an irrelevant consideration. An examination of the diversity of goods subject to export approval under the regulations, and the range of authorities involved, meant that no inference could be drawn that considerations were confined to trade or commerce matters.[98]

Judicial review might be refused because of a privative (or ouster) clause in the relevant legislation. Courts generally give these a narrow interpretation. However, a privative clause was ultimately determinative in a challenge to the building of a road through Daintree forest in northern Queensland. Two landowners near Cape Tribulation, at the northern end of the road, challenged the validity of the proclamation made under the Queensland *National Parks and Wildlife Act* 1975–1982, which had excluded a portion of land from a national park so that the road could be built. Section 24(1) of the Act provided that the Governor-in-Council might by proclamation exclude land from a national park for use as a road for public use when satisfied that it was desirable having due regard to the objects and purposes of the Act and to the public interest. Section 25 of the Act provided that the principal object and purpose of the Act was the proper management of national parks, and the cardinal principle to be observed was the permanent preservation to the greatest extent of their natural condition. It was said on behalf of the applicants that the decision had failed to have due regard to these objects and purposes, did not observe the principle of the preservation of national parks, did not consider the prejudicial effect of a road on the environment, and had failed to have due regard to the public interest including potential damage to rainforests and the Great Barrier Reef. The full court of the Queensland Supreme Court held that on the wording of section 24, the objects and purposes of the Act were not the sole or even the dominant consideration to be taken into account in making a proclamation under it, as opposed to managing national parks established by it. In any event, challenges on the basis of irrelevant considerations were barred by a privative clause in section 73(2), which said that no proclamation should be invalid on account of any non-compliance with matters preliminary to such proclamation. This, the court held, was not confined to procedural matters; the various irrelevant considerations pleaded by the plaintiffs were antecedent to the making of the proclamation, and thus could not constitute a basis for judicial review.[99]

2 Public rights

The second basis for individual action is the public rights and duties created by legislation. At the outset, it must be established that the legislation is justiciable. Part I of the present chapter identified three types of non-justiciable legislation—that setting out statutory goals, that concerned with intra-governmental arrangements, and that involving high-level policy-making. Then it must be shown that the legislation creates public rights and duties. The courts fairly readily conclude that legislation is enacted for the benefit of, or in the interests of, the public generally.

They discern in an Act some provision enacted for the benefit of, or in the interest of, the public generally. Such are provisions for the public health or comfort or safety, or for the orderly arrangement of cities or towns, or for keeping public corporations, created for particular purposes, within the ambit of their powers, and so forth. But the categories of cases in which the Courts will act are never closed, owing to the exigencies of society and the great variety of cases that arise... The nature and purpose of the duty or obligation must be considered and also the effect of its contravention upon the public generally.[100]

Finally, it must be established that there has been a breach of the public rights or obligations in the legislation. With some legislation, it is somewhat difficult to do this where, say, the legislation imposes a public duty to do what is 'reasonably practicable'.[101] But if a standard is relatively straightforward, the matter is easier. There are now a number of cases where the High Court has recognized that planning, building and heritage legislation confer public rights, so that a breach can be prevented by way of an injunction or a declaration obtained.[102] The main obstacle to enforcing public rights and obligations, as we shall see, is standing.

3 Private rights

The third method of enforcing legislation is to show that it confers private rights, so that breach gives an individual the right to sue for damages or to seek an injunction or declaration. Exceptionally, there may be an express provision for private rights in the legislation. Otherwise, the courts are slow to recognize an action for breach of statutory duty, as it is called, outside the field of health and safety legislation. In *Australian Conservation Foundation v. Commonwealth*,[103] no private rights were conferred because of the intra-governmental character of the legislation. In *Onus v. Alcoa of Australia Ltd*,[104] the same result was reached because there was nothing to suggest that the Relics Act was passed for the benefit of Aborigines only, rather than all Australians, even if it were assumed that 'relics' in the legislation were confined to Aboriginal relics. But there are a few Australian cases where it has been said that planning and building legislation confers private rights of action on landowners in relation to the building activity of neighbours.[105] Although couched in terms of legislative intention, it is clear that such decisions are based on policy grounds.

Standing

Before reaching the substantive legal issues, a court has to be satisfied as to the threshold issue of whether the applicant before it is the appropriate party to institute the proceedings. The doctrine of standing (*locus standi*) is especially important, since the courts have said that some individuals are not entitled to bring certain actions before them (although others might be permitted to do so). Standing is critical in public law, although it might also operate in private law.[106]

In the area of public law, the doctrine is important as regards the first two substantive law doctrines considered in the previous section. A private person or group must have standing to seek, say, an injunction or a declaration against an official or authority acting unlawfully (*ultra vires*, on the basis of irrelevant considerations, and so on) or against someone acting in breach of the public rights or duties created by legislation. When legislation confers private rights, standing is not the same barrier.

The test for standing is whether the applicant has a special interest in the subject matter of the action. The High Court held, for example, that the Australian Conservation Foundation did not have standing to seek declarations and injunctions against the Australian Government, on the basis that the Commonwealth had approved a proposal by a Japanese company to develop a tourist resort in Queensland in breach of its environmental impact legislation.[107] Neither the obvious commitment which the Foundation had to environmental protection, nor the fact that it had lodged an objection to the development, constituted special interest. Similarly, the court held that an ordinary member of the public did not have a special interest to seek an injunction against the construction of the Franklin Dam in Tasmania on the basis that this would be in breach of the Tasmanian *Rivers Pollution Act* 1881.[108] The status of taxpayer does not constitute special interest.[109] But neighbouring landholders will usually be able to establish that they are specially affected by a proposed development, which might adversely affect their enjoyment or the value of their land.[110] In addition, those with a commercial interest might have standing and be able to harness it for the environmental cause: thus the Fraser Island Defence Organisation Ltd was granted standing to challenge the legality of subdivision on the island because it had business interests in promoting tours there.[111]

An Attorney-General always has standing, as do individuals who obtain his or her fiat (approval), to take proceedings. The courts will not review the refusal of an Attorney-General to give a fiat.[112] There are a number of important environmental cases in which approval has been refused. Perhaps the best example concerns the flooding of Lake Pedder by the Tasmanian Hydro-Electric Commission. The Tasmanian Cabinet instructed the Attorney-General to refuse his fiat to a proposed action by conservationists challenging the legality of the flooding. He resigned, having previously announced that he would give his fiat, and the Premier, who replaced him, refused a fiat.[113] Legislation has conferred standing on a few public bodies, such as local authorities, equivalent to that of the Attorney-General, enabling them to enforce the public rights created by planning and environmental legislation.[114]

In specific areas legislation has widened the doctrine of standing for private persons and bodies. For example, 'any person' can bring proceedings to remedy or restrain a breach of the New South Wales *Environmental Planning and Assessment Act* 1979.[115] Similarly, any person can seek an injunction restraining breach of the *Trade Practices Act* 1974.[116] In *Phelps v. Western Mining Corp. Ltd*,[117] the full court of the Federal Court held that an ordinary citizen had standing to seek injunctions against members of the Australian Uranium Producers Forum on the basis that advertisements they had published contravened section 52 of that Act (misleading or deceptive conduct). The *Administrative Decisions (Judicial Review) Act* 1977 enables any person aggrieved to challenge a decision to which the Act applies. In one case, the Canberra Labor Club, with premises near Lake Ginninderra in Canberra, satisfied this test when seeking to suspend the operation of a ministerial decision to auction blocks between its premises and the lake. It objected that the impact on the foreshore environment would be destructive and the amenities of the area permanently reduced.[118] Both the Australian Conservation Foundation and the National Trust have been held to be a 'person aggrieved' within the Victorian *Environment Protection Act* 1970 and the *Town and Country Planning Act* 1961 respectively.[119]

Remedies and law enforcement

A number of brief, and diverse, points might be made. First, there are the limitations attached to traditional public law remedies. For example, an applicant might not obtain an injunction because of bars such as laches (that is, delay) or because an interlocutory injunction was not sought and, say, a developer has continued to (near) completion despite breach of planning or environmental legislation.[120] Second, claims made to enforce public rights created by legislation face the reluctance of the courts to grant an injunction to restrain a breach of a legislative provision with its own system of penalties.[121] One reason is that to do so would be, in effect, to punish persons without the protections of the criminal law (notably, trial by jury and proof beyond reasonable doubt) to which they might be entitled. But where the penalty in legislation is obviously so low that it is profitable for the defendant to continue to breach it, the High Court has said that an injunction is justified.[122] Third, while an injunction or declaration might be obtained in relation to breach of a public right, damages are not available under *Lord Cairns' Act* 1858 and its successors.[123]

Fourth, anyone can bring a private prosecution for breach of a statutory provision. But legislation might abrogate the right, as with some environmental protection legislation which makes the consent of a specified official a prerequisite to proceedings.[124] Moreover, the Government has in effect a monopoly over the institution and termination of prosecutions on indictment, and might also be able to terminate summary prosecutions.[125] The cost of the private prosecution must be a major factor in its rarity.

Finally, there is the issue of whether action can be taken against a public official or authority failing to enforce the law. As a general rule, there is no obligation on public officials or authorities to prosecute all offences brought to their attention. Legislation implicitly confers a discretion as to whether legal proceedings will be instituted. Just one example: section 103 of the *Conservation and Land Management Act* 1984 (Western Australia) provides that no person 'shall, without lawful authority, fell, cut, injure, destroy, obtain or remove any forest produce in, on, or from' certain land, including Crown land, land under a pastoral lease, land held as a mining tenement or a State forest or timber reserve. The penalty specified is $1000 or imprisonment for a year; on conviction an offender may also be liable for payment of the loss or damage.[126] Whether the Department of Conservation and Land Management will prosecute offenders in a particular case under this section turns on a range of considerations, including the individual involved, the harm caused and the resources available to the Department. There are decisions where the courts have said that they would grant mandamus to ensure that the law in such a case is enforced, for example, by ordering the withdrawal of an instruction that it not be enforced in certain circumstances.[127] In fact mandamus has never been granted in this type of case. Given the reasoning in these decisions, the circumstances where it would be granted have to be quite extreme. Otherwise, as was put in one English decision, it would enable individuals 'to call in question the exercise of management powers and involve the court itself in a management exercise'.[128]

IV PRIVATE LAW

Private law has some role in environmental protection. Restrictive covenants can be used to limit the use of neighbouring land. Apparently planning authorities in Victoria sometimes require developers to undertake to impose restrictive covenants upon the land when it is sold.[129] Restrictive covenants have also been used in legislation for the preservation of historic or architecturally meritorious buildings, the protection of the landscape, and the conservation of Aboriginal relics.[130] Similarly, landowners can insert clauses in leases, obliging their tenants to fulfil conditions about conservation. Much rural land in Australia is held as Crown leasehold, rather than as freehold, and the covenants have set out what leaseholders must do in the way of land management (for example, refraining from overstocking; keeping the land free of noxious weeds; not cutting timber without a licence).[131] Primarily, however, the covenants have been directed at the economic development of land rather than against its degradation.

Environmental protection through restrictive covenants and conditions in leases entails prevention. The concern below is with the extent to which remedial, rather than preventive action, can be taken in private law. However, some preliminary remarks are in order about procedural aspects of private law remedies.

Procedural impediments

The institutional limitations of the courts have been referred to already at various points in this book. The Wade case,[132] for instance, is a notorious illustration of the costs and delays sometimes associated with litigation. Here it is sufficient to refer briefly to two doctrinal impediments.

The first is standing. Only the actual possessors of private land have standing to sue in private nuisance or trespass for interference with it, even though others may be damaged, inconvenienced or annoyed. So, in a Victorian decision it was said that a husband was not an appropriate plaintiff to sue for nuisance from noise from a neighbouring house, since his wife, not he, owned it, and therefore he was only a licensee.[133] Generally speaking, however, standing is not an important obstacle in private law, unlike public law, for there will usually be some person who has standing (in the case mentioned, the wife).

The second is the class action. To the extent that parties can combine together with other parties in litigating an issue, a court can determine it in relation to all of them at the one time, thereby saving costs. The rules of Australian courts provide for joinder, where a claim arises out of the same transaction or series of transactions, and for the representative action, if plaintiffs on the one hand, or defendants on the other, have the same interest.[134] There have been examples of the representative action being used for environmental purposes, such as the six plaintiffs representing others in a Melbourne neighbourhood in a private nuisance action against a noisy car wash operation.[135] And there was the misguided, and ultimately ill-fated, attempt of the Conservation Council of Western Australia and others to bring a class action in a United States Court against United States mining companies, the activities of which were said to threaten a jarrah forest in Perth.[136]

But the courts have given a restrictive interpretation to the degree of identity between claims in relation to joinder.[137] In addition, they have interpreted the 'same interest' requirement narrowly to mean that persons must have the same interest in the same cause or matter. Thus a representative action is not possible where the individual claims arise out of separate contracts with another person or where the relief claimed is damages (at least if the damages need separate calculation).[138] On this interpretation a representative action would not apply to all those who purchased from the one developer land which later subsides, since each would have a separate contract and would have a separate claim for damages, although the contractual terms in each case might be identical. Victoria has sought to abrogate this rule by statute.[139]

Substantive law

Although there is no law of the environment, the common law provides a number of actions and remedies for individuals or groups of individuals against threats to the environment, such as in the case of pollution. As will be seen, their limitations are great mainly because their ambit is to protect private, rather than public, interests. If successful, the remedy will be damages or, in some cases, an injunction. The latter might have the effect of closing down an enterprise.[140]

Private nuisance is the most important common-law action. Shortly stated, it protects actual possessors of land against unreasonable interference with their use and enjoyment of the land. Where material damage results, the reasonableness of the defendant's activity and precautions are irrelevant; but where the complaint is rather of interference with the plaintiff's enjoyment of land, the circumstances are important. The High Court has said that the issue is to balance the right of the occupier to do what he or she likes on his land, and the right of the neighbour not to be interfered with. A useful test is what is reasonable according to the ordinary standards in that particular society.[141] Locality, the time and duration of the nuisance, the nature of the defendant's activity and his motives, all become relevant.

In applying these principles in England, the courts often dealt with environmental questions. Defendants who were responsible for the emission of vapours from a copper smelter destructive to the plaintiff's trees,[142] or noxious fumes and smells from gas retorts,[143] or who operated an oil storage and distribution plant,[144] were successfully sued in private nuisance. On the basis of the doctrine Australian courts have also held, in a number of cases, that defendants could not carry on their trade with impunity. For example, the possibility of an action in private nuisance has been recognized in cases involving the penetrating sound from a sawmill both in a peaceful rural setting and in a mainly residential area,[145] the noise from pneumatic drills outside business premises during office hours,[146] from a speedway[147] or quarry,[148] the emission of smoke or grit from a brickworks in a populated area[149] and of smoke and vapours from a brass foundry,[150] smells from a hide and tallow works[151] or of effluent from a gas works,[152] and damage to the plaintiff's moored yacht from tar seeping from the defendant's gasworks into a river via a council drain.[153]

There are difficulties, however, with private nuisance as an environmental remedy. While non-occupiers who create a nuisance as a result of being on land might be liable,[154] it has yet to be conclusively determined whether the doctrine is available for interference unconnected with the user of land (for example, from use of areas subject to public rights).[155] Moreover, liability for private nuisance probably does not arise for a single isolated incident, not constituting an undesirable state of affairs, although other doctrines considered below might be invoked. As indicated earlier, whether interference with the enjoyment of land constitutes private nuisance depends on circumstances such as locality, so that what is a private nuisance in a middle-class suburb might not be regarded as such in an industrial or working-class suburb.[156] Because the focus is on interference with an individual's land, the deterioration of the general environment in a neighbourhood is not covered by the doctrine. In some situations of interference with the enjoyment of land, what has been called the 'give and take' principle protects the defendant from action.[157] Also, a defendant might have acquired a prescriptive right to commit a nuisance as a result of long use, although a defendant cannot otherwise claim that the plaintiff has voluntarily come into the vicinity of a nuisance.[158]

As to proof of the existence of the nuisance, the courts have taken a commonsense view. Although expert evidence is admitted, a view of the site is usually taken. Town planning, zoning and other legislation may be helpful.[159] Once nuisance is established and it is serious enough to justify an injunction, it is not up to the court with its lack of scientific knowledge to suggest a solution; if the defendant cannot develop means of carrying on its business without continuing the nuisance, it must close down.[160] Usually a period of grace is given to enable the defendant to develop the means of preventing the nuisance.

Public nuisance arises when a person, who need have no interest in land, suffers damage beyond that suffered by other members of the community from a variety of acts, including what today is water, air and noise pollution.[161] If no person can show this special damage, the Attorney-General may bring the action, because of the general rule that actions in the public interest can be brought by the Attorney-General. There are a number of Australian cases. For example, the blasting and other noise emanating from a quarry in a 'singularly quiet and pleasant' bush and residential area was held to be a public nuisance, the full court of the New South Wales Supreme Court adopting the view that public nuisance can be established by proving a sufficiently large collection of private nuisances.[162] Where nauseating smells were produced by the defendant boiling offal on his poultry farm, Else-Mitchell J held that a public nuisance was created, necessitating an injunction.[163] Again, although at common law there has never been any protection of pleasant views or scenic beauty through an action for aesthetic nuisance,[164] a plaintiff was held entitled to damages where his view was obstructed because the defendant mistakenly erected his building on a dedicated public highway, thus being guilty of public nuisance.[165]

As with private nuisance, there are doctrinal drawbacks to public nuisance as a tool of environmental protection. Occupiers are not liable for a public nuisance which they do not create, unless they continue it with knowledge or means of knowledge of its existence. An exception may be if, owing to a want of repair, premises become a nuisance and cause damage to passers-by on a highway or to adjoining owners.[166] But in a leading High Court decision, a passer-by failed in his claim because he had not proved the source of oil pollution, which caused him to slip and fall on the footpath. Consequently, the court said, it could not conclude that the owner-occupier had failed in its duty to keep a structure in repair.[167] When the Black Mountain Tower case reached the High Court, Jacobs J said that it was not a public nuisance to increase traffic upon the highway by creating the tower as an attraction.[168] Moreover, there may be a statutory justification for a public nuisance, if it is an inevitable consequence of the performance of statutory duties or the exercise of statutory powers or authorities.[169]

At common law, owners of land abutting a stream or river had riparian rights. As such, they had a right to substantially unpolluted water, water whose natural qualities had not been affected.[170] If this right was impaired, an action lay. Hence a mine owner could not pump water from its mines into a river affecting its 'hardness',[171] while riparian owners were entitled to succeed against a company discharging effluent containing suspended organic matter, a corporation discharging sewage, and an electricity station raising the temperature of the water, even though there may have been an actionable right against only one, or none of the three individually.[172] Since the rights of riparian owners are regulated in Australia by legislation,[173] can a riparian owner complain of an interference with those rights constituted by pollution? The issue is still open.[174] It might be said that there is no intention manifest in the legislation to deprive persons of their rights to sue if the quality of water is impaired by pollution, even if the right to water flow is affected. Rather it might be said, the legislation gives the Crown new rights, not riparian rights, which are superior to, and which can be exercised in derogation of, private riparian rights, but until those new and superior rights are exercised, private rights continue to coexist.[175] There are some early Australian cases where riparian owners brought successful actions —where waters were polluted by mining operations[176] and wool-washing.[177]

The rule in *Rylands v. Fletcher*[178] imposes strict liability on non-natural users of land who accumulate substances likely to escape. The original doctrine has been refined by later cases, but the rule still has potentiality for a plaintiff if pollutants come from the defendant's land and alight on the plaintiff's land or, it seems, on his property nearby. Hence in a case where the defendant was an occupier of an oil storage and distribution centre, it was held that the doctrine of *Rylands v. Fletcher* applied to 'the sulphuric acid or sulphate in the smuts or oily drops wherever they alight: on washing hung out to dry, as well as on to a motor car in the street'.[179] But 'natural user' has been given an expansive interpretation; the rule might be confined to escape from land, and not cover oil from a ship; and the defendant might be able to point to statutory authorization of its activities.[180]

Trespass seems less applicable in the pollution context, requiring intention and directness. Where the captain of a tanker discharged oil in an estuary which washed up on a beach vested in the defendant corporation, the trial judge was inclined to think that constituted trespass, but in the Court of Appeal and House of Lords it was said that there was not the degree of directness necessary for trespass, the discharge occurring in the estuary.[181] However, a neighbour might be able to invoke it in the case of building and like operations.[182]

Property owners might acquire a right, by prescription, to light for the purposes of illumination, and possibly also to direct sunlight.[183] But it is doubtful whether an owner of a home with a solar heating system could use the doctrine to prevent adjacent building or other activity having the effect of blocking the sun's rays.[184]

V INDIVIDUALS AND ENVIRONMENTAL PROTECTION

Parts III and IV of this chapter examined how individuals might play a part in environmental protection through proceedings in the courts. Does the law say anything about how individuals otherwise participate in decisions affecting the environment?

External review

For some time there have been methods of non-judicial review of public and private decision-making, where environmental considerations might have some influence. Apart from special commissions of inquiry,[185] legislation regulating the development of resources, such as land and minerals, has given rise to quasi-judicial bodies such as land (and environment) courts, town planning appeal tribunals and mining wardens' courts. While traditionally the emphasis of these bodies has been on facilitating development, and adjusting competing private interests, there has been some momentum for introducing environmental factors into their decision-making.[186] Planning and environmental protection legislation sometimes gives individuals an avenue for raising third-party objections. For example, it is possible for any person who feels aggrieved to appeal against decisions regarding works approval granted under the Victorian *Environment Protection Act* 1970.[187] Nonetheless, the barriers to the environmentally minded having an influence on public and private decision-making are still significant. We look at one example here, the mining warden's court, which under the legislation of some States hears objections to the grant of mining interests.

Standing is the first obstacle to be surmounted. Only in Western Australia is a right to challenge before a mining warden given expressly to any member of the public at the exploration licence stage.[188] At the mining lease stage, some of the other States grant this right to object to any member of the public.[189] By this time, however, mining companies are in a strong position, having already expended money on exploration and discovered minerals in quantities worth mining. Otherwise, standing is usually confined, for example, to those with 'an estate or interest in land' in the area. In litigation concerning an application for a special prospector's licence at Precipitous Bluff in south-western Tasmania the High Court held that this phrase means an interest of a proprietary nature, which is something more than a right held as a member of the general public. Therefore, the conservationists who had initiated the case were held not to be competent objectors.[190]

Even if under the legislation objectors have standing, and can mount a challenge, they must first convince a mining warden of their case. Mining wardens are typically magistrates and therefore probably lack technical competence to assess environmental evidence. Moreover, in some jurisdictions they do not have the independence of a judge, which makes it difficult for them to resist applications from mining companies which are supported, if only tacitly, by government. Moreover, mining wardens have recommendatory powers only, with the final decision being made at the political level. If approval is granted, much depends on the adequacy of the conditions imposed as to reinstating, regrassing and so on, and on the extent to which these are enforced.

On the whole Australian mining legislation is concerned with encouraging mining, and environmental concerns have not been specifically taken into account. In the Precipitous Bluff decision, a majority of the High Court held that under the relevant legislation the warden was confined to considering matters going to the validity of the application, including compliance by the mining company with the requirements of the legislation.[191] By contrast, the mining regulations examined in *Sinclair v. Mining Warden at Maryborough*[192] indicated that the mining warden was to take the public interest into account in formulating a recommendation to the Minister about a grant of mining leases. The High Court granted mandamus on the basis that the mining warden in that case had misconceived his duty by applying the wrong test of public interest. The warden had thought, incorrectly, that since the environmentalists objecting to the mining leases were only a section of the public, he could not be satisfied that their grant was against public interest.

Public participation

Participation has been prominent as an issue in land use and environmental planning, where it has been the product of various forces, including the desire of some planning authorities to obtain more information to formulate plans better, and demands from some sections of the public to be able to influence the nature of their immediate environment. Legally the scope for public participation in planning decisions is less than might be thought to exist in the light of the extensive discussions of the matter. In general terms it seems that participation in planning is more concerned with protecting individual property rights than with creating a role for the public at large in plan-making, and, inasmuch as the public at large is involved, more with obtaining useful data from them or with informing them about tentative proposals than with enabling them to influence the formulation of plans.

Take the making of plans in New South Wales. Under the *Environmental Planning and Assessment Act* 1979, the Minister is given wide discretion as to how a draft State environmental planning policy is to be publicized and submissions from the public on it sought and considered.[193] With regional and local environmental plans, the statute is more specific.[194] Public notice of an intention to make these must be given, and the environmental study on which they are occasionally based opened for public inspection. Submissions must be considered, and then the draft plan publicly exhibited. Submissions can again be made, but it is in the discretion of the planning authority whether a public inquiry will be held to examine the proposed plan. By contrast with plan-making, the public has a much greater right to participate when a plan is being implemented. For instance, under the New South Wales Act, any person may object to an application for 'designated' development approval, and if still dissatisfied can appeal to the Land and Environment Court.[195]

It should not be surprising that there is relatively little public participation in plan-making. The public might only learn of a planning proposal by chance. There is generally no provision for the public to be assisted in preparing any objections they might have to a planning proposal. The way participation is structured also limits its effectiveness: it might occur after plans are formulated and decisions taken; it might be disjointed so that individuals do not see the connection between the various stages; and if it covers a large geographic area it will probably not be of great interest to individuals.[196]

Direct action

Direct action by environmentalists has had some success. The green bans in Sydney in the early 1970s are a well-known example.[197] Direct action had some role in the ultimate decision of the Federal government to legislate to halt the Gordon-below-Franklin dam in south-western Tasmania.[198] Conversely, demonstrations and sit-ins have failed in other cases, such as over the Daintree forest road in north Queensland.

Law becomes relevant in such cases primarily because of prosecutions which arise for trespass, picketing or public order offences. Sometimes those prosecuted can use the publicity of a court hearing to advance their views. But in some situations direct action can lead to changes in the law adverse to the interests of environmentalists. For example, the green ban placed on the construction of the Newport power station in Victoria was the catalyst for the *Vital State Projects Act* 1976, which creates offences such as boycotting a declared vital State project.[199] Another example is the enactment of legislation in Victoria, giving the chairman at general meetings of companies wide power to have persons removed.[200] The legislation was prompted after disruption at several general meetings of mining companies, by persons with small shareholdings, who used the occasions to object publicly to company policy on uranium mining and Aboriginal rights.[201]

VI CONCLUSION

At present there are conflicting views about the role of law in environmental protection. The view which has most support among economists and others is that there should be a switch from regulation to market-based incentives.[202] Little movement along these lines has been manifest in public policy. Diametrically opposed is the view that law ought to play a greater role in environmental protection.

But if it is regarded as important enough to introduce such a policy, is there any reason why mechanisms should not be created to ensure substantial compliance? Certainly there is some novelty about this suggestion. But a system of self-operating policy structures, along the lines of an enforceable rule of law, would avoid interinstitutional rivalry or conflict, lead to a greater degree of certainty and predictability in resource management and create a more stable regime for developer and conservationist alike.[203]

As against this, however, are contentions such as the need for flexibility and speed in the administration of environmental protection policy, and that goals might be better achieved in some instances by voluntary compliance rather than legal threats.[204]

These conflicting views have not been addressed directly in this chapter, although what has been said has some bearing on them. The first part of the chapter examined legislation which is neither regulatory nor directed at encouraging compliance with standards in other ways. This legislation is, as one writer has put it, 'administrative, discretionary and procedural rather than normative' in character.[205] Nonetheless, it performs several important functions, such as establishing procedures for producing plans against which public and private bodies will make decisions—decisions which will have legally enforceable consequences.

Many lawyers are unhappy when this legislation is not justiciable. As a matter of training, they have come to associate legislative effectiveness with enforceability in the courts, although they are also aware of the inflexibility, delay and focus on technicalities which can occur when courts are involved. It is generally accepted that the involvement of courts in environmental assessment in the United States caused too frequent an interference with governmental decision-making and the undue delay of acceptable development.[206] But effectiveness in most cases derives from political and administrative will. This became evident in the second part of the chapter: even where legislation is enforceable in the courts, it might rarely give rise to legal proceedings, because there is no political or administrative will to enforce it. Now possibly compliance might occur without legal proceedings, because the regulated are law-abiding, the threat of legal proceedings is always in the background, and so on, but it would seem that unless the threat is credible, many of those regulated will fail to comply with legislative standards.

The issue of legislative form, discussed in part II of the chapter, raised another issue of current debate. On the one hand the Oxford study *Policing Pollution*[207] questions the appropriateness of criminal law sanctions in what is said to be an area of morally neutral behaviour. Sanctions, it is said, ought only to be imposed after non-complaince with an abatement order. By contrast, the Law Reform Commission of Canada has recommended that a new and distinct offence of 'crime against the environment' be added to the Canadian Criminal Code. The role and justification for the offence, it is said, would be to repudiate and deter conduct which seriously compromises a fundamental societal value and right.[208] Although this issue was not directly joined here, one point which will have become apparent is that criminal law sanctions are only one of the legislative techniques used in environmental protection policy. Pollution control, for example, uses what can be described as administrative regulation. Planning, for example, rests heavily on the preventive technique of prior approval. Another point which should be made is that law has its limitations as an instrument of public policy, whether it takes the form of criminal sanctions, administrative regulation or prior approval. Planning is illustrative: not only is it negative in character, unable to encourage greatly particular sorts of development, but it pales into all insignificance alongside all the other economic and institutional forces which shape the Australian city and countryside.[209]

The third and fourth parts of the chapter focused on the role of the courts in environmental protection. While recognizing their limitations, environmental lawyers have generally had high expectations of the courts. *The Court as the Public Conscience*—the title of a publication of the Environmental Law Reform Group—encapsulates this perspective.[210] A standard text on environmental law concludes, quoting a United States authority, that litigation is of value because it provides an additional source of leverage in making decision-makers environmentally conscious.[211] The reality for environmentalists was far removed from this picture when the Precipitous Bluff case went to the High Court:[212] 'This complex and protracted litigation added to the bitterness of Tasmanian environmentalists, since at the end of it all, they were left without environmental rights and had the full costs of legal action levied against them.'[213]

Indeed historically the courts have not been able to prevent pollution and other environmental damage.[214] For the procedural, doctrinal and institutional reasons outlined, it should not be surprising that they are no less effective today. As McDougal noted in 1955, with reference to the law of nuisance:

. . . it may be emphasized that the courts come in only after the damage has been done, that they decide only as between the two parties and between them only so long as there has been no substantial change in conditions, that they do not have the staffs or technical aids necessary to efficient and continuous performance of planning functions, and that the only technical standards at their command are these elusive tort doctrines.[215]

CONCLUSION

Three major themes emerge from this study of law, government and public policy: first, there is the centrality of legislation; second, there is the relatively marginal role of the courts; and third, there is the importance of a theory of government in resolving important legal problems in the area of public policy.

A JURISPRUDENCE OF LEGISLATION?

We lack a jurisprudence of legislation. Lawyers adhere to the view of law as litigation, even though modern legal practice belies this. Typically, legal education concentrates on judicial decisions, even though legislation is as pertinent, and possibly more pertinent for most legal issues. Legislation is examined mainly through the cases interpreting it, not as a source of law in its own right.

Legislation has three key functions for public policy—first, legitimating public policy, second, spelling out the details of public policy in an authoritative manner, and third, attempting to change public attitudes on some issues. How efficacious is legislation in performing these tasks? The book suggests a framework for examining legislative efficacy. The first aspect is the political and social background of legislation; the second, its legal form; the third, its implementation; and the fourth, its impact.

The first aspect is important because there is no necessary coincidence of the intention behind the introduction or modification of particular legislation and how it operates. Legislation enacted with a particular goal in mind might be ineffective in practice. The failure can occur because political conflicts in evidence when it is enacted are reflected in its provisions. Alternatively, there might be a deliberate decision by the legislature to leave the matter general and have the relevant enforcement body resolve problems when they arise. The failure of legislation might also be rooted in the very understanding of the problem to which it is supposedly addressed.[1] It may be that the intention underlying legislation was vaguely formulated or that the forces behind it were at odds with each other. Often it is wrong to assume that the forces dominant in formulating legislation really intended to make any dent on what happens in practice. In this event legislation may be characterized more as symbolic than substantive, since from the outset the purpose may simply have been to assuage public opinion or to divert attention.

The second issue, legislative form, highlights certain salient features about the implementation of legislation. Those drawing up legislation might not foresee particular problems. This might be attributable to the difficulty common in legislation of capturing the future, especially if substantial legal and other talent can be employed to maximize avoidance. Ambiguities and gaps might arise simply because not enough attention is given to drafting, or be a product of drafting difficulties, accentuated in Australia by the constitutional problems associated with a federal system. At another level legislative design is shaped by the legal culture. One aspect is the tradition in which legislation is drafted, which partly reflects the relationship between the legislature and the courts. In Australia legislation must be very precisely drawn, despite the increased possibility of error this leads to, for the courts interpret it in a critical rather than a sympathetic manner. Another aspect is that just as institutions develop a momentum so too does legislative design, for once a particular approach is adopted there are incentives for it to be continued. Despite its defects, an approach may be continued because of lethargy, a reluctance to think out new legal approaches, or familiarity with the existing approach by its administrators and those affected. On the other hand, more fundamental issues may be at stake, for a change in legislative design may go to matters of substance, as where it would produce more extensive control.

Consideration of legislative technique goes part of the way to a better understanding of public policy. Broad criminal prohibitions are relatively simple to formulate and, in the main, to enforce. On the other hand, they are not always diligently enforced in practice, and when legal proceedings are taken the courts tend to impose minor penalties. If businesses are involved, they can treat these as an ordinary expense. With the regulation of conflict of interest, examined in Chapter 3, we saw a move away from the broad standards of the criminal law to techniques such as disclosure (*ad hoc* or systematic through registers) and administrative regulation (as with the post-separation employment of Commonwealth public servants). In many ways the traditional, criminal modes of regulation are irrelevant to many of the conflicts of interests in modern government.

Too often in the past Australian parliaments have simply enacted United Kingdom legislation without thought as to its appropriateness.[2] Whether a particular legislative technique is chosen by the policy-maker ought to depend on a finely tuned calculation of its potential efficacy, its cost, and perhaps its economic repercussions, for example, for the distribution of wealth. Take pollution controls, examined in Chapter 5.

Pollution standards are of three types: quality standards, which set the limits of pollutants in air or water in a given area; performance standards, which require that pollution does not exceed specific limits but leave the polluter to choose the abatement method; and specification standards, which require the installation of pollution control equipment meeting certain design requirements. Technical difficulties sometimes stand in the way of formulating pollution standards. Not only do a variety of production techniques have to be regulated, but it is also not easy to foresee the type of use to which machinery will be put. The complexity of the task is reduced by performance standards, which a manufacturer must meet in whatever way it can, as opposed to standards which actually specify the way a process is to be carried out. Performance standards, in transferring the burden to manufacturers, lessen the degree of regulatory control, minimize possible adverse effects on competition, and provide businesses with flexibility as well as the opportunity to participate in developing standards. On the other hand, more specific standards mandating modes of manufacture may be more easily enforceable, in that a particular method can be readily identified as in breach of legal requirements.

A further aspect of legislative form, its justiciability, emerged in Chapter 4 on the economy and Chapter 5 on the environment. As we saw, some legislation is not subject to scrutiny by the courts, for it does not confer rights or denote claims which individuals can assert against each other or the state. Nonetheless, non-justiciable legislation performs important functions: it may evidence a governmental commitment to a particular goal; it may give greater legitimacy to particular goals by incorporating them in statutory form; and, it may constitute bodies which will advise government, educate the public or provide access to public decision-making. A government which creates an equal opportunities commission with purely conciliatory powers is promoting certain social values in the community, and giving added force to those who might wish to argue for those values, notwithstanding their lack of enforceability.

The third factor in legislative efficacy, implementation, draws attention mainly to the operation of regulatory agencies. There is clear evidence of regulatory agencies failing to function in the manner expected —failing, as we saw with environmental protection legislation, to take action against important violations of the law. But it is too simplistic to assume that such failures are endemic to regulation, or that they are always capable of remedy. For example, regulation is only as strong as its legislative mandate, however well-endowed with resources and dedicated to legislative purpose a regulatory agency might be, and however compliant are those being regulated. The consequences of defective design of legislation might be that the regulatory agency cannot adequately enforce it, those whose behaviour it ostensibly regulates avoid its effects, and those who are supposed to benefit do not do so. Many instances of 'regulatory failure' are in fact a failure to achieve a legislative mandate which, despite popular perceptions, a regulatory agency was never given. Another important cause of failure is a shortage of financial or human resources. Moreover, the effectiveness of an agency may be subverted by pressures from the environment in which it operates. Government agencies take account of the distribution of power and influence in society, which does not receive explicit recognition in the law.[3]

Another aspect of implementation has to do with the role of courts. A common assumption amongst lawyers is that unless the courts have a role, legislation will never be properly implemented. The assumption is fallacious. First, there is important legislation which is non-justiciable. One type of non-justiciable legislation is the Appropriation Act, which has been characterized by the High Court as being intra-governmental in character.[4] Can it be seriously contended that legislation like this is not being properly implemented by those charged with the task, or that there would be improvement if the courts were involved? Second, if the courts are invoked, they do not always apply regulatory legislation sympathetically where this is inconsistent with common law principles or where it conflicts with private property rights. For example, as we saw with environmental protection legislation, the courts impose relatively low fines.

Examination of the fourth aspect of legislation efficacy, its impact, is hampered by methodological and empirical problems. This much can be definitely said. Understanding impact requires that attention be given to the factors already mentioned. For instance, is the legislation intended to be more a symbolic gesture, to persuade the public that a problem is being dealt with, than to have a real impact on behaviour? Then the indicia of impact must be identified. In many cases this means that proxies must be used: to what extent are administrative law decisions being incorporated into the manuals of government departments and agencies; are investors complaining about market losses and thus about the failure of prudential regulation; have these factories installed the equipment which reduces air pollution? Lawyers often use the wrong proxies: for example, the focus on case-law leads them to measure the success of the new administrative law in terms of the volume of cases, whereas the real issue is whether officials are affected in their everyday practices by its concerns. Finally, there are the indirect and unintended effects of legislation, some of which might be welcomed by the proponents of legislation, others of which may constitute new problems demanding resolution.

ROLE OF THE COURTS

Compared with legislation, the courts have a comparatively marginal role in public policy. This is not universally the case, for in some areas their decisions can approve or hinder major developments or allocate important benefits or burdens. For example, the High Court has had a profound effect on the incidence of individual and corporate taxation, by sanctioning tax avoidance schemes which could not possibly have been contemplated by the legislation. Moreover, the courts in a general sense provide an underpinning to the operation of markets with doctrines such as freedom of contract, the protection given to private property and the limits placed on governmental powers.

But on the whole the courts do not have a profound social or economic impact. One aspect is that while the courts make authoritative decisions, the range of matters which they handle is quite narrow. Not only do people have narrow perceptions of what courts do, affecting whether they conceptualize matters as a legal problem, but there are barriers to litigation such as cost, the attitude of lawyers and the chances of success on substantive legal grounds. The upshot is that personal injury litigation, debt recovery and family matters dominate Australian civil courts. Then, even if we concentrate on important adjudication we find that most cases have few repercussions other than for the parties involved. Moveover, the judicial solution is not necessarily final, for a matter may be relitigated in different form, or there might be legislation or administrative action to reverse its effects.

At various points we encountered other aspects to the limited impact of the courts. While private law doctrines such as nuisance can be used for environmental ends, their doctrinal origins mean that they have only a limited scope. With regard to the public sector, the occasional judicial review of administrative action can hardly rival the impact of the 'internal law' of bureaucracy. Although the constitutional decisions of the High Court have had a profound effect in particular instances, their overall impact on the dynamics of the Australian federal system has not been great. This is not to say that High Court decisions have never affected the federal balance—plainly they have in the financial arena— or that High Court decisions are not taken into account, on a day-to-day basis, by those in government responsible for drawing up legislation.

Rather, it is to say that in the broad sweep, the history of Australian federalism has been mainly a history of the dissociation between the High Court decisions about the scope of Commonwealth power on the one hand, and the actual exercise of that power by governments on the other.

It is appropriate to say a few words about the normative issue: what role should the courts play in public policy? Australian courts have yet to define, in a systematic fashion, their legitimate role in public policy matters. In the main the issue is ignored, treated as a simple matter of interpretation (whether of the constitution, or legislation such as the *Administrative Decisions (Judicial Review) Act* 1977), or buried in doctrines such as standing which are really directed at other matters. The issue is not straightforward. Judges are not directly responsible to anyone, although some are not averse to conjuring up 'the law' which they themselves have created to justify their conclusions. Their only accountability is through acceptance of their mode of principled decision-making. Separation of powers, which might form the basis for a theory of the legitimate area of judicial activity, has become in Australia a collection of arcane rules, mainly about where judicial power can be vested under the Australian constitution. Justiciability has been invoked in Australia in only a few instances to explain why a matter is incapable of adjudication.[5]

Take standing. The present rules on standing have been partly justified on the basis that otherwise busybodies, cranks and those actuated by malice will abuse the processes of the law and put others to great cost and to the inconvenience of defending the legality of their actions. However, various responses are open if abuse occurs, such as the rules about abuse of process and vexatious litigants. Then it is sometimes said that more liberal standing rules would lead to a flood of litigation. The notion of floodgates cannot be too readily disparaged—Lord Abinger's floodgates[6] have proved to be far from mythical in relation to the deluge of personal-injury litigation before Australian courts. But experience elsewhere suggests that more liberal rules of standing in the public law area would not have a great impact. Another justification for the present rules is said to be that the adversary system requires parties to have a personal stake in litigation, so that the strongest arguments possible are placed before a court. But it is clear that the issues can be presented to a court just as keenly by those who are motivated by intellectual or emotional considerations.

The only convincing justification for the present rules on standing is that otherwise the courts will be embroiled in issues which they are ill-suited to handle or will intrude on issues which are really political or economic in character. In other words, the justification has to do with the legitimate role of the courts, not the possibility of abuse, a flood of litigation or inadequate argument. Since standing is the only real barrier to litigation at present, its liberalization would have a profound effect on the role of the courts in society. Proponents of liberalization might justify this extended role by arguing that legislation is increasingly designed to support public values which go beyond the traditional concern of the law with property interests and liberty of the subject.[7] But this assumes that unless legal proceedings can be instituted, the ends of legislation will not be attained. A constant theme of this book has been that courts are only one (and certainly not a necessary) aspect of legislative efficacy.

The perceived failure of the courts as institutions has led to legislative and administrative schemes being substituted. The establishment of many tribunals has been prompted by the courts' unsympathetic handling of particular litigation. The new administrative law, for instance, grew from the conviction that the courts would be incapable of transcending the anachronisms and technicalities associated with judicial review of administrative action. The 'flight from the courts' has meant a decline in their importance, with decision-making and adjudication being vested elsewhere.

An important aspect of this failure has to do with judicial decision-making. Judicial decision-making combines conceptual and social reasoning. The exact mix is difficult to fathom and varies from case to case. Social reasoning entails a range of factors from the judges' own personal beliefs, through policy considerations, to general values embodied in the law. There is clearly an element of choice, its scope varying with the circumstances. Too often, however, the courts have been seen to make a choice favouring certain values, such as property rights or *laissez-faire* values, over others which would benefit a wider class of persons. Instead of working in partnership with the legislature, trying to give effect to underlying policies in legislation, the courts have been seen to give effect to contrary values.[8] Their demand for clear and unambiguous language in tax legislation, for instance, is seen not only to be impossible, but as a mask for reaching conclusions adverse to the public interest. It is this ideological dimension of the courts' activity which legislatures have reacted to in stripping them of functions and conferring these elsewhere.

Perhaps another dimension to the limited impact of the courts has to do with legal discourse. The language of judicial argument is not that of ordinary day life. Procedural, evidentiary and substantive rules distort the social and economic realities underlying litigation. Problems have to be pleaded in a particular way and only certain evidence is admissible, and then only in certain ways. Social and economic problems have to be transformed substantively—into legal form—before they can be dealt with by the courts. So the motor vehicle accident only becomes a personal injury case, involving assessment of the extent of the injuries and the loss suffered, *after* it is determined whether particular injuries, such as nervous shock, were reasonably foreseeable by the defendant and whether the person suffering it was sufficiently proximate to the defendant to claim successfully. The takeover battle in court has little, if anything, to do with the social or economic justification of the bid, but is a matter of whether, for instance, the bidder has set out in sufficient detail the financial resources to support the bid. If litigation is removed from the underlying social and economic realities, would it be surprising if it has little impact in the community?

A THEORY OF GOVERNMENT

Lawyers need a theory of government. Without it, they will adopt doctrines or suggest reforms with respect to public policy, in some cases drawn from other jurisdictions such as the United States, which are quite inappropriate to Australian conditions. But it is not for them to evolve their own theory of government; they must accept the principles of responsible and representative government. Courts do not have the legitimate authority to do otherwise. It is a dangerous practice on their part to assume, without evidence, that the theory of responsible and representative government is not working.[9] Their duty is to give effect to the theory in instances where it has a bearing on the issue before them. It is not to assume its failure and to arrogate to themselves review functions.

In broad terms the theory of representative and responsible government means that parliaments are accountable to the people, the ministry to Parliament, and the public sector to the ministry. In particular areas, such as government spending and revenue raising, the theory has been given expression in the constitution. The lines of accountability entailed by the theory can be supplemented by statute, as where horizontal lines of accountability are introduced for public agencies (for example, fiscal control). Thus stated, the theory relies on the mechanisms of political and administrative, rather than legal, accountability. Parliamentary and caucus committees scrutinize the acts of the ministry, public officials and statutory corporations. The financial controls institutionalized in the office of Auditor-General, the *Audit Act* 1901 and the attendant Finance Regulations all bear on the accountability of executive government. Although established in law, such instruments of accountability do not depend on the legal system for their vitality.

But the theory has legal ramifications. To take just one example: when legislation entrusts a power to the Governor-General or to a Governor, that means the Governor-General or the Governor acting on advice.[10] (In the very special case of the Australian constitution, there are reserve powers exercisable by the Governor-General acting without advice.) Any other interpretation would be inconsistent with the theory of responsible and representative government. Similarly, when legislation entrusts discretions to public officials or to statutory authorities, that does not mean that they can act contrary to government policy and directions (subject, of course, to any legislative provision which expressly, or by clear implication, means that they can do so). This follows because public officials and statutory authorities are part of the executive government; under the system of responsible and representative government, they cannot have independent discretions unless legislation specifically authorizes this.

This theory of government does not correspond with that of other countries. The theory of government in the United States is quite different: for example, it has a notion of the separation of powers and the courts can legitimately interfere with legislative and administrative actions on the basis of far-reaching principles drawn from vague constitutional mandates. There are no counterparts in Australia. Another instance is that constitutional conventions are far less central to the operation of Australian government than to government in Britain. What are conventions in Britain are sometimes embodied in constitution or legislation in Australia. Moreover, conventions which are peculiarly Australian, relating for instance to the Senate or to the Governor-General, are fiercely contested in their application.

What, then, is the proper role of the judiciary, consistent with this theory of government, in areas of public policy? There would seem to be three principles which should guide the courts. First, the theory demands deference to legislation, and an attempt to give effect to its terms and purposes, recognizing that statutory language will often be open-textured because of the problem of capturing the future. A corollary is that in areas where the legislature is active, the courts should be reluctant to tread. Second, a lack of institutional competence is an important limitation on judicial activity. The main factor in this is that litigation is distorting, because it focuses on the individual case, rather than on the whole range of cases of which the instant case is but one. In the main, courts do not have the breadth of vision and expertise of administrators and are not as attuned to legislative policies. Third, in the constitutional sphere the High Court ought to confine itself to the policing of the federal division. There is something radically wrong when the Court can regard as unconstitutional the fundamental policy of a major political party.[11] The Court should be slow in drawing out implications from the constitution about individual rights. These will either be trite or will lead to the introduction of particular political philosophies dressed up in legal terminology, as has happened with section 92 of the constitution.

ABBREVIATIONS

ABLR	Australian Business Law Review	FLR	Federal Law Reports
AC	Appeal Cases	F Supp.	Federal Supplement Cases (US)
ACLR	Australian Company Law Reports	Harv. Int. LJ	Harvard International Law Journal
A Crim. R	Australian Criminal Reports	HLC	House of Lords Cases
ACTR	Australian Capital Territory Reports	Int. J Soc. L	International Journal of the Sociology of Law
ALD	Administrative Law Decisions	J Leg. Stud.	Journal of Legal Studies
ALJ	Australian Law Journal	JP & EL	Journal of Planning & Environment Law
ALJR	Australian Law Journal Reports	KB	King's Bench Cases
All ER	All England Reports	L & Soc. R	Law and Society Review
ALR	Australian Law Reports	Law Inst. J	Law Institute Journal
AQ	Australian Quarterly	LGRA	Local Government Reports of Australia
ATPR	Australian Trade Practices Reports		
CLR	Commonwealth Law Reports	LRPC	Law Reports Privy Council
Ch.D/Ch.	Chancery Cases		
Colum. LR	Columbia Law Review	MLR	Modern Law Review
EPLJ	Environment and Planning Law Journal	NSWLR/NSWR	New South Wales Reports
ER	English Reports	NTR	Northern Territory Reports
Fed. LR	Federal Law Review		

QB	Queen's Bench Reports		
QLJ	Queensland Law Journal	UQLJ	University of Queensland Law Journal
QSR/Qd R	Queensland Reports	VLR/VR	Victorian Reports
SASR	South Australian State Reports	WAR	Western Australian Reports
SR (NSW)	State Reports (New South Wales)	Wis. LR	Wisconsin Law Review
Tas. LR	Tasmanian Law	WLR	Weekly Law Reports

NOTES AND REFERENCES

Introduction

1 Private persons might exercise a delegated legislative power, for example, the disciplinary power conferred on the legal and medical professions under State legislation.
2 For example, *A. v. Hayden (No. 2)* (1984) 56 ALR 82, 87, 94, 112, 120, 128.
3 See J. Sigler & B. Beede, *The Legal Sources of Public Policy*, pp. 3–4.
4 For example, S. Barnes & M. Blakeney, *Advertising Regulation*, pp. 449–72.
5 Cf. L. Friedman, *The Legal System*, p. 93.
6 D. Miers & A. Page, *Legislation*, p. 211.
7 R. Cotterell, *The Sociology of Law*, pp. 57–60.
8 An Australian study is P. O'Malley, *Law, Capitalism and Democracy*, pp. 5, 56–62.
9 For example, the New South Wales *Crown Lands Alienation Act* 1861 and *Crown Lands Occupation Act* 1861; the Victorian *Mining Statute* 1865; and the Queensland *Post and Telegraph Act* 1891. See D. Baker, 'The Origins of Robertson's Land Acts' (1958) 8 *Historical Studies* 166; A. Lang & M. Crommelin, *Australian Mining and Petroleum Laws*, pp. 1–7; P. Gribble, *What Hath God Wrought: The Story of the Electric Telegraph — Queensland*, esp. Chapter 7. See generally N. Butlin, 'Colonial Socialism in Australia 1860–1900', in H. Aitken (ed.), *The State and Economic Growth*.
10 J. Hurst, *Dealing with Statutes*, p. 10.

1 Legislation

1 The remainder of this paragraph, and the following two paragraphs, are derived from my *Legal Foundations of the Welfare State*, pp. 104–5.
2 J. Griffiths, 'Is Law Important?' (1979) 54 New York University LR 339.
3 For instance, see the account of why the Lunacy Acts 1878 and 1898 of New South Wales went unamended: S. Garton, 'Bad or Mad? Developments in Incarceration in N.S.W. 1880–1920', in Sydney Labour History Group, *What Rough Beast?*, pp. 104–6.

4 See pp. 95–6 below.
5 *Constitution Act* 1902 (New South Wales), s.5A. See R. Lumb, *The Constitutions of the Australian States*, 4th edn, p. 52.
6 For example, House of Representatives, *Standing Orders*, nos. 211–69.
7 See John Uhr, 'Parliament and Public Administration', in J. Nethercote, *Parliament and Bureaucracy*, pp. 34–40, 52–5.
8 *Victoria v. Commonwealth* (1975) 134 CLR 81, 164, 181.
9 G. Lindell, 'Duty to Exercise Judicial Review', in L. Zines (ed.), *Commentaries on the Australian Constitution*, p. 168; P. Hanks, *Australian Constitutional Law*, 3rd edn, pp. 142–3.
10 *Victoria v. Commonwealth* (1975) 134 CLR 81. See also *Western Australia v. Commonwealth* (1975) 134 CLR 201 and H. Renfree, *The Executive Power of the Commonwealth of Australia,* pp. 164–8.
11 *Attorney-General for New South Wales v. Trethowan* [1932] AC 526. The extent to which Australian parliaments can adopt such 'manner and form' requirements is discussed in basic texts such as Hanks, op. cit.
12 J. Pettifer (ed.), *House of Representatives Practice*, p. 308; J. Odgers, *Australian Senate Practice*, 5th edn, p. 298.
13 Money bills are discussed on pp. 95–6, 108–10, 113–14 below.
14 Department of the Prime Minister and Cabinet, *Legislation Handbook*.
15 L. Curtis & G. Kolts, 'The Role of the Government Lawyer in the Protection of Citizens' Rights' (1975) 49 ALJ 335, 341–3.
16 *Watson v. Lee* (1979) 144 CLR 374, 378, 383, 397, 404.
17 See D. Pearce, *Delegated Legislation*, pp. 100–2. Consultation is generally required in relation to statutory rules in Victoria: *Subordinate Legislation Act* 1962, ss.11, 12, Schedule 2 para. 3(e), Schedule 3.
18 For example, *Acts Interpretation Act* 1901 (Commonwealth), s.48(1)(a), (b). The requirement is mandatory. See *Golden-Brown v. Hunt* (1972) 19 FLR 438; *Watson v. Lee* (1979) 144 CLR 374.
19 For example, *Acts Interpretation Act* 1901, s.48(1)(c), (3).
20 For example, see ibid., ss.48(4)–(6). Parliamentary scrutiny is dealt with in J. Odgers, op. cit., pp. 460–6; D. Pearce, op. cit., pp. 28–78, 81–91; S. Hotop, *Principles of Australian Administrative Law*, 6th edn, pp. 130–9; G. Reid, 'Parliament and Delegated Legislation', in J. Nethercote (ed.), op. cit. See also Legal and Constitutional Committee (Parliament of Victoria), *Report on the Subordinate Legislation (Deregulation) Bill*.
21 *Dignan v. Australian Steamships Pty Ltd* (1931) 45 CLR 188. The political background to the case is dealt with in Geoffrey Sawer, *Australian Federal Politics and Law 1929–1949*, pp. 30–1, 37.
22 There is some discussion of such models in R. Tomasic, 'The Sociology of Legislation', in R. Tomasic (ed.), *Legislation and Society in Australia*; P. O'Malley, *Law, Capitalism and Democracy,* chapter 2.
23 See S. Peltzman, 'Toward a More General Theory of Regulation' (1976) 19 J Law & Econ. 211. An Australian example is Peter L. Swan, 'Is Law Reform Too Important to be Left to the Lawyers?' in R. Cranston & A. Schick (eds), *Law and Economics*, pp. 18–20. Contrast A. Fels, 'The Political Economy of Regulation' (1982) 5 UNSWLJ 29.
24 See W. Carson, 'Hostages to History: Some Aspects of the Occupational Health and Safety Debate in Historical Perspective', in B. Creighton & N.

Gunningham (eds), *The Industrial Relations of Occupational Health and Safety*, p. 65; Hugh Collins, 'Capitalist Discipline and Corporatist Law' (1982) 11 *Industrial Law J* 78, 85–7.

25 A useful account is G. Hawker, R. Smith & P. Weller, *Politics and Policy in Australia*.

26 See the survey in G. Sawer, 'Who Controls the Law in Australia?: Instigators of Change, and the Obstacles Confronting Them', in A. Hambly & J. Goldring, (eds), *Australian Lawyers and Social Change*.

27 See S. Ross, *Politics of Law Reform*; M. Kirby, *Reform the Law*; Senate Standing Committee on Constitutional and Legal Affairs, *Reforming the Law*.

28 On the role of the legal profession: T. Halliday, 'Prospects of Power: Legal Associations and Government 1970–1990', in *Power in Australia: Directions of Change*.

29 For example, *The Trade Practices Act Proposals for Change* (Canberra, 1984) (which contained proposed amending legislation); Companies and Securities Legislation (Miscellaneous Amendments) Bill (No. 2) 1984, Exposure Draft; Companies and Securities Legislation (Miscellaneous Amendments) Bill 1985, Second Exposure Draft.

30 P. Loveday, *Promoting Industry*, pp. 76–8; K. Campbell, 'Australian Farm Organisations and Agricultural Policy' (1966) 10 *Australian Journal of Agricultural Economics* 112, 117–20; T. Matthews, 'Interest Group Access to the Australian Government Bureaucracy', in *Royal Commission on Australian Government Administration, Appendixes*, vol. 2, p. 344.

31 For example, R. Stewart, 'The Politics of the Accord. Does Corporatism Explain It?' (1985) 20 *Politics* 26. The Accord is contained in Department of Employment and Industrial Relations, *Prices and Incomes Policy. The Third Progress Report on Government Initiatives*.

32 A. Parkin and A. Graycar, 'The South Australian Council of Social Service', in R. Scott (ed.), *Interest Groups and Public Policy*, p. 29.

33 Senate Select Committee on Securities and Exchange, *Australian Securities Markets and Their Regulation*.

34 R. Sackville, 'Residential Tenancies in Victoria: A Study of Consultation' in *Consultation and Government*.

35 See H. Wootten, 'The Future of the Conservation Movement' (1985) 13 *Habitat* 25; R. Roddewig, *Green Bans*.

36 Cf. M. Sawer, 'The Origins of Affirmative Action in the United States', in M. Sawer (ed.), *Program for Change*.

37 F. Brennan, *Too Much Order With Too Little Law*, pp. 121–39. There is a general discussion of direct action and legal change in R. Cranston, *Legal Foundations of the Welfare State*, pp. 283–6, 296–300, 315–19.

38 N. Gunningham and W. Creighton, 'Industrial Safety Law in Social and Political Perspective', in R. Tomasic (ed.), *Legislation and Society in Australia* pp. 162–4; Jennifer Doran, 'Implementing the Victorian Government's Policy on Occupational Health and Safety—1982–1984' in W. Creighton & N. Gunningham (eds), op. cit., p. 155; William M. Castleden et al., 'Changes in Tobacco Advertising in Western Australian Newspapers...' (1985) 142 Medical Journal of Australia 305.

39 A. Hopkins, *Crime Law and Business*, p. 90.

40 A. Heatley, 'Aboriginal Land Rights in the Northern Territory', in R. Scott (ed.), op. cit., pp. 49, 52.

41 See J. Nieuwenhuysen & M. Williams-Wynn, *Professions in the Marketplace*.

42 J. Hagan, 'Employers, Trade Unions and the First Victorian Factory Acts' (1961) 7 Labour History 3, 5, 9.

43 M. Armstrong, *Broadcasting Law and Policy in Australia*, p. 38.

44 Interestingly, one travel agent was quoted as follows in relation to the proposal: 'One of the motivations for the self-regulation is simply that agents are feeling the pinch. It's a tough business with very thin margins, and I think they want to limit the competition.' (Australian Business, 19 November 1981, p. 29). On advertising self-regulation: M. Blakeney & S. Barnes, 'Industry Self-Regulation: An Alternative to Deregulation?' (1982) 5 UNSWLJ 133.

45 This part is based on my 'Reform through Legislation: The Dimension of Legislative Technique' (1979) 73 Northwestern ULR 873. Reprinted by special permission. Copyright © 1979 by Northwestern University School of Law.

46 V. Aubert, 'Some Social Functions of Legislation' (1967) 10 Acta Sociologica 98, 102, 108–9. See also L. Fuller, *Anatomy of the Law*, p. 37.

47 H. Hart, *Punishment and Responsibility*, p. 23.

48 H. Mannheim, *Criminal Justice and Social Reconstruction*, pp. 166–7.

49 See C. Howard, *Strict Responsibility*.

50 D. Gifford, 'Communication of Legal Standards, Policy Development, and Effective Conduct Regulation' (1971) 56 Cornell LR 409, 435–7.

51 F. Zimring & G. Hawkins, *Deterrence*, p. 355.

52 J. Landis, *The Administrative Process*, pp. 30, 35.

53 W. Whitford, 'The Functions of Disclosure Regulation in Consumer Transactions' (1973) Wisc. LR 400.

54 J. Romans, 'Moral Suasion as an Instrument of Economic Policy' (1966) 56 *American Economic Review* 1220, 1221 (emphasis in original).

55 N. Gunningham, *Safeguarding the Worker*, pp. 323–4, 328.

56 L. Friedman & S. Macaulay, *Law and the Behavioural Sciences*, p. 297.

57 S. Barnes & M. Blakeney, *Advertising Regulation*, p. 21.

58 For example, *Petroleum (Submerged Lands) Act* 1967, Part III, Division 3; *Broadcasting and Television Act* 1942, Part IIIB. Breyer argues that this is better regarded as allocation under a public interest standard, not as licensing: S. Breyer, *Regulation and Its Reform*, ch. 4.

59 As with medicines: see L. Darvall, 'Prescription Drug Advertising. Legal and Voluntary Controls', in A. Duggan & L. Darvall (eds), *Consumer Protection Law and Theory*, pp. 42–3.

60 M. Friedman, *Capitalism and Freedom*, pp. 144–5.

61 On lodgment of the memorandum, articles (if any) and other documents, the National Companies and Securities Commission shall register the company: *Companies Act* 1981, s.35(1).

62 There are some examples in A. Duggan, 'Occupational Licensing and Related Forms of Control', in D. Galligan (ed.), *Essays in Legal Theory*, pp. 53–4.

63 See the examples in J. Goldring & L. Maher, *Consumer Protection Law in Australia*, chapter 6.

64 R. Arens & H. Lasswell, *In Defense of Public Order*, pp. 224–5.
65 Australian governments have sometimes had a 'buy-Australia' policy in contracting: K. Puri, *Australian Government Contracts. Law and Practice*, pp. 100–1.
66 Y. Grbich & J. Grbich, 'Tax Expenditures as a Regulatory Tool: Targeting Superannuation Dollars' in R. Tomasic (ed.), *Business Regulation in Australia*. See generally on incentives: J. Brigham & D. Brown (eds), *Policy Implementation*; J. Robertson & P. Treitelbaum, 'Optimising Legal Impact: A Case Study in Search of a Theory' (1973) Wisc. LR 665.
67 *Companies Act* and *Codes* 1981, ss.35(6), 263, 360. An exempt proprietary company need not lodge accounts if it appoints an auditor: s.264.
68 See Australian Law Reform Commission, *Access to Courts—I. Standing: Public Interest Suits*, Working Paper no. 7, 1977, pp. 99–102.
69 *Cooney v. Ku-Ring-Gai Corporation* (1963) 114 CLR 582. On standing, see pp. 158–9. Courts are reluctant to grant injunctions in aid of the criminal law, except when the offence is frequently repeated, especially in disregard of an inadequate penalty, or in cases of emergency: *Commonwealth of Australia v. John Fairfax and Sons Ltd* (1980) 147 CLR 39, 49–50; (1980) 32 ALR 485, 491; *Attorney-General (Qld) ex rel. Kerr v. T.* (1983) 57 ALJR 285; (1983) 46 ALR 275.
70 *Hornsby Building Information Centre Pty Ltd v. Sydney Building Information Centre Ltd* (1978) 140 CLR 216.
71 *R. v. Commissioner of Police of the Metropolis ex p. Blackburn* [1968] 2 QB 118; *R. v. McAulay ex p. Fardell* (1979) 2 NTR 22.
72 There was a surprising utilization of the masters and servants legislation by workers in the nineteenth century in New South Wales: See A. Merritt, 'The Historical Role of Law in the Regulation of Employment—Abstentionist or Interventionist' (1982) 1 Australian Journal of Law and Society 56, 83.
73 The authorities are canvassed in P. Finn, 'A Road Not Taken: The Boyce Plaintiff and Lord Cairns' Act' (1983) 57 ALJ 493, 495–8; F. Trindade & P. Cane, *The Law of Torts in Australia*, pp. 580–94.
74 Notably, the Royal Commission on the Activities of the Federated Ship Painters and Dockers Union. But see *Final Report* vol. 1, p. 163.
75 The remainder of Part I draws on my 'Regulation and Deregulation: General Issues' (1982) 5 UNSWLJ 1.
76 J. Landis, *The Administrative Process*. Cf. J. Freedman, *Crisis and Legitimacy*, pp. 46–56.
77 R. Wettenhall & P. Bayne, 'Administrative Aspects of Regulation', in R. Tomasic (ed.), *Business Regulation in Australia*.
78 The Confederation of Australian Industry has criticized the arrangement whereby companies and securities legislation is administered by eight 'autonomous' bodies—the National Companies and Securities Commission and the corporate affairs commissions of the States and the Australian Capital Territory. See (1985) *Reform* 95.
79 The classic statement is K. Davis, *Discretionary Justice*. See also R. Kagan, *Regulatory Justice*, pp. 13, 16; J. Jowell, *Law and Bureaucracy*, pp. 22–4.
80 An argument vastly overstated in E. Bardach & R. Kagan, *Going by the Book*.
81 Performance standards for air or water pollution, for example, fix the

maximum concentration of a pollutant allowed from a given source, whereas a specification standard would require the polluter to incorporate particular apparatus to control pollution. See J. Braithwaite, 'The Limits of Economism in Controlling Harmful Corporate Conduct' (1981–82) 16 L & Soc. R 481.

82 *Phosphate Cooperative Co. of Australia Ltd v. Environment Protection Authority* (1977) 138 CLR 134; (1977) 18 ALR 210.

83 See Attorney-General's Department, *Prosecution Policy of the Commonwealth.*

84 See p. 5 above.

85 G. Robinson, E. Gellhorn, H. Bruff, *The Administrative Process*, 2nd edn, pp. 30–2, 127–8, 180–2, 419–31.

86 See J. Braithwaite & P. Grabosky, *Of Manners Gentle*. See also J. Braithwaite, *To Punish or Persuade: Enforcement of Coal Mine Safety*; J. Braithwaite & P. Grabosky, *Occupational Health and Safety Enforcement in Australia*, pp. 29–31, 41–7; J. Braithwaite & S. Vale, 'Law Enforcement by Australian Consumer Affairs Agencies' (1985) 18 Australian and New Zealand Journal of Criminology 147; A. Hopkins & N. Parnell, 'Why Coal Mine Safety Regulations in Australia are Not Enforced' (1984) 12 International Journal of Sociology of Law 179, 188–93; J. Telfer, 'The Policing of Companies' (1983) 1 Companies and Securities Law Journal 243; J. Wade, 'Corporate Affairs Office—Victoria', ibid. 2, 1984, p. 38; J. Braithwaite, 'An Exploratory Study of Used Car Fraud' in P. Wilson & J. Braithwaite, *Two Faces of Deviance*; A. Hopkins, *A Working Paper on White Collar Crime in Australia.*

87 The seminal article on 'mobilization' of law is D. Black, 'The Mobilisation of Law' (1973) 2 J Leg. Studies 125.

88 A. Stone, *Economic Regulation and the Public Interest*, pp. 183–4.

89 S. Weaver, *Decision to Prosecute*, pp. 22–3.

90 M. Lipsky, *Street-Level Bureaucracy*, p. 51.

91 K. Marx, *Capital*, vol. 1, p. 494. The legislation Marx was referring to was presumably the *Factory and Workshop Act* 1871, 34 & 35 Vict., c. 104.

92 W. Gormley, 'A Test of the Revolving Door Hypothesis at the F.C.C.' (1979) 23 Am. J Pol. Sci. 665.

93 S. Breyer & R. Stewart, *Administrative Law and Regulatory Policy*, Ch. 8; P. Quirk, 'Food and Drug Administration', in J. Wilson (ed.), *The Politics of Regulation*, pp. 204–5.

94 On the perception that business is basically law-abiding: R. Kriegler, *Working for the Company*, p. 65; R. Cranston, *Regulating Business*, pp. 32–9, 122.

95 K. Hawkins, *Environment and Enforcement*, pp. xiii-xiv, 10–14, 127, 153, 195–207.

96 For example, the direction to the Trade Practices Commission in its *Annual Report 1980–1981*, pp. 12–13, and the limited staff resources of the National Companies and Securities Commission: *Fifth Annual Report and Financial Statements 1st July 1983 to 30th June 1984*, p. 54. See also P. Russ & L. Tanner, *The Politics of Pollution*, p. 42; O. Hughes, 'Bauxite Mining and Jarrah Forests in Western Australia', in R. Scott (ed.), *Interest Groups and Public Policy*, p. 184; V. Venturini, *Malpractice*, pp. 193–204, 277–8, 290–3, 348.

97 See R. Melnick, *Regulation and the Courts.*

98 Compare the decision of Taylor CJ at CL in *R. v. McMahon* (1976) 2 ACLR

543 with that of the Court of Criminal Appeal in *R. v. M & Ors* (1979) 4 ACLR 610. On the approach of the courts to the *Companies (Acquisition of Shares) Act* 1980, and corresponding state takeover codes, see C. Maxwell, 'The New Takeover Code and the NCSC: Policy Objectives and Legislative Strategies for Business Regulation' (1982) 5 UNSW LJ 93, 106–110. Cf. *Bond Corporation Holdings Ltd v. Grace Bros Holdings Ltd* (1983) 48 ACTR 3, 32; (1983) 8 ACLR 61, 86.

99 For example, compare *Eva v. Mazda Motors (Sales) Pty Ltd* (1977) ATPR 40–020; (1977) TPRS 304.48 and *R v. Wattle Gully Gold Mines N.L.* [1980] VR 622. Compare generally the relatively high fines imposed for breaches of the *Trade Practices Act* 1974 (Cth) with the relatively low fines imposed by State magistrates' courts for breaches of health and safety at work legislation: Trade Practices Commission, *Annual Report 1983–84*, Schedule II; J. Braithwaite & P. Grabosky, *Occupational Health and Safety Enforcement in Australia*, pp. 13–24. Powell J has said:

> I am no unrestrained advocate of rigid legislative control over the myriad aspects of the commercial life of the community—for nearly every such form of control carries with it a cost factor which the community may be neither willing, nor able, to bear. This notwithstanding, it seems to me that, the Parliament having adopted, in the form of the *Securities Industry Act*, a policy of seeking (inter alia) to protect investors and prospective investors on the stock exchange from being defrauded or being taken down by such activities as insider trading, consideration might, in the light of the view which I have taken as to the, apparently, inadequate nature of one of the forms of protection devised, well be given to the question whether some greater or other form of protection is now called for.

Daly v. Sydney Stock Exchange Ltd (1981) Australian Securities Law Cases 76–008, at pp. 86, 187.

100 M. Olson, *The Logic of Collective Action*, is the classic statement.

101 P. Sabatier, 'Social Movements and Regulatory Agencies: Toward A More Adequate—and Less Pessimistic—Theory of "Clientele Capture"' (1975) 6 Policy Sciences 301.

102 See P. MacAvoy, *The Regulated Industries and the Economy*, pp. 100–1; B. Ackerman & W. Hassler, *Clean Coal Dirty Air*.

103 P. Sands, 'How Effective is Safety Legislation?' (1968) 11 Journal of Law and Economics 165; R. Smith, 'The Impact of OSHA Inspections on Manufacturing Injury Rates' (1979) 14 Journal of Human Resources 145.

104 B. Whiting, 'OSHA's Enforcement Policy' (1980) 31 Labour Law J 259; M. Lewis-Beck & J. Alford, 'Can Government Regulate Safety? The Coal Mine Example' (1980) 74 American Political Science Review 745.

105 My own attempt at an empirical study is contained in *Regulating Business*, ch. 6.

106 J. Forbes, *The Divided Legal Profession in Australia*, pp. 115–30.

107 M. Clark, *A History of Australia*, vol. 4, p. 167.

108 Federal Office of Road Safety, *Summary of National Road Crash Statistics*, pp. 5–6.

109 H. Ross, *Deterring the Drinking Driver*, p. 84.

110 Summarized in J. Braithwaite & P. Grabosky, *Occupational Health and Safety Enforcement in Australia*, p. 4.

111 P. Williams, Class Conflict and the Decline of Residential Landlordism, p. 12.

112 *Reform of the Australian Tax System. Draft White Paper*, ch. 3; Royal Commission on the Activities of the Federated Ship Painters and Dockers Union, Interim Reports nos 3 & 4; R. Gyles, QC, *Final Report to the Attorney-General for the Period 1 July 1984 to 21 September 1984*, Commonwealth Parliamentary Papers no. 12, 1985; *Report to the Attorney-General for the Year Ended 30 June 1984*, Parliamentary Papers no. 258, 1984; R. Redlich, *Annual Report of the Special Prosecutor 1983–84*, Parliamentary Papers no. 203, 1984; *Report of Inspectors Appointed to Investigate the Particular Affairs of Navillus Pty Ltd and 922 Other Companies* (the McCabe-La Franchi Report).

113 A. Hopkins, *The Impact of Prosecutions under the Trade Practices Act*. See also B. Fisse & J. Braithwaite, *The Impact of Publicity on Corporate Offenders*, pp. 121–3, and chs 7–9.

114 The Australian Commissioner of Taxation has commented:

> Most taxpayers comply voluntarily. They submit fair and accurate tax returns, and with employers, tax agents and practitioners, they assist Australian Taxation Office staff in their endeavours to gather in for the Government and the community, revenue from tax collections which are vital to the welfare and running of this country. In the vast majority of cases the legislation has worked and the money has been collected.

(*Sixty-third Report 1983–84*, Parliamentary Papers no. 77, 1984, p. 6.) A poll of 2000 Australians for the *Sydney Morning Herald* in 1985 found that sixteen per cent thought understating income in their tax return acceptable (down from twenty per cent in 1972), sixteen per cent thought smoking marihuana acceptable (nine per cent in 1972) and only three per cent thought drink-driving acceptable. *Sydney Morning Herald*, 19 August 1985, p. 1.

115 See S. Lloyd-Bostock, 'Explaining Compliance With Imposed Law', in S. Burman & B. Harrell-Bond (eds), *The Imposition of Law*; J. Tapp & F. Levine, 'Legal Socialisation: Strategies for an Ethical Legality' (1974) 27 Stanford LR 1.

116 In addition to the references in footnote 20, there is some Australian evidence in P. Grabosky (ed.), *Corporate Harm, Corporate Crime* (forthcoming, 1986); P. Grabosky, 'Corporate Crime in Australia: An Agenda for Research', *Australian and New Zealand Journal of Criminology* 17, 1984, pp. 95, 97; R. Purvis, *Corporate Crime*; T. Sykes, *The Money Miners*.

117 W. Chambliss, 'Types of Deviance and the Effectiveness of Legal Sanctions' [1967] Wisc. LR 703, 712–7.

118 *Max Weber on Law in Economy and Society*, p. 38.

119 See S. Macaulay, *Private Government*, p. 31.

120 See K. Llewellyn, 'A Realistic Jurisprudence—The Next Step' (1930) 30 Columbia LR 431, 458.

121 D. Vaughan, *Controlling Unlawful Organisational Behaviour*.

122 Leading Australian businessman, Robert Holmes à Court, has been quoted as saying 'I require everyone to meticulously stay within both the letter and the spirit of all statutory requirements and to co-operate totally with the regulatory bodies' (*Weekend Australian*, 23–24 February 1985, p. 23).

123 See generally O. Mendelsohn & M. Lippman, 'The Emergence of the Corporate Law Firm in Australia' (1979) 3 UNSWLJ 78, 84–90.

124 Two examples:

'The legislation in New South Wales and Queensland relating to blood alcohol levels and driving have continued to have a serious effect on the hotel industry': *Castlemaine Tooheys Ltd Annual Report*, 1984, p. 4.

'Deposit legislation [an environmental measure], by adding to the price of canned beverages, reduces the amount sold and therefore the demand for aluminium can stock': *Comalco Ltd Annual Report*, 1983, p. 8.

But a perusal of the annual reports of Australian companies will produce few such examples.

125 Australian examples of the approach are R. Albon & G. Lindsay (eds), *Occupational Regulation and the Public Interest*; P. Swan, 'The Economics of Law', (1984) 67 Australian Economic Review 92; R. Albon, 'Lawyers and the Rental Market for Housing: A Critical Appraisal' in R. Cranston & A. Schick (eds), *Law and Economics*.

126 See further my 'Consumer Protection and Economic Theory' in A. Duggan & L. Darvall (eds), *Consumer Protection Law and Theory*; A. Duggan, *The Economics of Consumer Protection*.

127 Compare S. Peltzman, 'The Effects of Automobile Safety Regulation', (1975) 83 Journal of Political Economy 677 with L. Robertson, 'A Critical Analysis of Peltzman's "The Effects of Automobile Safety Regulation"' (1977) 11 Journal of Economic Issues 587.

128 Confederation of Australian Industry, 'Government Regulation in Australia, Paper 1, Introduction: The Federal Government, 1980'.

129 For example, J. Pincus & G. Withers, 'Economics of Regulation' in F. Gruen (ed.), *Surveys of Australian Economics*, p. 56; M. Green & N. Waitzman, *Business War on the Law*, pp. 32–47.

130 Tabb, 'Government Regulations: Two Sides to the Story' (1980) 23 Challenge 40, 48.

131 J. Grant, 'The Economic Costs and Benefits of the Australian Trade Practices Legislation', in R. Tomasic (ed.), *Business Regulation in Australia*, p. 339. Benefits were assessed in terms of price rises avoided and costs in terms of the cost of the Trade Practices Commission and legal costs for businesses (offset by savings—e.g., members of trade associations do not have to spend time discussing pricing matters).

132 See the suggestions in B. Fisse, 'Reconstructing Corporate Criminal Law: Deterrence, Retribution, Fault, and Sanctions' (1983) 56 S. Calif. LR 1141.

133 See K. Hawkins, *Environment and Enforcement*, pp. 198–200, 202, 205. Contrast R. Cranston, *Regulating Business*, pp. 170–1. See also N. Gunningham, Safeguarding the Worker, pp. 265–74, 313–22.

134 At present the government funds certain independent bodies (e.g., the Australian Federation of Consumer Organisations Inc.), but a government agency would probably have greater clout and attract more resources. Cf. recommendation for a General Counsel for Grievances: Commonwealth Administrative Review Committee, *Report*, p. 93.

135 *Freedom of Information Act* 1982 (Commonwealth); *Freedom of Information Act* 1982 (Victoria).

136 For example, any person may apply for an injunction under the *Trade Practices Act* 1974 (s.80); the *Administrative Appeals Tribunal Act* 1975 (Commonwealth) gives standing to any person whose interests are affected

by a decision (s.27). See *Re Control Investments Pty Ltd and Australian Broadcasting Tribunal* (No. 1) (1980) 3 ALD 74.

137 For example, *Trade Practices Act* 1974, s.170; *Administrative Appeals Tribunal Act* 1975, s.69.

138 *Subordinate Legislation Act* 1962, ss.3A, 11, 13(4), 14(1)(k), Schedules 1 & 2. (The sunset provision is ten years for statutory rules made after 1 July 1982.) See Legal and Constitutional Committee, *Report on the Subordinate Legislation (Deregulation) Bill*. In mid-1984, a Business Regulation Review Unit was established in the Federal Department of Industry, Technology and Commerce to scrutinize proposals for new regulations and examine existing regulations which affect business.

139 For example, *Ministerial Statement, Review of Commonwealth Functions*, 30 April 1981, pp. 10–15 (the so-called 'Razor Gang').

140 For example, S. Breyer, *Regulation and Its Reform*, pp. 156–88 and passim; M. Baram, *Alternatives to Regulation*.

141 See generally R. Stewart & C. Sunstein, 'Public Programs and Private Rights' (1982) 95 Harv. LR 1193.

2   The Courts

1 The literature is vast: see, in particular, R. Dworkin, *Taking Rights Seriously*, esp. pp. 81–149; N. MacCormick, *Legal Reasoning and Legal Theory*; J. Bell, *Policy Arguments in Judicial Decisions*.

2 Again, there is an academic industry: R. Abel, 'A Comparative Theory of Dispute Institutions in Society' (1973) 8 L & Soc. R 217; L. Nader & H. Todd (eds), *The Disputing Process* are examples.

3 W. Murphy, *Congress and the Court* and G. Schubert, *The Judicial Mind* are representative of the different approaches within this tradition. Studies at the local level are K. Dolbeare, *Trial Courts in Urban Politics*; M. Levin, *Urban Politics and the Criminal Courts*.

4 M. Cain, 'Where Are the Disputes? A Study of a First Instance Civil Court in the U.K.', in M. Cain & K. Kulcsar (eds), *Disputes and the Law*, p. 130.

5 For example, G. Tullock, *Trials on Trial*.

6 Cf. the systems analysis of political science, notably D. Easton, *A Framework for Political Analysis*.

7 S. Daniels, 'Ladders and Bushes: The Problem of Caseloads and Studying Court Activities over Time' (1984) American Bar Foundation Research Journal 751; L. Friedman & R. Percival, 'A Tale of Two Courts: Litigation in Alameda and San Benito Counties' (1976) 10 L & Soc. R 267; R. Lempert, 'More Tales of Two Courts: Exploring Changes in the "Dispute Settlement Function" of Trial Courts' (1978) 13 L & Soc. R 91.

8 W. Felstiner, R. Abel & A. Sarat, 'The Emergence and Transformation of Disputes' (1980–81) 15 L & Soc. R 631.

9 J. FitzGerald, 'Grievances, Disputes and Outcomes' (1983) 1 Law in Context 15. The terminology 'problem', 'grievance', 'claim' and 'dispute' is as used in this study.

10 *Bank of New South Wales v. Commonwealth* (1948) 76 CLR 1.

11 *Commonwealth v. Tasmania* (1983) 46 ALR 625.

12 Attorney-General's Department, *Legal Aid Task Force*, pp. 45–8, 63–85.

13 D. Black, *The Behaviour of Law*, pp. 27–8. R. Cranston, *Legal Foundations of the Welfare State*, pp. 51–62, 77–8, 131–2.

14 R. Cranston et al. *Delays & Efficiency in Civil Litigation*, p. 23.

15 C. Howard, *Australia's Constitution*, p. 2.

16 S. Macaulay, 'Lawyers and Consumer Protection Laws' (1979) 14 L & Soc. R 115.

17 Explicitly recognized in the 'floodgates' argument; e.g., *Winterbottom v. Wright* (1842) 10 M&W, 109; 152 ER 402.

18 Various comments of Sir Owen Dixon (*R. v. Foster ex p. Commonwealth Life (Amalgamated) Assurances Ltd* (1952) 85 CLR 138, 155; *R. v. Wright ex p. Waterside Workers' Federation of Australian* (1955) 93 CLR 528, 542) encouraged the successful challenge which became the Boilermakers' case (*R. v. Kirby ex p. Boilermakers' Society of Australia* (1956) 94 CLR 254). Following *Western Australia v. Commonwealth* (1975) 134 CLR 201, McTiernan J retired and Aickin J was appointed. In *Attorney-General (NSW) ex. rel. McKellar v. Commonwealth* (1977) 139 CLR 527, Barwick CJ hinted at p. 532 that it was appropriate for the decision to be relitigated, which it was: *Queensland v. Commonwealth* (1977) 139 CLR 585. I am grateful to Professor Leslie Zines for these references.

19 These results (unpublished) are derived from R. Cranston et al., op. cit.

20 An example is *Onus v. Alcoa of Australia Ltd* (1981) 149 CLR 27. Similarly, constitutional claims are brought by individuals on behalf of groups; thus *Uebergang v. Australian Wheat Board* (1980) 145 CLR 266, litigation under section 92 of the constitution, was supported by 'The Ninety-Two Association' based in northern New South Wales and southern Queensland.

21 J. Pullen, N. Young & S. Geddes, *Court Surveys and Studies 1978–1984*, pp. 239–41.

22 For example, *Marsh v. Adamson* (1985) 59 ALR 629; *Burton v. Murphy* [1983] 2 Qd R 321; *Attorney-General (NSW) v. Grant* (1976) 135 CLR 587 respectively. Note that the 'other' category in Table 4 includes building societies and credit unions; these are mainly mortgage default and debt claims akin to those brought by businesses.

23 The table, and the following paragraph, are taken from R. Cranston et al., op. cit., pp. 25–6. Copyright is in the Australian Institute of Judicial Administration Incorporated.

24 There might also have been legal advantages: e.g., *Renouf v. Federal Capital Press of Australia Pty Ltd* (1977) 17 ACTR 35, 58–9.

25 J. Pullen et al., op. cit., pp. 168, 238.

26 D. Legge, 'Patients' Rights' in *We've Got No Choice!*, pp. 41–2.

27 Cf. *North Eastern Dairy Co. Ltd v. Dairy Industry Authority of NSW* (1975) 134 CLR 559, 621–2; *Clark King and Co. Pty Ltd v. Australian Wheat Board* (1978) 140 CLR 120, 189–93.

28 B. Yngresson & L. Mather, 'Courts, Moots, and the Disputing Process' in K. Boyum & L. Mather, *Empirical Theories About Courts*, p. 64.

29 (1975) 132 CLR 164. See C. Howard. 'Public Law and Common Law', in D. Galligan (ed.), *Essays in Legal Theory*, pp. 8–13.

30 At p. 173.

31 *Wildsmith v. Dainford Ltd* (1983) 51 ALR 24. Cf. e.g., *Sanrod Pty Ltd v. Dainford Ltd* (1984) 54 ALR 179.

32 *Munna Beach Apartments Pty Ltd v. Kennedy* (1982) 7 ACLR 257.

33 *Dainford Ltd v. Smith* (1985) 58 ALR 285.

34 *Sunbird Plaza Pty Ltd v. Boheto Pty Ltd* [1983] 1 Qd R 248.

35 *Chan v. Dainford Ltd* (1985) 58 ALR 623.

36 *Stack v. Coast Securities (No. 9) Pty Ltd* (1983) 49 ALR 193.

37 For example, *Re Myer Retail Investments Pty Ltd and the Companies Act* (1983) 48 ACTR 41.

38 For example, *Wright Heaton Ltd v. PDS Rural Products Ltd* [1982] 2 NSWLR 301.

39 *National Companies and Securities Commission v. News Corporation Ltd* (1984) 58 ALJR 308; 52 ALR 417.

40 *News Corporation Ltd v. National Companies and Securities Commission* (1984) 52 ALR 277; 57 ALR 550.

41 R. Cranston et al., op. cit., p. 23. Other findings are gathered by F. Zemans, 'Framework for Analysis of Legal Mobilisation' [1982] ABF Res. J 989, 1062–3.

42 See, for example, 'Minute of Judgment by Consent' (1976) 14 Law Soc. J 12.

43 For example, Supreme Court Rules (New South Wales), pt 13, 17.

44 R. Cranston et al., op. cit., pp. 27–8; J. Pullen et al., op. cit., pp. 176, 180, 231, 236–8.

45 See, for example, B. Kercher & M. Noone, *Remedies*, p. 23. The Australian Law Reform Commission was examining the matter as part of its debt recovery and insolvency reference. One aspect was an empirical study of default summons in the New South Wales District Court and Court of Petty Sessions: W. Tearle, *Debt Recovery and Insolvency: Research Paper No. 1: Default Summons Survey*, 1982.

46 See *Field v. Commissioner for Railways of New South Wales* (1955) 99 CLR 285.

47 R. Mnookin & L. Kornhauser, 'Bargaining in the Shadow of the Law: The Case of Divorce' (1979) 88 Yale LJ 950.

48 For example, Supreme Court Rules (New South Wales), pt 22.

49 R. Cranston et al., op. cit., p. 61.

50 The decision to settle is reciprocal in character: the plaintiff with a high probability of success is usually matched by a defendant with a low probability.

51 For general discussions of settlement: D. Black, 'Social Control as a Dependant Variable', in D. Black (ed.), *Toward a General Theory of Social Control*, pp. 22–3; D. Harris, et al., *Compensation and Support for Illness and Injury*, pp. 93–112; H. Ross, *Settled Out of Court*.

52 On adjudication: see M. Eisenberg, 'Participation, Responsiveness, and the Consultative Process' (1978) 92 Harv LR 410; L. Fuller, *The Principles of Social Order*, pp. 86–124; H. Hart & A. Sacks, The Legal Process, pp. 662–9; P. O'Malley, *Law, Capitalism and Democracy*, pp. 121–47; W. Simon, 'The Ideology of Advocacy' (1978) Wisc. LR 29. Cf. R. Abel, 'Theories of Litigation in Society' (1980) 6 *Jahrbuch für Rechtssoziologie und Rechtstheorie* 165, 171–7.

53 This paragraph derives from R. Cranston et al., op. cit., pp. 146–51.

54 K. Llewellyn, 'A Realistic Jurisprudence—The Next Step' (1930) 30 Colum. LR 431, 437–8.

55 R. Summers, 'Law, Adjudicative Processes, and Civil Justice', in G. Hughes (ed.), *Law, Reason, and Justice*, pp. 176–8.

56 Twining notes the variety of perspectives on trials: '[T]rials are referred to as forensic lotteries or degradation ceremonies or licensed battles or conveyor belts. See 'Evidence and Legal Theory' (1984) 47 MLR 261, 274. See, also, M. Weinberg, 'Evidence Scholarship and Theories of Adjudication', in D. Galligan (ed.), *Essays in Legal Theory*.

57 Alternative approaches, such as the use of presumptions, are discussed in M. Shapiro, *Courts*, pp. 11–12.

58 *Acts Interpretation Act* 1901, s.15AA.

59 A. Mason, 'The Role of Counsel and Appellate Advocacy' (1984) 13 Leg. Rep. 4, 5.

60 For example, *Shaddock L. & Associates Pty Ltd v. Parramatta City Council* (1981) 150 CLR 225, 252; *Baker v. Campbell* (1983) 57 ALJR 749, 758; 49 ALR 385, 402; *Onus v. Alcoa of Australia Ltd* (1981) 149 CLR 27, 35.

61 F. Kitto, 'Why Write Judgments' in *Judicial Essays*. See also G. Barwick, 'Judiciary Law: Some Observations Thereon' (1980) 33 Current Legal Problems 239, 240, 244; O. Dixon, *Jesting Pilate*, pp. 155, 158, 160–4; R.W. Fox, 'The Judicial Contribution' in A. Tay & E. Kamenka (eds), *Law-making in Australia*, K. Jacobs, 'Lawyers' Reasoning: Some Extra-Judicial Reflections' (1967) 5 Sydney LR 425.

62 *Reform the Law* pp. 38–40; *The Judges*.

63 For example, *Commonwealth v. Tasmania* (1983) 57 ALJR 451, 457; 46 ALR 625, 633; *Clunies-Ross v. Commonwealth* (1984) 58 ALJR 554, 557; 55 ALR 609, 614.

64 *State Government Insurance Commission v. Trigwell* (1979) 142 CLR 617, 633.

65 For example, A. Blackshield, 'The High Court: Change and Decay' (1980) 5 Legal Service Bulletin 107, 113; G. Evans, 'The Most Dangerous Branch?' in A. Hambly & J. Goldring (eds), *Australian Lawyers and Social Change*.

66 Cf. the sophisticated argument in M. Detmold, *The Australian Commonwealth*, esp. pp. 4–7, 262.

67 *National Commercial Banking Co. of Australia Ltd v. Robert Bushby Ltd* [1984] 1 NSWLR 559, 577.

68 *Day v. Bank of New South Wales* (1978) 19 ALR 32, 45.

69 H. Luntz et al., op. cit., pp. 350–2.

70 For example, *Consumer Claims Tribunals Act* 1974 (New South Wales), s.23(2).

71 This paragraph is derived from R. Cranston et al., op. cit., pp. 32, 185–8.

72 Australian Law Reform Commission, *Community Law Reform: Domestic Violence in the ACT*, pp. 42–3.

73 See especially M. Feeley, 'Power, Impact, and the Supreme Court', in T. Becker & M. Feeley (eds), *The Impact of Supreme Court Decisions*, 2nd edn; W. Muir, *Law and Attitude Change*.

74 *Bank of New South Wales v. Commonwealth* (1948) 76 CLR 1.

75 *Australian Communist Party v. Commonwealth* (1951) 83 CLR 1.

76 *Commonwealth v. Tasmania* (1983) 57 ALJR 450; 46 ALR 625.

77 Notably in *Curran v. Federal Commissioner of Taxation* (1974) 131 CLR 409. See Y. Grbich, 'Problems of Tax Avoidance in Australia', in J. Head (ed.), *Taxation Issues of the 1980s*.

78 See A. Hutchinson, 'The Rise and Ruse of Administrative Law and Scholarship' (1985) 48 MLR 293, 317.

79 *Public Service Board 58th Annual Report 1981–82*, pp. 2–3; *Public Service Act* 1922, s.50D(2).

80 The conclusion of authors working from quite different standpoints: R. Epstein, 'The Social Consequences of Common Law Rules' (1982) 95 Harv. LR 1717, 1744–51; J. Hurst, 'The Functions of Courts in the United States, 1950–1980' (1980–81) 15 L & Soc. R 401, 448–9; R. Unger, 'The Critical Legal Studies Movement' (1983) 96 Harv. LR 561, 581. Interviews with 370 persons in elite positions in Australia in 1975 revealed that judges were not regarded as having great influence. Conciliation and arbitration commission judges might have been regarded as more influential: J. Higley, D. Deacon & D. Smart, *Elites in Australia*, pp. 70, 188, 230.

81 M. Galanter, 'Justice in Many Rooms: Courts, Private Ordering, and Indigenous Law' (1981) 19 J Leg. Pluralism 1, 11–15.

82 *Onus v. Alcoa of Australia Ltd* (1981) 149 CLR 27.

83 (1981) 150 CLR 402.

84 (1983) 152 CLR 359.

85 (1981) 150 CLR 225.

86 Commonwealth Ombudsman, *Fifth Annual Report 1981–82*, p. 20.

87 R. Cranston, 'Consumer Protection and Economic Theory', in A. Duggan & L. Darvall (eds), *Consumer Protection Law and Theory*, pp. 244–5; New South Wales Law Reform Commission, *Accident Compensation* (1984), vol. 1, paras 3.7–3.10; 3.37–3.39.

88 R. Pullan, *Guilty Secrets*, pp. 25–30, 126–31.

89 (1977) 51 ALJR 463; 13 ALR 1.

90 Commonwealth Ombudsman, *Second Annual Report 1979*, p. 29; Commonwealth Ombudsman, *Third Annual Report 1979–80*, p. 21; Commonwealth Ombudsman, *Fourth Annual Report 1980–81*, p. 3.

91 *Motor Vehicles (Third Party Insurance) Act* 1942, pt IIIA.

92 *Social Security Act* 1947, s.120A.

93 *Repatriation Commission v. O'Brien* (1985) 59 ALJR 363; 58 ALR 119; *Veterans' Entitlements Act* 1985, s.119(3).

94 See Senate Select Committee on Private Hospitals and Nursing Homes, *Private Nursing Homes in Australia*, pp. 46–51.

95 *Searle v. Wallbank* [1947] AC 341.

96 *Animals Act* 1977, s.7(2)(b).

97 *Piro v. W. Foster & Co. Ltd* (1943) 68 CLR 313; *Statutory Duties (Contributory Negligence) Act* 1945.

98 [1957] AC 555. See H. Luntz et al., op. cit., p. 1100.

3   Government

1 The term is used here to describe the written constitution embodied in section 9 of the United Kingdom *Commonwealth of Australia Constitution Act*

(63 & 64 Vic., c. 12), as amended by referenda in 1906, 1910, 1928, 1946, 1967 and 1977.

2 For example, *Amalgamated Society of Engineers v. Adelaide Steamship Co. Ltd* (1920) 28 CLR 129, 146–8; *Young v. Williams* (1916) 21 CLR 145, 147; *Re Skyring's Application* (1984) 59 ALJR 123. The earlier authorities are discussed in H. Evatt, *Certain Aspects of the Royal Prerogative*, pp. 18–35.

3 See generally J. Goldring, 'Public Law and Accountability of Government' (1985) 15 FLR 1. Cf. B. Jinks, 'The "New Administrative Law"' (1982) 41 AJ Pub. Admin. 209.

4 See R. Parker, 'Responsible Government in Australia', in P. Weller & D. Jaensch (eds), *Responsible Government in Australia*, p. 12.

5 For example, *Commonwealth Electoral Act* 1918, pt IV.

6 *Commonwealth Electoral Act* 1918, pt. XX; *Election Funding Act* 1981 (NSW). See E. Chaples, 'Election Finance in New South Wales' (1983) 55 AQ 66. For the limited controls on campaign expenditure: C. Hughes, Party Finance and Compulsory Voting.

7 The leading discussion is G. Winterton, *Parliament, the Executive and the Governor-General*, pp. 71–110.

8 See E. Campbell, 'Appearance of Officials as Witnesses before Parliamentary Committees' in J. Nethercote (ed.), *Parliament and Bureaucracy*; E. Campbell, 'Parliament and the Executive', in L. Zines (ed.), *Commentaries on the Australian Constitution*.

9 *Cudgen Rutile (No. 2) Pty Ltd v. Chalk* [1975] AC 520; (1974) 49 ALJR 23; 4 ALR 438 and cases cited there.

10 S.25(2) (amended 1984). See E. Campbell, 'Ministers, Public Servants and the Executive Branch', in G. Evans (ed.), *Labor and the Constitution 1972–1975*, pp. 147–8.

11 Public Service Board, Personnel Management Manual, vol. 3, pt 3, pp. 6–7.

12 *Carltona Ltd v. Commissioners of Works* [1943] 2 All ER 560; *O'Reilly v. Commissioners of the State Bank of Victoria* (1983) 57 ALJR 342; 44 ALR 27. Whether this is possible with legislative power was left open in *Foley v. Padley* (1984) 58 ALJR 454; 54 ALR 609.

13 *A. v. Hayden (No. 2)* (1984) 59 ALJR 6; 56 ALR 82.

14 *R. v. Smith ex p. Mole Engineering Pty Ltd* (1981) 147 CLR 340 turned on particular statutory provisions. It is not uncommon in Acts to provide that delegation of a power does not prevent the exercise of the power by the delegator: *Social Security Act* 1947, s.8(2). This is the result of the caution of drafters; it should not be taken as acknowledgment that the law generally is that the delegation of power prevents the delegator from exercising it.

15 *Ansett Transport Industries (Operations) Pty Ltd v. Commonwealth* (1977) 139 CLR 54, 82 per Mason J. Gibbs & Aickin JJ leave the matter open (pp. 62, 116); *R. v. Anderson ex p. Ipec-Air Pty Ltd* (1965) 113 CLR 177, 192, 202 per Kitto & Menzies JJ: Taylor and Owen JJ leave the matter open.

16 See the views of Barwick CJ and Murphy J in *Anderson* (at pp. 61–2; 87); Windeyer J in *Ipec* (at p. 204); and *Zachariassen v. Commonwealth* (1917) 24 CLR 166, 180. The qualifications would be if acting on the policy or direction were somehow unlawful; if the officer were under a duty to act judicially; or if the officer were directly answerable to parliament (in which case accountability would be unimpaired). The rule would include a

direction on a matter of fact. It also applies to statutory authorities (see pp. 124–5 below).

17 P. Finn, *Law and Government in Colonial Australia*; *Royal Commission on Australian Government Administration*, pp. 84–6.

18 Parliamentarians are approached not infrequently about legal grievances/ disputes: J. FitzGerald, 'Grievances, Disputes & Outcomes' (1983) 1 Law in Context 15, 33.

19 *Arthur Yates & Co. Pty Ltd v. Vegetable Seeds Committee* (1945) 72 CLR 37, 66.

20 R. Parker, 'Statesmen in Disguise' (1981) 40 AJ Pub. Admin. 1, 3; R. Parker, 'The Meaning of Responsible Government' (1976) 11 Politics 178, 184.

21 For example, on the reform of parliaments: G. Reid, 'The Changing Political Framework' (1980) 24 Quadrant 5, 6–7; on administrative accountability through greater monitoring of budgets, policy, programmes and efficiency: H. Emy, 'The Public Service and Political Control', in *Royal Commission in Australian Government Administration*, vol. 1, Appendix, pp. 15–63.

22 For example, *Municipal Council of Sydney v. Harris* (1912) 14 CLR 1; *Scurr v. Brisbane City Council* (1973) 133 CLR 242; *Parisienne Basket Shoes Pty Ltd v. Whyte* (1938) 59 CLR 369. A good example of what can be done to a privative clause is *Ex p. Wurth*; *Re Tully* (1954) 55 SR (NSW) 47.

23 Explicitly recognized in the natural justice area: *Salemi v. Mackellar (No. 2)* (1977) 137 CLR 396 (as to whether the principle applies); *Heatley v. Tasmanian Racing and Gaming Commission* (1977) 137 CLR 487, 514 (as to the requirements entailed; for example, whether an oral hearing is necessary).

24 Cf. *Minister for Immigration and Ethnic Affairs v. Pochi* (1980) 31 ALR 666, 689 per Deane J.

25 *R. v. Toohey ex p. Northern Land Council* (1981) 151 CLR 170, 186. *Murphyores Incorporated Pty Ltd v. Commonwealth* (1976) 136 CLR 1, 12.

26 *Arthur Yates & Co. Pty Ltd v. Vegetable Seeds Committee* (1945) 72 CLR 37, 68.

27 *R. v. Trebilco* (1936) 56 CLR 20, 32.

28 *Bread Manufacturers of New South Wales v. Evans* (1981) 56 ALJR 89, 96; 38 ALR 93, 106.

29 *de Smith's Judicial Review of Administrative Action*, 4th edn, pp. 89, 112, 117, 146, 418.

30 For example, *R. v. Toohey ex p. Northern Land Council* (1981) 151 CLR 170, 192, 222.

31 A. Blackshield, 'The Courts and Judicial Review', in S. Encel et al. (eds), *Change the Rules!*, p. 139.

32 See generally D. Galligan, 'Judicial Review and Democratic Principles' (1983) 57 ALJ 69.

33 Cf. J. Freedman, *Crisis and Legitimacy*, pp. 45–6, 253–4.

34 *Green v. Daniels* (1977) 51 ALJR 463; 13 ALR 1 seems to be the only Australian case.

35 See M. Aronson & H. Whitmore, *Public Torts and Contracts*, pp. 77–86.

36 See T. Daintith, 'Legal Analysis of Economic Policy' (1982) 9 JL & Society 191, 215.

37 P. Craig, *Administrative Law*, pp. 34–5.

38 For example, *ACT Health Authority v. Berkeley Cleaning Group Pty Ltd*

(1985) 60 ALR 284; *Harris v. Director-General of Social Security* (1985) 59 ALJR 194; 57 ALR 729.

39 *Attorney-General for the Northern Territory v. Kearney* (1985) 59 ALJR 749; 61 ALR 55.

40 There were 51 immigration decisions in 1982–83 (43 Federal Court) and 52 in 1983–84 (41 Federal Court): Department of Immigration and Ethnic Affairs *Review of Activities 1983–84*, Parliamentary Paper no. 82, 1985, p. 53.

41 *Administrative Appeals Tribunal Act* 1975, s.43(1), (6).

42 *Drake v. Minister for Immigration and Ethnic Affairs* (1979) 24 ALR 577, 590, 602.

43 Contra J. Sharpe, 'Acting under Dictation and the Administrative Appeals Tribunal's Policy-Review Powers' (1985) 15 FLR 109, 114.

44 *Re Drake and Minister for Immigration and Ethnic Affairs (No. 2)* (1979) 2 ALD 634, 645.

45 The Administrative Review Council, to its shame, abandoned its one attempt to study the matter.

46 T. Brennan, 'Lessons for Brian Howe' (1985) 10 Legal Service Bulletin 20. Cf. J. Morgan. 'Late Claims', p. 23.

47 J. Griffiths, Australian Administrative Law: Institutions, Reforms and Impact, pp. 17, 43.

48 The issues in this paragraph are discussed at length in R. Cranston, *Legal Foundations of the Welfare State*, pp. 252–69.

49 P. Hanks, *Australian Constitutional Law*, 3rd edn, pp. 181–8.

50 This refers mainly to powers of the executive government, recognized by the common law, to act without statutory authority. Among present-day prerogative powers are those to conduct foreign relations, to regulate the disposition of the armed forces, to grant pardons and to confer honours. Legislation has supplanted many prerogative powers. While the courts can determine the limits of the prerogative, it has been thought that they cannot review the propriety or the adequacy of the grounds upon which they are exercised: *R. v. Toohey ex. p. Northern Land Council* (1981) 151 CLR 170, 217–21. Cf. *Council of Civil Service Unions v. Minister for the Civil Service* [1985] AC 374. See generally G. Winterton, *Parliament, the Executive and the Governor-General*, ch. 6.

51 Governing the admissibility, in legal proceedings, of evidence, especially government documents: *Sankey v. Whitlam* (1978) 142 CLR 1; *Alister v. R.* (1983) 58 ALJR 97; 50 ALR 41.

52 See R. Lumb, *The Constitutions of the Australian States*, 4th edn.

53 On the latter: G. Curnow & C. Saunders, *Quangos*.

54 Notably, *Sutherland Shire Council v. Heyman* (1985) 59 ALJR 564; 60 ALR 1.

55 *Dunlop v. Woollahra Municipal Council* (1981) 33 ALR 621, 630; [1981] 1 NSWLR 76, 84. See generally M. Aronson & H. Whitmore, *Public Torts and Contracts*, pp. 120–31.

56 R. Van Munster, 'Changes in Administrative Arrangements and their Implementation', in *Royal Commission on Australian Government Administration, Appendixes*, vol. 1, pp. 409–25.

57 *Murphyores Incorporated Pty Ltd v. Commonwealth* (1976) 136 CLR 1; *Common-*

wealth v. Tasmania (1983) 57 ALJR 450; 46 ALR 625.

58 *Australian National Airways Pty Ltd v. Commonwealth* (1945) 71 CLR 29. See also *Bank of New South Wales v. Commonwealth* (1948) 76 CLR 1.

59 For example, *Fountain v. Alexander* (1982) 150 CLR 615; *In the Marriage of Cormick; Salmon, Respondent* (1984) 59 ALJR 151; 56 ALR 245.

60 *Attorney-General (Vic.) ex rel. Dale v. Commonwealth* (1945) 71 CLR 237; *Victoria v. Commonwealth* (1975) 134 CLR 338.

61 Leading recent cases include *North Eastern Dairy Co. Ltd v. Dairy Industry Authority of NSW* (1975) 134 CLR 559; *Clark King & Co. Pty Ltd v. Australian Wheat Board* (1978) 140 CLR 120; *Permewan Wright Consolidated Pty Ltd v. Trewhitt* (1979) 145 CLR 1; *Uebergang v. Australian Wheat Board* (1980) 145 CLR 266; *Australian Coarse Grains Pool Pty Ltd v. Barley Marketing Board (No. 2)* (1985) 59 ALJR 516; 59 ALR 641.

62 See p. 115 below.

63 *Amalgamated Society of Engineers v. Adelaide Steamship Co. Ltd* (1920) 28 CLR 129.

64 This recalls Wheare's definition of federalism: K. Wheare, *Federal Government*, p. 11.

65 See L. Zines, *The High Court and the Constitution*, 2nd edn, ch. 1.

66 D. Wright, *Shadow of Dispute*, pp. 75–106.

67 *Victoria v. Commonwealth* (1926) 38 CLR 399.

68 *Deputy Federal Commissioner of Taxation (NSW) v. W.R. Moran Pty Ltd* (1939) 61 CLR 735, affirmed (1940) 63 CLR 338; *South Australia v. Commonwealth* (1942) 65 CLR 373; *Victoria v. Commonwealth* (1957) 99 CLR 575; *Attorney-General (Vic.) ex rel. Black v. Commonwealth* (1981) 146 CLR 559. See R. Cranston, 'From Co-operative to Coercive Federalism and Back?' (1979) 10 Fed. LR *121*, 129–135.

69 R. Mathews, *The Changing Pattern of Australian Federalism*, pp. 16–17.

70 *New South Wales v. Commonwealth (No. 1)* (1932) 46 CLR 155; *The Garnishee Cases Nos. 2 and 3* are at (1932) 46 CLR 235, 246. See G. Sawer, *Australian Federal Politics and Law 1929–1949*, pp. 65–66.

71 J. Lang, *Why I Fight!*, pp. 213–14. Cf. W. Wynes, *Legislative, Executive and Judicial Powers in Australia*, 5th edn, p. 361. Cf. D. Clark, 'Was Lang Right?' in H. Radi and P. Spearitt (eds), *Jack Lang*, pp. 144–8, 158–9.

72 *South Australia v. Commonwealth* (1942) 65 CLR 373.

73 At p. 429.

74 J. Maxwell, *Commonwealth-State Financial Relations in Australia*; R. Mathews & W. Jay, *Federal Finance*, chs 8–9; J. Holmes & C. Sharman, *The Australian Federal System*, ch. 6.

75 M. Crommelin & G. Evans, 'Explorations and Adventures with Commonwealth Powers', in G. Evans (ed.), *Labor and the Constitution 1972–1975*, p. 40.

76 The term seems slightly more accurate than 'co-operative federalism', indicating that the Federal government is more powerful than the States: G. Sawer, *Modern Federalism*, 2nd edn, pp. 104–7.

77 R. Leach, *Interstate Relations in Australia*, ch. 3; D. Provost, Inter-Governmental Co-operation in Australia; K. Wiltshire, *Administrative Federalism*.

78 R. Cranston, 'Uniform Laws in Australia' (1971) 30 Public Admin. 229.

79 *Senate Select Committee on Off-Shore Petroleum Resources*, pp. 232–3. Exam-

ples of joint statutory corporations are the Joint Coal Board (*Coal Industry Act 1946*) (Cth) and the Albury-Wodonga Development Corporation (*Albury-Wodonga Development Act* 1973) (Cth).

80 See D. Rose, 'The Commonwealth Places (Application of Laws) Act 1970' (1971) 4 Fed. LR 263.

81 See D. Jaensch (ed.), *The Politics of New Federalism.*

82 (1975) 135 CLR 337.

83 *Commonwealth v. Tasmania* (1983) 57 ALJR 450; 46 ALR 625. See the symposium Sawer et al., (1984) 14 Fed. LR 199–302.

84 In this regard see esp. *Kirmani v. Captain Cook Cruises Pty Ltd* (1985) 59 ALJR 265; 58 ALR 29.

85 'Environment Minister Explains his "Consensus" Approach to the Future of Cape Tribulation', Habitat, Aug. 1984, p. 30. Failure to pursue national Aboriginal land rights might also be seen in this light.

86 G. Marshall, *Constitutional Conventions*, pp. 1, 4–6.

87 This, and some of the succeeding paragraphs, are taken from a comment at (1976) Pub. L 217–221 written by myself and Professor Denis Galligan. I am grateful to Professor Galligan for his generous permission to reproduce these; he should not be taken to agree with any of the present agruments.

88 G. Winterton, op. cit., pp. 14–16.

89 Notably *Victoria v. Commonwealth* (1975) 134 CLR 81, 156; *Western Australia v. Commonwealth* (1975) 134 CLR 201, 278.

90 Popular accounts include P. Kelly, *The Unmaking of Gough* (subsequently published as *The Dismissal*), L. Oakes, *Crash Through or Crash*. Key protagonists have also published accounts—see G. Whitlam, *The Truth of the Matter*. Works by Sir Garfield Barwick and Sir John Kerr are cited below.

91 Set out in G. Sawer, *Federation Under Strain*, Appendix I.

92 *Report from the Joint Committee on Constitutional Review*, 1959, p. 43.

93 Australian Constitutional Convention, Standing Committee D, Special Report to Executive Committee, *The Senate and Supply*, p. 14; cf. the legal opinion obtained by the committee: pp. 68–70.

94 I am grateful to Colin A. Hughes for this information.

95 Sawer, *Federation under Strain*, p. 181.

96 R. Eggleston & E. St John, *Constitutional Seminar*, pp. 5–9, 19–22.

97 See esp. *Victoria v. Commonwealth* (1975) 134 CLR 81, 121, 143, 168, 185; G. Sawer, *Federation under Strain*, pp. 111–21.

98 The letter was signed by Professors Sawer, Zines, Castles and Howard, and published in various newspapers 11 October 1975. See also C. Howard & C. Saunders, 'The Blocking of the Budget and Dismissal of the Government' in G. Evans (ed.), *Labor and the Constitution 1972–1975*, pp. 265–7.

99 Quoted P. Hanks, *Australian Constitutional Law*, 3rd edn, p. 138. See also Australian Constitutional Convention, Standing Committee D, Special Report to Executive Committee, *The Senate and Supply*, pp. 42–3.

100 J. Richardson, 'The Legislative Power of the Senate in Respect of Money Bills' (1976) 50 ALJ 273, 280. The period of the Scullin government might provide examples: see G. Sawer, *Australian Federal Politics and Law 1929–1949*, pp. 1–38.

101 G. Barwick, *Sir John Did His Duty*, pp. 41, 43. See also J. Kerr, *Matters for Judgment*, pp. 307, 312ff; D. O'Connell, 'The Dissolution of the Australian

Parliament: 11 November 1975' (1976) 57 The Parliamentarian 1.

102 Ibid., pp. 46, 49.

103 L. Cooray, *Conventions, The Australian Constitution and the Future*, p. 122.

104 See esp. G. Barwick, op. cit., p. 85; J. Kerr, op. cit., p. 339.

105 J. Kerr, op. cit., pp. 362-3. See also pp. 217, 222; G. Barwick, op. cit., ch. 4.

106 For example, L. Cooray, op. cit., 52, 134-9. Cf. J. Kerr, ibid., 334-5.

107 L. Cooray, ibid., p. 137; G. Whitlam, *The Whitlam Government 1972-1975*, p. 734.

108 Their legality is discussed in G. Sawer, *Federation Under Strain*, Appendix 3; G. Barwick, 'The Economics of the 1975 Constitutional Crisis', Quadrant, March 1985, p. 37.

109 See S. de Smith, *Constitutional and Administrative Law*, 2nd edn, p. 104; H. Evatt, *The King and His Dominion Governors*, 2nd edn; E. Forsey, *The Royal Power of Dissolution of Parliament in the British Commonwealth*, pp. 270-1; I. Jennings, *Cabinet Government*, 3rd edn, p. 412.

110 There is a precedent in Victoria in 1865 of a ministry continuing in office for several months without supply: *Alcock v. Fergie* (1867) 4 WW & a'B(L) 285. But the case is of doubtful value: it was a colonial government in a different era.

111 See R. Cranston & D. Galligan, 'Comment' (1976) Pub. L 217, pp. 218-20.

112 There is some discussion in H. Renfree, *The Executive Power of the Commonwealth of Australia*, pp. 60-3.

113 Quoted J. McMillan, G. Evans, H. Storey, *Australia's Constitution*, p. 198.

114 *Cameron v. Hogan* (1934) 51 CLR 358. Cf. *McKinnon v. Grogan* [1974] 1 NSWLR 295; *Harrison v. Hearn* [1972] 1 NSWLR 428. Where money or property is involved, as with faction fights, the courts intervene: e.g., *Burton v. Murphy* [1983] 2 Qd R 321. Dr C.A. Hughes has suggested to me that the registration of parties, under public funding legislation, and the notion of 'approved names' for use on ballot papers, might lead to greater judicial intervention.

115 See p. 81 above.

116 S. Walker, *Contempt of Parliament and the Media*; Joint Select Committee on Parliamentary Privilege, *Final Report*.

117 The Australian constitution does not require equality in electorates: *Attorney-General (Cth) ex rel. McKinlay v. Commonwealth* (1975) 135 CLR 1. The Australian Bill of Rights will provide for equality, but not directly bind the States: Bill of Rights, Article 6(b). See generally Shane Marshall, 'Electoral Equality and the Law' [1979] Oracle 26. For one example of electoral inequality: C. Hughes, *The Government of Queensland*, pp. 88-104.

118 See pp. 158-9 as to the availability of injunctions and *Webster v. Dobson* [1967] VR 253. See also P.D. Finn, 'Electoral Corruption and Malpractice' (1977) Fed. LR 194, 217-8.

119 United States Code, vol. 2, 267.

120 Department of the Special Minister of State, *Registration of Lobbyists. Guidelines*, 1985. The guidelines define registerable activities.

121 Much of what follows derives from R. Cranston, 'Regulating Conflict of Interest of Public Officials' (1979) 12 Vanderbilt J Transnational L 215.

122 Cf. A. Heidenheimer, *Political Corruption*, pp. 363-4.

123 C. Friedrich, *The Pathology of Politics*, p. 155.
124 For problems in identifying conflict of interest: R. Cranston, 'Regulating Conflict...', op. cit., pp. 219–20.
125 *R. v. White* (1875) 13 SCR (NSW) 322; *R. v. Boston* (1923) 33 CLR 386. See also *R. v. Connolly* [1922] QSR 278; *Speaker of the Legislative Assembly of Victoria v. Glass* (1871) LR 3 PC 560.
126 See note 125 above.
127 *Royal Commission on Standards of Conduct in Public Life*, Command Papers 6524, 1976, p. 98.
128 S.73 A(1). Those bribing the member are caught by sub-section (2).
129 *Public Duty and Private Interest. Report of the Committee of Inquiry*, p. 127.
130 Public officer in this context clearly includes a cabinet minister, as illustrated by *R. v. Vaughan* (1769) 98 ER 308, involving the First Lord of the Treasury: See also *R. v. Whitaker* [1914] 3 KB 1283; *R. v. Jones* [1946] VLR 300.
131 *Crimes Act* 1914 (Commonwealth), s.73; *Williams v. R.* (1979) 23 ALR 369. See also *Secret Commissions Act* 1905 (Commonwealth), s.4. Some State parliamentarians are subject to bribery legislation: Queensland Criminal Code ss.59–60; Tasmanian Criminal Code ss.71–72.
132 *Report of the Royal Commission [on] Allegations of Corruption Relating to Dealings with Certain Crown Leaseholds in Queensland*, 1956, p. 129.
133 See *Hilton v. Wells* (1985) 59 ALR 281.
134 D. Hickie, *The Prince and the Premier*.
135 R. Fitzgerald, *From 1915 to the Early 1980s*, pp. 271, 475.
136 J. Pettifer (ed.), *House of Representatives Practice*, pp. 173–4. Standing order 326 prohibits members sitting on a committee if personally interested in the inquiry.
137 *House of Representatives, Debates*, 8 October 1984, p. 1877.
138 *Common Informers (Parliamentary Disqualifications) Act* 1975, S.3(1). Legislative power for this derives from section 47 of the constitution.
139 See H. Hallam, *The Constitutional History of England*.
140 T. May, *The Law, Privileges, Proceedings and Usage of Parliament*, 17th edn, pp. 209–10.
141 Few have reached the courts, but see *In re the Warrego Election Petition (Bowman v. Hood)* (1899) 9 QLJ 272. Cf. *Clydesdale v. Hughes* (1934) 51 CLR 518; and note 'Gair affair' (1974) 48 ALJ 221. See also Western Australian Law Reform Commission, *Offices of Profit under the Crown*.
142 Suggested by Senate Standing Committee on Constitutional and Legal Affairs, *The Constitutional Qualifications of Members of Parliament*.
143 *In re Samuel* [1913] AC 514, 524.
144 S.44(v). Similar provisions in Australian State constitutions have been considered by the courts but have never been held to disqualify a member of parliament. Most of the decisions seem justified in terms of legislative purpose: *Proudfoot v. Proctor* (1887) 8 LR (NSW) 459; *Hobler v. Jones* [1959] QSR 609. See also the so-called *Tasmanian Members' Case* (1933) 6 ALJ 322, 365 (MPs borrowing from government bank; receiving loans under veterans' repatriation scheme prior to election). But *Miles v, McIlwraith* (1883) 8 AC 120 is less acceptable.
     Note that there are similar provisions for public servants: for example, *R. v. Clarke* (1957) 60 WALR 83.

145 *In re Webster* (1975) 132 CLR 270. See also G. Evans, 'Pecuniary Interests of Members of Parliament under the Australian Constitution' (1975) 49 ALJ 464.
146 *R. v. Boston* (1923) 33 CLR 386, 393, 399–400; *Horne v. Barber* (1920) 27 CLR 494, 500–1; *Wilkinson v. Osborne* (1915) 21 CLR 89, 98–99; *R. v. Jones* [1946] VLR 300. See P. Finn, 'Public Officers: Some Personal Liabilities' (1977) 51 ALJ 313.
147 For example, the Victorian lands case in Australia: *Report of the Board of Inquiry into Certain Land Purchases by the Housing Commission and Questions Arising Therefrom*, Vict. Parliamentary Paper no. 6, 1978; the Commonwealth meat scandal: Royal Commission into Australian Meat Industry, *Report*.
148 See Joint Committee on Pecuniary Interests of Members of Parliament, *Declaration of Interests*, pp. 15–17, 19–21.
149 *House of Representatives, Debates*, 13 February 1986, 425. *Constitution Act 1902* (NSW), s.14A; *Members of Parliament (Register of Interests) Act 1978* (Vic.); *Members of Parliament (Register of Interests) Act 1983* (SA). At the time of writing, the Commonwealth government was intending to act, but faced opposition in the Senate.
150 *Cabinet Handbook*, p. 4. In addition, ministers must make specific declarations of interest at meetings of cabinet, etc.
151 Secretaries or equivalent declare to their minister.
152 For example, *Industries Assistance Commission Act 1973*, s.20; *Trade Practices Act 1974*, s.17.
153 Public Service Board, Personnel Management Manual, paras 3.19–3.36. See also Public Service Regulations, reg. 37.
154 Public Service Board, paras 3.39–3.35. See also *Crimes Act 1914*, s.70(2), dealing with use of official information.
155 Some Australian examples of the 'revolving door' are listed in G. Whitlam, *The Whitlam Government*, p. 706.
156 *Canberra Times*, 18 December 1985.
157 *Cabinet Handbook*, p. 4.
158 Public Service Board, Personnel Management Manual, para. 3.9.
159 *Members of Parliament (Register of Interests) Act 1978*, s.3; Public Service Board, Personnel Management Manual, pp. 24–5.
160 See Kernaghan, 'Codes of Ethics and Public Administration' (1980) 59 Pub. Admin. 207; C. Hughes, 'Administrative Ethics' (1980) AJ Pub. Admin. 454.

4   The Economy

1 *Victoria v. Commonwealth* (1975) 134 CLR 338, 392. For the States: P. Hanks, *Australian Constitutional Law*, 3rd edn, p. 198.
2 See the discussion C. Saunders, 'Parliamentary Appropriation' in *Current Constitutional Problems in Australia*, pp. 6–9, 17–18, 19.
3 See p. 89 above.
4 *Osborne v. Commonwealth* (1911) 12 CLR 321, 336, 352, 355, 365, 373; *Buchanan v. Commonwealth* (1913) 16 CLR 315, 329.

5 J. Pettifer (ed.), *House of Representatives Practice*, pp. 355–63. On legal interpretation of the 'ordinary annual services of government' and enforcement of s.54, see D. Pearce, 'Legislative Power of the Senate', in L. Zines (ed.), *Commentaries on the Australian Constitution*, pp. 130–7.

6 *Audit Act* 1901, pt IX; *New South Wales v. Commonwealth* (1908) 7 CLR 179.

7 See *Audit Act* 1901, pt VIII; J. Quick & R. Garran, *The Annotated Constitution of the Australian Commonwealth*, p. 811. Cf. E. Campbell, 'Parliamentary Appropriations' (1971) 4 Adel. LR 145, 148–9. On the use of the Loan Fund for Consolidated Revenue Fund purposes: *Loan (Temporary Revenue Deficits) Act* 1953.

8 *Maguire v. Simpson* (1977) 139 CLR 362, 398.

9 *New South Wales v. Bardolph* (1934) 52 CLR 455. See E. Campbell, 'Federal Contract Law' (1970) 44 ALJ 580, 586.

10 *Estimates of Expenditure and Receipts of the Commonwealth Public Account 1985–86, Budget Paper No. 5*, Parliamentary Paper no. 254, 1985, p. 5. Table 5, p. 30ff. lists the legislation.

11 E. Campbell, 'Parliamentary Appropriations', p. 156.

12 Its duties are set out in the *Public Accounts Committee Act* 1951, s.8(1).

13 J. Uhr, 'Parliament and Public Administration', in J. Nethercote, *Parliament and Bureaucracy*, pp. 40–2.

14 *Public Works Committee Act* 1969, s.17(3).

15 B. McCallum, *The Public Service Manager*, p. 149.

16 *Audit Act* 1901, pts II, VI, VII, XI; Audit Regulations, Schedules. See generally *Royal Commission on Australian Government Administration*, Appendix 4F.

17 S.32. The public account comprises the bank accounts of the Commonwealth: *Audit Act* 1901, s.21.

18 Cf. E. Campbell, 'The Federal Spending Power' (1968) 8 WA LR 443, 451–8.

19 S.34(1)–(2).

20 S.34(3).

21 S.69.

22 See esp. pt IIA, III. See also *Hawker Pacific Pty Ltd v. Freeland* (1983) 52 ALR 185.

23 Reg. 133. This can be deducted from salary: *Audit Act* 1901, s.71(4).

24 *Victoria v. Commonwealth* (1975) 134 CLR 338, 387, *per* Stephen J.

25 At pp. 385, 396, 410–11.

26 E. Campbell, 'Private Claims on Public Funds' (1969) 3 U Tas. LR 138, 139–40.

27 S.7(1)(f). Section 7(3) provides that the financial assistance shall be provided out of money appropriated by Parliament for the purpose.

28 *British Oxygen Co. Ltd v. Minister of Technology* [1971] AC 610.

29 Ss.3(1), 5, 6.

30 *Green v. Daniels* (1977) 51 ALJR 463; 13 ALR 1.

31 *Administrative Appeals Tribunal Act* 1975, ss.25, 26, 44. An updated list of bodies subject to the AAT is included as an appendix to each annual report of the Administrative Review Council.

32 For example: *PAP Printers & Publishers Pty Ltd v. Minister for Business and Consumer Affairs* (1982) 42 ALR 377; *Export Development Grants Board v. Michell Carbonised Wool Exports Pty Ltd* (1985) 59 ALJR 602; 59 ALR 729; *Harris v. Director-General of Social Security* (1985) 59 ALJR 194; 57 ALJ 729.

33 *Commonwealth v. Colonial Combing Spinning and Weaving Co. Ltd* (1922) 31 CLR 421, 444–5.

34 P. Hanks, *Australian Constitutional Law*, pp. 183–8.

35 House of Representatives, Standing Orders 292, 298. See also J. Odgers, *Australian Senate Practice*, 5th edn, pp. 369ff.

36 D. Rose, 'Discrimination, Uniformity and Preference' in L. Zines (ed.), *Commentaries on the Australian Constitution*, pp. 193–210.

37 *Commissioner of Taxation v. Clyne* (1958) 100 CLR 246.

38 *Moore v. Commonwealth* (1951) 82 CLR 547, 569.

39 *Income Tax (Rates) Act* 1982; *Income Tax (Individuals) Act* 1985; *Income Tax (Companies, Corporate Unit Trusts and Superannuation Funds) Act* 1985; *Medicare Levy Act* 1985.

40 The exact division presently used might not be constitutionally required: *Re Dymond* (1959) 101 CLR 11.

41 *Osborne v. Commonwealth* (1911) 12 CLR 321.

42 *Fairfax v. Federal Commissioner of Taxation* (1965) 114 CLR 1.

43 *Income Tax Assessment Act* 1936, pt III, divn 10, 10AA, 10BA.

44 Economic Planning Advisory Council, *Tax Expenditures in Australia*; Y. Grbich & J. Grbich, 'Tax Expenditures as a Regulatory Tool' in R. Tomasic (ed.), *Business Regulation in Australia*. For some empirical evidence of effects: I. Phillips, 'Using the Tax System to Influence Private and Corporate Investment' (1984) 1 Aust. Tax Forum 313.

45 *South Australia v. Commonwealth* (1942) 65 CLR 373.

46 C. Howard, *Australian Federal Constitutional Law*, 3rd edn, pp. 416–41.

47 See *Hematite Petroleum Pty Ltd v. State of Victoria* (1983) 57 ALJR 591, 595; 47 ALR 641, 649.

48 R. Mathews, 'The Commonwealth-State Financial Contract', in J. Aldred & J. Wilkes (eds), *A Fractured Federation?*.

49 *Deputy Federal Commissioner of Taxation v. Brown* (1958) 100 CLR 32, 40–1. See *MacCormick v. Commissioner of Taxation* (1984) 58 ALJR 268, 273; 52 ALR 53, 63; *Deputy Commissioner of Taxation v. Truhold Benefit Pty Ltd* (1985) 59 ALJR 507, 509; 59 ALR 431.

50 Ss.185, 186.

51 S.187.

52 But they do not decide in favour of taxpayers as much as courts: B. Andrew & F. Gul, 'An Analysis of Taxation Board of Review and Court Decisions 1980–1983' (1985) 14 Aust. Tax Rev. 172.

53 S.196(1)–(2).

54 Ss.196(5), 200, 200A. Certain decisions can be taken straight from the Commissioner to the Federal Court: *Administrative Decisions (Judicial Review) Act* 1977, Schedule 1.

55 p. 47 (Table 1).

56 Government bills—the Taxation (Unpaid Company Tax) Assessment Amendment Bills 1983 Nos 1, 2, 3, 4, 1985—have been defeated in the Senate.

57 I. Spry, 'Retrospective Legislation for Company Tax' (1982) 11 Aust. Tax Rev. 152, 156; editorial, ibid., 191, 193–4.
58 Editorial, ibid., 191, 193–4.
59 M. Graetz, 'Retroactivity Revisited' (1985) 98 Harv. LR 1820, 1822.
60 See I. Wallschutzky, 'Towards a Definition of the Term "Tax Avoidance"' (1985) 14 Aust. Tax Rev. 48, 55–6.
61 For example, *Federal Commissioner of Taxation v. Westraders Pty Ltd* (1980) 144 CLR 55.
62 *Inland Revenue Commissioners v. Duke of Westminster* [1936] AC 1.
63 An excellent study is G. Lehmann, 'The Income Tax Judgments of Sir Garfield Barwick' (1983) 9 Monash ULR 115. See also R. Parsons, *Income Taxation in Australia*, pp. 844–5.
64 In *Westraders*, however, Barwick CJ left legalisms to one side at one point when he said that the approach in *Duke of Westminster* was 'basic to the maintenance of a free society' (p. 60).
65 *Cooper Brookes (Wollongong) Pty Ltd v. Federal Commissioner of Taxation* (1981) 147 CLR 297; *Federal Commissioner of Taxation v. Whitfords Beach Pty Ltd* (1982) 150 CLR 355 are examples.
66 One of the most vigorous was from the then president of the ACTU, R.J.L. Hawke. He was reported as saying:

> For too long, reformist governments... have accepted a situation that the High Court of Australia can sit there in splendid and unrealistic isolation from the mainstream of events and make decisions which can be catastrophic for the welfare of this country. In this day and age I can't think of a greater obscenity than the decision of the High Court in respect of the Curran case. It defies all logic and commonsense. Yet salary and wage earners in this country are having greater impositions put upon them in respect of taxation because people are allowed to escape their rightful obligations, in a fiscal sense, to society by the totally unacceptable decisions of that High Court. *Canberra Times* 28 July 1979, p. 1.

Critical editorials include *Financial Review* 23 September 1980; *Sydney Morning Herald* 19 March 1981.
67 *Reform of the Australian Tax System*, p. 240.
68 Y. Grbich, 'Problems of Tax Avoidance in Australia', in J. Head (ed.), *Taxation Issues of the 1980s*, pp. 414–5.
69 *Curran v. Federal Commissioner of Taxation* (1974) 131 CLR 409; *Federal Commissioner of Taxation v. Patcorp Investments Ltd* (1976) 140 CLR 247; *Slutzkin v. Federal Commissioner of Taxation* (1977) 140 CLR 314; *Federal Commissioner of Taxation v. Westraders Pty Ltd* (1980) 144 CLR 55.
70 *Reform of the Australian Tax System*, p. 37.
71 Notably, *Income Tax Assessment Act* 1936, as amended in pt IVA.
72 M. Aronson & H. Whitmore, *Public Torts and Contracts*, pp. 187ff.; E. Campbell, 'Commonwealth Contracts' (1970) 44 ALJ 14.
73 Ss.55, 57(1)(2).
74 For example, *Housing Assistance Act* 1984, s.14; *Loan Act* 1984, s.4; *States (Works and Housing) Assistance Act* 1985, s.16.
75 For example, *Loan (International Bank for Reconstruction and Development) Act* 1962, s.9 (Snowy Mountain scheme loan); *Loans (Australian Industry Development Corporation) Act* 1974, s.8; *Loans (Australian National Airlines Commission) Act* 1976, s.8; *Loans (Qantas Airways Limited) Act* 1976, s.9.

76 Ss.6, 4 respectively. See also *Audit Act* 1901, s.57(3).

77 See p. 89 above; E. Campbell, 'Federal Contract Law' (1970) 44 ALJ 580.

78 Amended 1944, 1966, 1976. The Agreement is set out as Appendix D of *The Australian Constitution Annotated*; R. Gilbert, *The Future of the Australian Loan Council*.

79 *Sankey v. Whitlam* (1978) 142 CLR 1, 85–91; *Tasmanian Wilderness Society Inc. v. Fraser* (1982) 153 CLR 270, 275–6.

80 S.105A(4).

81 Cl. 3(8), 5(1)(a), (3), 6(1)(a), (3).

82 M. Crommelin & G. Evans, 'Explorations and Adventures with Commonwealth Powers' in G. Evans (ed.), *Labor and the Constitution 1972–1975*, pp. 57–61; P. Hanks, *Australian Constitutional Law*, pp. 195–7; G. Sawer, *Federation under Strain*, pp. 74–83.

83 See R. Mathews & W. Jay, *Federal Finance*, pp. 202–7; R. Scott, *The Australian Loan Council and Public Investment*, pp. 10–11.

84 R. Mathews, *The Australian Loan Council*, p. 19.

85 A. Prowse & E. Morey, *The Financial Agreement and the Future of the Loan Council*, pp. 6–7. This method of financing gave a private body participating with a tax-exempt public body a tax advantage—at the expense of Commonwealth revenue. See *Income Tax Assessment Act* 1936, s.23(d).

86 *Payments to or for the States...and Local Government Authorities 1985–86*, Budget Paper no. 7, Parliamentary Paper no. 256, 1985, p. 38. See generally Advisory Council for Inter-Government Relations, *The Australian Loan Council and Inter-Governmental Relations*.

87 Ibid. pp. 42–3.

88 *Loan (International Bank for Reconstruction and Development) Act* 1950; *Loan (International Bank for Reconstruction and Development) Act* 1962.

89 The *Treasury Bills Act* 1914 is no longer used. As will be seen, Treasury bills are issued under the first-mentioned Act. A somewhat dated outline of some of the matters discussed in the text is contained in *Parliamentary Handbook on Commonwealth Government Financial Affairs*, 1977.

90 The description of these is taken from *Australian Financial System. Report of the Review Group*, pp. 326–8. See also A. Cohen & L. Scott-Kemmis, 'Techniques for the Marketing of Public Sector Debt Instruments', in *Australian Financial System Inquiry. Commissioned Studies and Selected Papers*, pp. 10–13.

91 S.4. See Commonwealth Inscribed Stock Act Regulations, reg. 6A.

92 S.6.

93 S.11.

94 S.12.

95 S.13.

96 S.15; reg. 10(1).

97 S.17; reg. 22A(2), Form 14.

98 S.18.

99 Ss.24, 27–30.

100 Ss.48–51.

101 Ss.51H, 51J.

102 J. Bain, 'Government Debt and the Capital Market' in R. Mathews (ed.), *Public Sector Borrowing in Australia*, p. 48.

103 P. Esler, 'Government Regulation of the Short-Term Money Market' (1982) 13 Commercial L Assoc. Bull. 75; M. Cashion, 'The Short Term Money Market in Australia and its Regulation' (1977) 2 UNSWLJ 90.

104 H. Dalton, *Principles of Public Finance*, 10th edn, pp. 275–81. Cf. J. Keynes, *The General Theory of Employment, Interest and Money*, pp. 100–2.

105 Cl. 12B, 12C.

106 See R. Cranston 'Business Regulation: Problems of Policy' (1980) 2 Labor Forum 14. The Commonwealth Bank, and state enterprises in Queensland, were products of this.

107 The classic statement is F. Eggleston, *State Socialism in Victoria*.

108 D. Corbett, *Politics and the Airlines*, p. 86; *Australian National Airways Pty Ltd v. Commonwealth* (1945) 71 CLR 29.

109 See p. 74 above.

110 See the first half-dozen papers in G. Whitlam, *On Australia's Constitution*.

111 S. Brogden, *Australia's Two-Airline Policy*, p. 96; H. Poulton, *Law, History and Politics of the Australian Two Airline System*, pp. 137ff.

112 Senate Standing Committee on Finance and Government Operations, *Statutory Authorities of the Commonwealth, Second Report*, p. 9. An updated list of such bodies is contained in the *Fifth Report*, 1982, Appendix 5.

113 *Fifth Report*, ibid., p. 23.

114 Ibid., ch. 9.

115 See L. Zines, 'Federal Public Corporations in Australia' in W. Friedmann & J. Garner (eds), *Government Enterprise*, pp. 230–2.

116 For example, *Australian National Airlines Act* 1945, s.25; *Australian Shipping Commission Act* 1956, s.17.

117 For an example of explicit exclusion: *Australian Industry Development Corporation Act* 1970, s.9.

118 *Australian Coastal Shipping Commission v. O'Reilly* (1962) 107 CLR 46, 54–5, 60, 69. And see pp. 82–3 above. Section 61 of the Australian Constitution, the executive power, does not affect this conclusion: P. Finn & G. Lindell, 'The Accountability of Statutory Authorities' in Senate Standing Committee on Finance and Government Operations, *Fifth Report*, Appendix 4 (cf. J. Goldring 'Accountability of Commonwealth Statutory Authorities and "Responsible Government"' (1980) 11 Fed. LR 353).

119 That pragmatic manner is outlined in P. Finn, *Law and Colonial Government in Australia*.

120 *Walker v. Wimborne* (1976) 137 CLR 1.

121 *Levin v. Clark* [1962] NSWR 686, 700; *Re Broadcasting Station 2GB Pty Ltd* [1964–5] NSWR 1648, 1663.

122 *Ngurli Ltd v. McCann* (1953) 90 CLR 425, 438–9.

123 For example, R. Harding, *Outside Interference*, pp. 190–1.

124 For example, *Commonwealth Banks Act* 1959, s.24. See also pp. 101–4 above.

125 AUSSAT Pty Ltd is a peculiar case, since the *Satellite Communications Act* 1984 deems a principal object of the company, imposes obligations on its directors, prevents it becoming a public company, limits its shareholding and provides for its winding up only after parliamentary resolution: ss.6(2), 8, 11, 12, 13.

126 *Victoria v. Commonwealth* (1975) 134 CLR 338, 362, 379, 396, 405–6.

127 (1977) 139 CLR 117.

128 See at pp. 138, 145, 157.
129 See T. Daintith, 'The Mixed Enterprise in the United Kingdom', in W. Friedmann & J. Garner (eds), *Government Enterprise*, pp. 53–78; W. Friedmann & G. Kalmanoff, *Joint International Business Ventures*, p. 125.
130 See *Commonwealth v. Bogle* (1953) 89 CLR 229, 252, 261–2.
131 For example, *Helicopter Utilities Pty Ltd v. Australian National Airlines Commission* (1961) 80 WN (NSW) 48.
132 Schedule 2, (k).
133 For the Ombudsman: D. Pearce, *Comonwealth Administrative Law*, p. 178.
134 M. Sexton & L. Maher, 'Competitive Public Enterprises with Federal Government Participation' (1976) 50 ALJ 209, 223–4.
135 K. Wiltshire, *An Introduction to Australian Public Administration*, p. 71.
136 See E. Russell, 'Ministerial and Parliamentary Accountability of Public Bodies', in G. Curnow & C. Saunders (eds), *Quangos*, pp. 43–4; M. Forrest, 'Reporting and Review of Quangos', loc. cit., pp. 85–8, 97–9.
137 The enterprises seem to see it this way: R. Wettenhall, 'Report on Statutory Authorities', in *Royal Commission on Australian Government Administration*, vol. 1, Appendix, pp. 338, 357.
138 For example, *Portfolio Program Estimates 1985–86*, Budget Paper no. 6, Parliamentary Paper no. 255, 1985, Tables 1, 3.
139 For example, *Report of the Auditor-General Upon Audits, Examinations and Inspections...*, Parliamentary Paper no. 64, 1985.
140 Senate Standing Committee on Finance and Government Operations, *The Australian Dairy Corporation and its Asian Subsidiaries*, p. 311.
141 For proprietary companies, this is a matter of common law; for public companies see *Companies Act* 1981, ss.223, 225.
142 *Companies Act* 1981, ss.280–2.
143 J. Stanford, *Money, Banking and Economic Activity*, p. 35.
144 See now *Currency Act* 1965. The States must not coin money: Constitution, s.115.
145 *Australian Notes Act* 1910. See now *Reserve Bank Act* 1959, s.44. *Re Skyring's Application (No. 2)* (1985) 59 ALJR 561; 58 ALR 629.
146 *Banking Act* 1959, pt IV. By proclamation, no longer in force.
147 In addition to other legislation mentioned in this paragraph, see for example *Crimes Act* 1914, pts IV–V.
148 Ss.7–9; Schedule I; Banking Regulations, reg. 2.
149 *Yango Pastoral Co. Pty Ltd v. First Chicago Australia Ltd* (1978) 139 CLR 410.
150 *Australian Financial System. Report of the Review Group*, pp. 48–50.
151 *Commissioners of the State Savings Bank of Victoria v. Permewan, Wright & Co. Ltd* (1914) 19 CLR 457; *Australian Independent Distributors Ltd v. Winter* (1964) 112 CLR 443.
152 See House of Representatives, *Debates*, 17 April 1985, p. 1283.
153 Banking (Savings Banks) Regulations.
154 Financial Corporations (Statistics) Regulations.
155 See generally K. Davis & M. Lewis, 'Monetary Policy' in F. Gruen (ed.), *Survey of Australian Economics*, pp. 70–9.
156 See *Reserve Bank of Australia, Report and Financial Statements 30 June 1984*, pp. 12–14.

157 D. Flint, *Foreign Investment Law in Australia*, p. 278.
158 *Clyne v. Director of Public Prosecutions* (1984) 58 ALJR 493; 55 ALR 9. See also reg. 41 (prohibiting contracts to avoid the regulations); reg. 42(2)–(3) (forfeiture) reg. 43 (divestiture); reg. 45 (civil validity not affected by breach); *R. v. Waterhouse* (1984) 14 A Crim. R 163.
159 *Watson v. Lee* (1979) 144 CLR 374, 400–1.
160 See D. Flint, op. cit., pp. 289, 297ff. Particular authorizations and exemptions are apparently not gazetted: p. 289.
161 E. Sieper & G. Fane, 'Exchange Control and Exchange Rate Policy' in *Australian Financial System Inquiry. Commissioned Studies and Selected Papers*, pt 2, p. 135.
162 See pp. 83–5 above.
163 *Australian Financial System. Final Report of the Committee of Inquiry*, pp. 75, 306–8.
164 Banking (Savings Banks) Regulations, reg. 5(4).
165 *Australian Financial System. Report of the Review Group*, p. 101.
166 The forces behind, as opposed to the justifications for, regulation are dealt with at pp. 7–10 above.
167 House of Representatives, *Debates*, vol. 37, 1962, pp. 3102–4; vol. 46, 1965, pp. 1655–6; Senate, *Debates*, vol. 60, 1974, p. 541.
168 A. Kneese & C. Schultz, *Pollution, Prices and Public Policy*; A. Kahn, *The Economics of Regulation: Principles and Institutions*: K. Kapp, *The Social Costs of Business Enterprise*, chs 4–5.
169 N. Gunningham, *Safeguarding the Worker*, pp. 283–4.
170 See S. Breyer, *Regulation and its Reform*, pp. 26–8.
171 *Foreign Takeovers Act* 1975; *Broadcasting Act* 1942, s.90G. See R. Cranston, 'Foreign Investment Restrictions' (1973) 14 Harv. Int. LJ 345.
172 Perhaps the *Petroleum Retail Marketing Franchise Act* 1980 is an example. See *Mobil Oil Australia Ltd v. Brindle* (1985) 62 ALR 89.
173 Some regulation has not been given a direct legal form: for example, the foreign investment guidelines.
174 Ss.18–21.
175 D. Flint, *Foreign Investment Law in Australia*, p. 85.
176 *Industries Assistance Commission Act* 1973, s.22(1). On temporary assistance see s.29A.
177 *Prices Surveillance Act* 1983, s.17(3).
178 *Companies (Acquisition of Shares) Act* 1980, ss.57–8.
179 S.59. See *OPSM Industries Ltd v. NCSC* (1982) 7 ACLR 192; NCSC, *Release 105: Companies (Acquisition of Shares) Act and Codes: Discretions Vested in the Commission*, effective 1 July 1981.
180 *Roberts v. Hopwood* [1925] AC 578; *Prescott v. Birmingham Corporation* [1955] Ch. 210; *Bromley LBC v. Greater London Council* [1983] 1 AC 768.
181 *R. and Attorney-General (Cmth) v. Associated Northern Collieries* (1911) 14 CLR 387. See D. Stalley, 'Federal Control of Monopoly in Australia' (1956–59) 3 UQLJ 258, 271–6, 278–89.
182 M. Blakeney, *Price Discrimination Law*, pp. 7–8. See also M. Brunt, 'Lawyers and Competition Policy' in A. Hambly & J. Goldring (eds), *Australian Lawyers and Social Change*, p. 272.

183 *Moorgate Tobacco Co. Ltd v. Philip Morris Ltd (No. 2)* (1984) 59 ALJR 77, 88; 56 ALR 193, 214.
184 Note that certain practices are prohibited outright: for example, price fixing (s.45A); product forcing (s.47(6)–(9)); resale price maintenance (s.48).
185 S.45(2). The market in which the anti-competitive effect is to be gauged is specified: ss.4E, 45(3). See N. Norman & P. Williams, 'The Analysis of Market and Competition under the Trade Practices Act' (1983) 11 ABLR 396.
186 S.47. The relevant market is defined in s.47(3).
187 S.49.
188 *Tillmanns Butcheries Pty Ltd v. Australasian Meat Industry Employees' Union* (1979) 42 FLR 331, 348; 27 ALR 367, 382. See also at p. 338 and p. 374, *per* Bowen CJ.
189 Ss.90, 93, 101A, 102.
190 *Re Queensland Co-operative Milling Association Ltd* (1976) 25 FLR 169; *Re Rural Traders Co-operative (WA) Ltd* (1979) 37 FLR 244.
191 S.46.
192 S.50.
193 *Trade Practices Commission v. Ansett Transport Industries (Operations) Pty Ltd* (1978) 32 FLR 305, 318; 20 ALR 31, 42.
194 For example, N. Gunningham, *Safeguarding the Worker*, pp. 100–2.
195 (1977) 138 CLR 134.
196 At p. 148.
197 On the latter: *Industries Assistance Commission Annual Report 1980–1*, pp. 23ff.
198 For earlier measures: J. Warhurst, *Jobs or Dogma?*, pp. 182–208.
199 C. Hodgekiss, 'Conglomerate Mergers', p. 28. See also J. Nieuwenhuysen & N. Norman, *Australian Competition and Prices Policy*, pp. 40–2; *Trade Practices Act Review Committee*, p. 4.
200 Cf. P. Davey, 'Frozen Vegetables: Before and After Restrictive Practices', in J. Nieuwenhuysen (ed.), *Australian Trade Practices*, pp. 52–6.
201 R. Bannerman, 'Points from Experience 1967–1984', Trade Practices Commission, *Annual Report 1983–84*, Appendix, p. 191.
202 M. Kirby, *Domestic Airline Regulation*.
203 See pp. 37–8 above.
204 P. Atiyah, *The Rise and Fall of Freedom of Contract*. Australian judges apply English decisions in this area.
205 J. Fleming, *The Law of Torts*, 6th edn, p. 485.
206 *Hughes and Vale Pty Ltd v. New South Wales (No. 1)* (1953) 87 CLR 49.
207 *Samuels v. Readers' Digest Association Pty Ltd* (1969) 120 CLR 1; *O'Sullivan v. Miracle Foods (SA) Pty Ltd* (1966) 115 CLR 177; *North Eastern Dairy Co. Ltd v. Dairy Industry Authority of New South Wales* (1975) 134 CLR 559.
208 *North Eastern Dairy Co. Ltd v. Dairy Industry Authority of NSW* (1975) 134 CLR 559, 615.
209 *Uebergang v. Australian Wheat Board* (1980) 145 CLR 266, 300.
210 See G. Walker, 'The Constitutional Protection of Property Rights', in M. James (ed.), *The Constitutional Challenge*, pp. 138, 148–57.
211 *Trade Practices Commission v. Tooth & Co. Ltd* (1979) 142 CLR 397, 403, 452.

212 K. Hancock, 'The Wages of the Workers' (1969) 11 J Indust. Rel. 17, 23.
213 E. Sykes & H. Glasbeck, *Labour Law in Australia*, pp. 590–616.
214 J. Isaac, 'The Function of the Court' in J. Niland & J. Isaac (eds), *Australian Labour Economics Readings*, p. 52; R. Hawke, 'The Commonwealth Arbitration Court' (1956) 3 West A. Annual LR 422, 476.
215 See the remarks on the 1960 credit squeeze: *Queensland Bacon Pty Ltd v. Rees* (1966) 115 CLR 266, 278.
216 C. Rowley & A. Peacock, *Welfare Economics*, pp. 155–6.
217 R. Posner, 'Some Uses and Abuses of Economics in Law' (1979) 46 University of Chicago Law Review 281, 288–9. There is a hint of this in *Insurance Contracts. Treasury Submission to the Law Reform Commission*, p. 39.
218 P. Rubin, 'Why is the Common Law Efficient' (1977) 6 J Leg. Stud. 51. See P. Kenny, 'Economic Analysis and Efficiency in the Common Law' in R. Cranston & A. Schick (eds), *Law and Economics*.
219 (1979) 142 CLR 563.
220 At pp. 575–6.
221 D. Partlett, 'Economics Analysis in the Law of Torts', in R. Cranston & A. Schick (eds), ibid., pp. 61–2.
222 See the authorities: H. Luntz, A. Hambly, R. Hayes, *Torts*, pp. 356–7.
223 G. Calabresi, *The Costs of Accidents*.
224 Cf. P. Swan, 'The Economics of Law', (1984) 67 Australian Economic Review, pp. 99–101.
225 See R. Cotterrell, *The Sociology of Law*, p. 54.
226 For example, the one-line appropriation does not mean an absence of accountability, because a detailed breakdown of spending is often provided to Parliament: *Royal Commission on Australian Government Administration*, vol. 4, Appendix, pp. 106–114, 144–5; P. Weller & J. Cutt, *Treasury Control in Australia*, p. 74.

5 The Environment

1 See D. Horne, *Money Made Us*, Penguin, Melbourne, 1976, pp. 26–7, 34–6, 64, 146–9; J. Powell, *Environmental Management in Australia, 1788–1914*, pp. 30–41, 60–71, 89–94.
2 See H. Wootten, 'The Future of the Conservation Movement' (1985) 13 Habitat 25–6.
3 See K. MacDonald, 'The Negotiation and Enforcement of Agreements with State Governments Relating to the Development of Mineral Ventures' (1977) 1 Australian Mining and Petroleum Law Journal 29, 36; L. Warnick, 'State Agreements—The Legal Effect of Statutory Endorsement' (1982) 4 Australian Mining and Petroleum Law Journal 1; L. Warnick, 'The Roxby Downs Indenture' [1983] Australian Mining and Petroleum Law Association Yearbook 84.
4 L. Zines, 'The Environment and the Constitution', in R. Mathews (ed.), *Federalism and the Environment*. See also Z. Lipman, 'Cape Tribulation: The Legal Issues' (1985) 2 EPLJ 206.
5 *Commonwealth v. Tasmania* (1983) 57 ALJR 450; 46 ALR 625.

6 For example, *Associated Minerals Consolidated Ltd v. Wyong Shire Council* [1975] AC 538; (1974) 48 ALJR 464. See D. Fisher, *Environmental Law in Australia*, ch. 2.

7 D. Pearce, *Statutory Interpretation in Australia*, 2nd edn, pp. 50–2.

8 *News Corporation Ltd v. National Companies and Securities Commission* (1984) 52 ALR 277, 279; *Kavvadias v. Commonwealth Ombudsman* (1984) 52 ALR 728 (cf. Australian Law Reform Commission, *Standing in Public Interest Litigation*, p. 22).

9 *Municipal Officers' Association of Australia v. Lancaster* (1981) 37 ALR 559.

10 R. Cotterrell, *The Sociology of Law*, pp. 57–61.

11 *Australian Conservation Foundation v. Commonwealth* (1980) 146 CLR 493, 546. It might be different if individual rights, for instance to promotion, were affected.

12 House of Representatives Standing Committee on Environment and Conservation, *Administration of the Environment Protection (Impact of Proposals) Act 1974*, Parliamentary Paper no. 188, 1985, pp. 11–15.

13 See R. Cranston, 'From Co-operative to Coercive Federalism and Back?' (1979) 10 Fed. LR 121, 127.

14 S.7. The national estate is defined as components of the natural or cultural environment which have aesthetic, historic, scientific or social significance or other special value for future generations as well as for the present community: s.4.

15 Under the Act, ministers must ensure that departments and authorities do not take action which adversely affects listed areas unless satisfied that there are no prudent and feasible alternatives and that all reasonable measures are taken to minimize the adverse effects: s.30(1). This section may be justiciable: *Tasmanian Wilderness Society Inc. v. Fraser* (1982) 153 CLR 270.

16 Thus excluding *certiorari* and prohibition: *R. v. Electricity Commissioners ex p. London Electricity Joint Committee Company (1920) Ltd* [1924] 1 KB 171, 205; *R. v. Collins ex p. ACTU–Solo Enterprises Pty Ltd* (1976) 50 ALJR 471.

17 Thus excluding mandamus: *R. v. Anderson ex p. Ipec-Air Pty Ltd* (1965) 113 CLR 177; *Water Conservation and Irrigation Commission (NSW) v. Browning* (1947) 74 CLR 492. Injunction and declaration would seem to be similarly excluded: see esp. *Johnco Nominees Pty Ltd v. Albury-Wodonga (New South Wales) Corporation* [1977] 1 NSWLR 43.

18 *Lamb v. Moss* (1983) 49 ALR 533, 556. The court said that it had a wide discretion to grant or refuse relief if its expansive view of reviewable decisions led to a proliferation of cases (at p. 557).

19 *Evans v. Friemann* (1981) 35 ALR 428, 431.

20 S.7A(2).

21 S.8CA.

22 Ss.8E, 18(2AA), 8F. See G. Morris and M. Barker, *Planning and Environment Service (Victoria)*, pp. 2051–2, 2211–2.

23 S.6. See generally D. Fisher, 'The Federal Environment Protection Procedures' (1977) 8 Fed. LR 164; R. Fowler, 'The Prospects of Judicial Review in Relation to Federal Environmental Impact Statement Legislation' (1977) 11 Melb. ULR 1; R. Fowler, 'Legislative Bases for Environmental Impact Assessment' (1985) 2 EPLJ 200.

24 S.7. Whether the procedures are made by regulation or order would seem to be irrelevant.

25 S.8.

26 Ss.6(1), 8. *Canberra Labor Club Ltd v. Hodgman* (1982) 47 ALR 781. Cf. the position in New South Wales: *F. Hannan Pty Ltd v. Electricity Commission of New South Wales* [1983] 3 NSWLR 282; D. Farrier, 'Environmental Assessment in New South Wales' (1984) 1 EPLJ 151.

27 Cf. *Murphyores Inc. Pty Ltd v. Commonwealth* (1976) 136 CLR 1.

28 For example, *Church of Scientology Inc. v. Woodward* (1982) 57 ALJR 42; 43 ALR 587.

29 For example, *Green v. Daniels* (1977) 51 ALJR 463.

30 S.3(2). See G. Bates, 'The Tasmanian Dam Case and Its Significance in Environmental Law' (1984) 1 EPLJ 325, 327–30.

31 *Sutherland Shire Council v. Heyman* (1985) 59 ALJR 564, 577; 60 ALR 1, 26.

32 For example, *Padfield v. Minister of Agriculture, Fisheries and Food* [1968] AC 997.

33 [1975] AC 520; (1974) 49 ALJR 22.

34 At pp. 536, 26 respectively.

35 *Sutherland Shire Council v. Heyman* (1985) 59 ALJR 564, 582; 60 ALR 1, 34–5.

36 M. Cannon, *Life in the Cities*, pp. 154–75; A. Mayne, *Fever, Squalor and Vice*, pp. 41–2, 220–1.

37 J. Gawler, *A Roof Over My Head*, pt 2; P. Ryan, 'The Regulation of Land-use and Planning in Australia', in R. Tomasic (ed.), *Business Regulation in Australia*, p. 243.

38 C. Porter, *Environmental Impact Assessment*, pp. 23–9. See also *Senate Select Committee on Air Pollution Part I*, Parliamentary Paper no. 91, 1969; *National Estate. Report of the Committee of Inquiry*.

39 Cf. R. Fowler, *Environmental Impact Assessment, Planning and Pollution Measures in Australia*, p. 246.

40 Ss.150–3.

41 Now ss. 186–90.

42 NSW: *Prevention of Oil Pollution of Navigable Waters Act* 1960–1969. Vic.: *Navigable Waters (Oil Pollution) Act* 1960. Qld: *Pollution of Waters by Oil Act* 1973. SA: *Prevention of Pollution of Waters by Oil Act* 1961–1975. WA: *Prevention of Pollution of Waters by Oil Act* 1960–1973. Tas.: *Oil Pollution Act* 1961–1964. See also Commonwealth legislation: *Protection of the Sea (Discharge of Oil from Ships) Act* 1981; *Protection of the Sea (Civil Liability) Act* 1981; *Protection of the Sea (Powers of Intervention) Act* 1981.

43 But for fines to be imposed, there need to be prosecutions: see Public Interest Research Group, *Legalized Pollution*, pp. 45, 51–2.

44 See *Nicholson v. Fremantle Port Authority* [1969] WAR 27.

45 Incorporated in *Environment Protection Act* 1970, as· s.42B(2).

46 S.42B(3)–(5).

47 S.42B(7).

48 S.42B(8), (11).

49 *Goodes v. General Motors-Holden's Pty Ltd* [1972] VR 386; *Majury v. Sunbeam Corporation Ltd* [1974] 1 NSWLR 659. See D. Fisher 'Environment Protec-

tion and the Criminal Law' (1981) 5 Crim. LJ 184, 191–201.

50 *Window v. The Phosphate Co-operative Co. of Australia Ltd* [1983] 2 VR 287.
51 S.63(2).
52 For example, *Local Government Act* 1919 (NSW), s.289B-C.
53 For example, *Environment Protection Act* 1970 (Vic.), s.31A(1)–(2).
54 S.31A(7).
55 S.39(2)(a).
56 S.48B(2).
57 Ss.16(1), 20C(1)(2), 33B, 38, 40, 44, 46.
58 S.18.
59 G. Morris & M. Barker, *Planning and Environment Service (Victoria)*, pp. 6506, 6512–3; Commonwealth/State Transport Secretariat, *Report on the Development of a Long-term National Motor Vehicle Emissions Strategy*, pp. 60–3.
60 For example, Clean Air Regulations 1964 (NSW), pt IV; Clean Water Regulations 1972 (NSW), pt III.
61 C. Arup, 'Technology, Society and the Functions of Traffic Noise Laws' (1981) 4 UNSWLJ 29, 48–9, 52.
62 S.26(e). See P. Ryan, 'Tree Preservation Orders in New South Wales' (1984) 1 EPLJ 178, 183.
63 S.126(2).
64 R. Chapman, Environment Protection: The Law and Administration in Australia, p. 9.
65 But not a life tenant: see P. Butt, *Introduction to Land Law*, pp. 80–1.
66 L. Stein, *Urban Legal Problems*, pp. 130–80.
67 See generally A. Fogg, *Australian Town Planning Law*, 2nd edn.
68 There is considerable litigation over whether an alteration or extension of a non-conforming use is significant enough to make the use unlawful. For example: *Shire of Perth v. O'Keefe* (1963) 110 CLR 529; *Woollahra Municipal Council v. Banool Developments Pty Ltd* (1973) 129 CLR 138; *Eaton & Sons Pty Ltd v. Warringah Shire Council* (1972) 129 CLR 270.
69 W. Herd, 'The Balance of Private and Public Interests in the Control of Non-Conforming Uses' (1982) 12 UQLJ 29, 31.
70 M. Auster, 'Spot Zoning' (1984) 1 EPLJ 347, 351.
71 T. Bryant, 'Conditioned Town Planning Permits' (1979) 12 Melb. ULR 139. Where a zoning scheme is incorporated in delegated legislation, a statutory empowering provision to prohibit will enable conditions to be imposed.
72 For example *Dorrestijn v. South Australian Planning Commission* (1984) 59 ALJR 105; 56 ALR 295; *Kentucky Fried Chicken Pty Ltd v. Gantidis* (1979) 140 CLR 675.
73 For example, *Environmental Planning and Assessment Act* 1979 (NSW), s.90(1).
74 For example, *Lloyd v. Robinson* (1962) 107 CLR 142; *Cardwell Shire Council v. King Ranch Australia Pty Ltd* (1984) 58 ALJR 386; 53 ALR 632.
75 A. Nott, *Environmental Planning and Development Law (NSW)*, pp. 92–3.
76 *Heath Signs Pty Ltd v. Parramatta City Council* (1983) 50 LGRA 376.
77 NSW: *National Parks and Wildlife Act* 1974. Vic: *Wildlife Act* 1975. Qld: *Fauna Conservation Act* 1974. SA: *National Parks and Wildlife Act* 1972–74. WA:

Wildlife Conservation Act 1950–1984. Tas: *National Parks and Wildlife Act* 1978. NT: *Wildlife Conservation and Control Ordinance* 1962–1975. ACT: *Nature Conservation Ordinance* 1980. See G. Bates, *Environmental Law in Australia*, pp. 103–17.

78 See W. Poole, *Management of Kangaroo Harvesting in Australia* (1984). A threat to legislative effectiveness is the protection given to the interstate trade in fauna by the High Court's interpretation of s.92 of the Australian constitution: *Fergusson v. Stevenson* (1951) 84 CLR 421.

79 S.20(1).

80 S.4(1). See *The Phosphate Co-operative Company of Australia Ltd v. Environment Protection Authority* (1977) 138 CLR 134, 146.

81 S.20(11).

82 S.20(1), (2).

83 S.19A.

84 S.46A.

85 M. Barker, 'Pollution Control' (1984) 1 EPLJ 101.

86 P. Russ and L. Tanner, *The Politics of Pollution*, pp. 24–5, 50.

87 Ibid., pp. 52–4.

88 P. Grabosky & J. Braithwaite, *Of Manners Gentle*, p. 38.

89 Ibid., p. 40.

90 Ibid., pp. 40–9 (see esp. Table 7, p. 48). See also M. Hollick, 'The Role of Statute Law in Environmental Management' (1985) 2 EPLJ 116, 119–20. There are no Australian studies of how environmental protection officers in the field make judgments about prosecution in terms, say, of a discharger's power to prevent pollution and its economic capacity (cf. K. Hawkins, *Environment and Enforcement*, pp. 73–5).

91 *Western Suburbs* [Victoria] *Planning and Environment Action Program Investigation Working Paper*, vol. 1, pp. 46–8, Appendix I, pp. 6–7, cited in G. Morris & M. Barker, *Planning and Environment Service (Victoria)* p. 2463.

92 See *Protean (Holdings) Ltd v. Environment Protection Authority* [1977] VR 51. But cf. the Phosphate Co-operative case (see note 80 above).

93 *Walker v. Shire of Flinders* [1984] VR 409.

94 P. Grabosky & J. Braithwaite, *Of Manners Gentle*, p. 48.

95 See pp. 83–4.

96 *Attorney-General (NSW) ex rel. Franklins Stores Pty Ltd v. Lizelle Pty Ltd* [1977] 2 NSWLR 955, 964.

97 *Scurr v. Brisbane City Council* (1973) 133 CLR 242, 255–6.

98 *Murphyores Incorporated Pty Ltd v. Commonwealth* (1976) 136 CLR 1. See also *Evans v. Forestry Commission of New South Wales* (1982) 48 LGRA 266 (consideration of environmental factors in grant of clearing licences under Forestry Act 1916 (NSW); *National Trust of Australia (Vic.) v. Australian Temperance and General Mutual Life Assurance Society Ltd* [1976] VR 592 (non-consideration of historical character of building in planning approval).

99 *Truelove v. Queensland* [1985] Australian Current Law 669.

100 *Ramsay v. Aberfoyle Manufacturing Co. (Australia) Pty Ltd* (1935) 54 CLR 220, 249 *per* Starke J.

101 Cf. *State of Queensland v. Australian Communications Commission* (1985) 59 ALJR 562; 59 ALR 243.

102 *Cooney v. Ku-Ring-Gai Municipal Council* (1963) 114 CLR 582; *Day v. Pinglen Pty Ltd* (1981) 148 CLR 289; *Onus v. Alcoa of Australia Ltd* (1981) 149 CLR 27.

103 (1980) 146 CLR 493.

104 (1981) 149 CLR 27.

105 *Anderson v. Mackellar County Council* (1968) 69 SR (NSW) 444; *Dajon Investments Pty Ltd v. Talbot* [1969] VR 603. cf. *Thorne v. Doug Wade Consultants Pty Ltd* [1985] VR 433.

106 See *Oldham v. Lawson (No. 1)* [1976] VR 654.

107 (1980) 146 CLR 493.

108 *Everyone v. State of Tasmania* (1983) 49 ALR 381. See also *Ingram v. Commonwealth* (1980) 54 ALJR 395 (no standing to challenge policy on nuclear weapons on ground of breach of international law).

109 *Anderson v. Commonwealth* (1932) 47 CLR 50; *Logan Downs Pty Ltd v. Federal Commissioner of Taxation* (1965) 112 CLR 177.

110 *Day v. Pinglen Pty Ltd* (1981) 148 CLR 289; cf. *Thorne v. Doug Wade Consultants Pty Ltd* [1985] VR 433.

111 *Fraser Island Defence Organisation Ltd v. Hervey Bay Town Council* [1983] 2 Qd R 72.

112 See *R. v. Toohey ex p. Northern Land Council* (1981) 151 CLR 170, 218–20.

113 T. Hundloe, 'Heads They Win, Tails We Lose: Environment and the Law', in P. Wilson & J. Braithwaite (eds), *Two Faces of Deviance*, pp. 145–6. Another example was the Mt Etna case: Australian Law Reform Commission, *Standing in Public Interest Litigation*, pp. 90–1. But in the Black Mountain Tower Case the Attorney-General gave his fiat: see *Kent v. Cavanagh* (1973) 1 ACTR 43; *Johnson v. Kent* (1975) 132 CLR 164; W. Hancock, *The Battle of Black Mountain*.

114 *Cooney v. Ku-Ring-Gai Municipal Council* (1963) 114 CLR 582; *City of Prahran v. Cameron* [1972] VR 90.

115 S.123. Between 1979 and 1984, 35 such actions were commenced: Australian Law Reform Commission, p. 107.

116 S.80(1)(c). cf. 'any member of the Aboriginal race': *World Heritage Properties Conservation Act* 1983, ss.13(7), 14(5).

117 (1978) 20 ALR 183.

118 *Canberra Labor Club Ltd v. Hodgman* (1982) 47 ALR 781.

119 *Australian Conservation Foundation v. Environment Protection Appeal Board* [1983] 1 VR 385; *National Trust of Australia (Vic.) v. Australian Temperance and General Mutual Life Assurance Society Ltd* [1976] VR 592.

120 *Day v. Pinglen Pty Ltd* (1981) 148 CLR 289.

121 *Ramsay v. Aberfoyle Manufacturing Co. (Australia) Pty Ltd* (1935) 54 CLR 230; *Commonwealth of Australia v. John Fairfax & Sons Ltd* (1980) 147 CLR 39, 49–50; *Attorney-General (Queensland) ex rel. Kerr v. T.* (1983) 57 ALJR 285; 46 ALR 275. See also *Gouriet v. Union of Post Office Workers* [1978] AC 435.

122 *Cooney v. Ku-Ring-Gai Municipal Council* (1963) 114 CLR 582.

123 *Wentworth v. Woollahra Municipal Council* (1982) 149 CLR 672; *Wentworth v. Woollahra Municipal Council (No. 3)* (1984) 59 ALJR 36; 56 ALR 233; *Thorne v. Doug Wade Consultants Pty Ltd* [1985] VR 433.

124 For example, *Clean Waters Act* 1970 (NSW), s.33(2), (2A).

125 See Australian Law Reform Commission, *Standing in Public Interest Litiga-tion*, pp. 188–93; G. Morris & M. Barker, *Planning and Environment Service (Victoria)*, p. 2454.
126 S.110.
127 *R. v. McAulay ex p. Fardell* (1979) 2 NTR 22; *R. v. Commissioner of Police of the Metropolis ex p. Blackburn* [1968] 2 QB 118. But *certiorari* was granted in *R. v. London County Council ex p. The Entertainments Protection Association Ltd* [1931] 2 KB 215.
128 *Inland Revenue Commissioners v. National Federation of Self-Employed and Small Businesses Ltd* [1982] AC 617, 635.
129 A. Bradbrook & M. Neave, *Easements and Restrictive Covenants in Australia*, p. 201. See also *Commission of Inquiry into Land Tenures. Final Report*, Parliamentary Paper no. 151, 1976, pp. 45–53.
130 Ibid., p. 200.
131 J. Bradsen & R. Fowler, 'Land Degradation—Legal and Institutional Con-straints', in *Land Degradation and Public Policy*, pt IV(3).
132 *Thorne v. Doug Wade Consultants Pty Ltd* [1985] VR 433. The case involved private individuals seeking to bring a public law claim about planning approval. Costs were some $¾ million; the case was heard over some 36 days.
133 *Oldham v. Lawson (No. 1)* [1976] VR 654.
134 T. Pinos, 'Class Actions in Victoria' (1984) 58 Law Inst. J 955–6.
135 *McLeod v. Rub-A-Dub Car Wash (Malvern) Pty Ltd* 1972, unreported, Victorian Supreme Court, cited P. Alston, 'Representative Class Actions in Environmental Litigation' (1973) 9 Melb. ULR 307, 311 n.
136 *Conservation Council of Western Australia, Inc. v. Aluminium Company of America* (1981) 518 F. Supp. 270. Not surprisingly, the court held that it had no jurisdiction.
137 *Payne v. Young* (1980) 145 CLR 609.
138 *Clark v. University of Melbourne* [1978] VR 457.
139 *Supreme Court Act* 1958, s.62(1C). On class actions generally: see R. Cranston, *Consumers and the Law*, 2nd edn, pp. 94–101; M. Kirby, *Reform the Law*, pp. 156–70.
140 Cf. *St Helen's Smelting Co. v. Tipping* (1865) 11 HLC 642.
141 *Elston v. Dore* (1982) 149 CLR 480, 488.
142 *St Helen's Smelting Co. v. Tipping* (1865) 11 HLC 642.
143 *Wood v. Conway Corporation* [1914] 2 Ch. 47.
144 *Halsey v. Esso Petroleum Co. Ltd* [1961] 1 WLR 683; [1961] 2 All ER 145.
145 *Dunstan v. King* [1948] VLR 269 (Barry J admitted evidence of decibel readings); *Spencer v. Silva* [1942] SASR 213.
146 *Daily Telegraph Co. Ltd v. Stuart* (1928) 28 SR (NSW) 291.
147 *Field v. South Australian Soccer Association* [1953] SASR 224.
148 *Wilkinson v. Co-operative Estates Ltd* [1919] 15 Tas. LR 22. See also *Munro v. Southern Dairies Ltd* [1955] VLR 332 (smell and noise from suburban dairy).
149 *McKell v. Rider* (1908) 5 CLR 480.
150 *Don Brass Foundary Pty Ltd v. Stead* (1948) 48 SR (NSW) 482.
151 *Harkess v. Woodhead* [1950] SASR 54.
152 *Bode v. Wollongong Gas Light Co. Ltd* (1910) 10 SR (NSW) 566.

153 *L'Estrange v. Brisbane Gas Co.* [1928] QSR 180.
154 *Fennell v. Robson Excavations Pty Ltd* [1977] 2 NSWLR 486.
155 H. Luntz, A. Hambly, R. Hayes, *Torts*, p. 931. Public nuisance might be available.
156 *Sturges v. Bridgman* (1879) 11 Ch.D 852. See the discussion of *Kidman v. Page* [1959] Qd R 53 in C. Arup, 'Technology, Society and Functions of Traffic Noise Law' (1981) 4 UNSWLJ 29, 39.
157 *Clarey v. Principal and Council of the Women's College* (1953) 90 CLR 170.
158 *Miller v. Jackson* [1977] QB 966.
159 *Harkess v. Woodhead* [1950] SASR 54 (noxious trade regulations); *L'Estrange v. Brisbane Gas Co.* [1928] QSR 180, 190 (Navigation Act gave plaintiff right to own yacht, and thus right to moor it in unpolluted water).
160 Cf. *Footscray Corporation v. Maize Products Pty Ltd* (1942) 67 CLR 301; *Wilkinson v. Co-operative Estates Limited* (1919) 15 Tas. LR 22.
161 Public nuisance is dealt with in s.230 (Qld); s.207 (WA); s.140 (Tas.) of the respective criminal codes. See *Smith v. Cornish* (1971) 23 LGRA 87.
162 *Farley & Lewers Ltd. v. Attorney-General* [1963] NSWR 1624.
163 *Baulkham Hills Shire Council v. A.V. Walsh Pty Ltd* (1968) 15 LGRA 338.
164 *Campbell v. Paddington Corporation* [1911] 1 KB 869.
165 *Owen v. O'Connor* [1964] NSWR 1312.
166 *Wringe v. Cohen* [1940] 1 KB 229, 233.
167 *Cartwright v. McLaine & Long Pty Ltd* (1979) 143 CLR 549.
168 *Johnson v. Kent* (1975) 132 CLR 164, 173–4, disagreeing with the trial judge. In *Kent v. Johnson* (1973) 21 FLR 177 at p. 209 the trial judge had also said:

> In my opinion a substantial deleterious unlawful interference with the nature and quality of the reserve as a park for one to use and enjoy as such as a member of the public would constitute a public nuisance. Injury to the flora and fauna seems to me to be the same class of interference with public rights as would be the fouling of a public swimming pool.

The matter was not argued on appeal.
169 *York Bros (Trading) Pty Ltd v. Commissioner of Main Roads* [1983] 1 NSWLR 391. Powell J said:

> Where, however, the duty is imposed, or the power or authority conferred, in general terms, then, prima facie, it was not the intention of the legislature that the rights of others should be invaded as a consequence of the performance of the duty or the exercise of the power or authority, and such an invasion may be justified only if it can be demonstrated that the work was reasonably necessary, that it was properly performed in all respects, and that, if it resulted in damage, there was, in the light of the scientific knowledge then available no reasonable way in which the end directed or permitted could have been achieved without doing the damage which in fact resulted (pp. 397–8).

170 S. Hobday, *Coulson and Forbes on the Law of Waters*, 6th edn, pp. 191–201.
171 *John Young v. Bankier Distillery* [1893] AC 691.
172 *Pride of Derby and Derbyshire Angling Association Ltd v. British Celanese Ltd* [1952] 1 All ER 1326. On appeal: [1953] Ch. 149.
173 NSW: *Water Act* 1912. Vic.: *Water Act* 1958. Qld: *Water Act* 1926–1983. SA: *Waters Resources Act* 1976. WA: *Rights in Water and Irrigation Act* 1914. Tas: *Water Act* 1957.

174 See S. Clark & I. Renard, 'The Riparian Doctrine and Australian Legislation' (1970) 7 Melb. ULR 475; P. Davis, "Nationalisation" of Water Use Rights by the Australian States' (1975) 9 UQLJ 2.

175 *Thorpes Ltd v. Grant Pastoral Co. Pty Ltd* (1955) 92 CLR 317, 331; *Nalder v. Commissioner for Railways* [1983] 1 Qd R 620; *Rapoff v. Velios* [1975] WAR 27.

176 *Lomax v. Jervis* (1885) 6 LR (NSW) 237.

177 *Hood v. Corporation of Sydney* (1860) 2 Legge 1294; *While v. Taylor* (1874) 8 SALR 1.

178 (1868) LR 3 HL 330.

179 *Halsey v. Esso Petroleum Co. Ltd* [1961] 1 WLR 683, 692.

180 *Kara Pty Ltd v. Rhodes* [1966] VR 77; *Miller Steamship Co. Pty Ltd v. Overseas Tankship (UK) Ltd.* [1963] NSWR 737, 764; *Benning v. Wong* (1969) 122 CLR 249 respectively.

181 *Esso Petroleum Co. Ltd v. Southport Corporation* [1956] AC 218, 225 (Devlin J), 242, 244.

182 Cf. *Stoneman v. Lyons* (1975) 133 CLR 550.

183 *Colls v. Home and Colonial Stores* [1904] AC 179; *Allen v. Greenwood* [1980] Ch. 119.

184 See generally A. Bradbrook, *Solar Energy and the Law*.

185 See D. Fisher, 'Environmental Planning, Public Enquiries and the Law' (1978) 52 ALJ 13.

186 See D. Fisher, *Environmental Law in Australia*, ch. 5.

187 S.33B(1). See also A. Fogg, 'Third Party Objections and Appeals in Development Control Decisions under Town Planning Legislation' (1985) 2 EPLJ 4.

188 *Mining Act* 1978, ss.42, 59.

189 For example, NSW: *Mining Act* 1973, s.112.

190 *Stow v. Mineral Holdings (Australia) Pty Ltd* (1977) 51 ALJR 672; 14 ALR 397. The four objectors were the secretary of the Tasmanian Conservation Trust, a person acting on behalf of the South-West Committee, a person who stated merely his interest in the preservation of the area, and the secretary of the Launceston Walking Club.

191 Ibid.

192 (1975) 132 CLR 473.

193 S.39(2).

194 Ss.42, 47, 49, 58, 66, 68. See J. Woodward, 'Environmental Enquiries in New South Wales' (1984) 1 EPLJ 317.

195 Ss.84, 87, 90(1)(p), 95, 98.

196 T. Logan & E. Ogilvy, 'The Statutory Planning Framework' in P. Troy (ed.), *Equity in the City*, p. 181.

197 R. Roddewig, *Green Bans*.

198 See M. Sornarajah (ed.), *The South West Dam Dispute*, pp. 8–9, 13–4, 124–44 (G. Bates, E. Braybrooke, K. Warner).

199 A. Gilpin, *The Australian Environment*, pp. 66–71.

200 *Summary Offences Act* 1966, s.17(3)–(4) (inserted 1981). Until then, companies had to rely on changing their articles, thus enabling their directors to refuse to register small shareholdings (less than, say, 100 shares); seeking a

court order prior to the meeting (see s.246 of the *Companies Act* 1981); or on the ordinary criminal law (for example, trespass). (A trespass prosecution, arising out of the EZ Industries Ltd general meeting in 1979, failed: *Australian*, 29 March 1980.)

201 Direct action is examined at length in R. Cranston, *Legal Foundations of the Welfare State*, ch. 7.

202 See M. Barker, 'Environmental Quality Control: Regulation or Incentives?' (1984) 1 EPLJ 222.

203 D. Fisher, 'The Policy of Resource Use and Conservation: Means for Its Implementation' (1985) 2 EPLJ 191, 198.

204 See D. Fisher, *Environmental Law in Australia*, p. 143. An example might be the forest practices code, made under the *Forest Practices Act* 1985 (Tas.).

205 D. Whalan, 'The Structure and Nature of Australian Environmental Law' (1977) 8 Fed. LR 294, 313.

206 R. Stewart & J. Krier, *Environmental Law and Policy*, 2nd edn, pp. 808–9.

207 G. Richardson, A. Ogus & P. Burrows, *Policing Pollution*, pp. 197–9.

208 Law Reform Commission of Canada, *Crimes Against the Environment*, Working Paper no. 44, Ottawa, 1985.

209 M. Neutze, *Australian Urban Policy*, p. 167; M. Neutze, *Urban Development in Australia*, 2nd edn, pp. 223–4, ch. 9.

210 R. Chapman & D. Roebuck, *The Court as the Public Conscience* (but see p. 47 for a more sober assessment than the title indicates).

211 G. Bates, *Environmental Law in Australia*, p. 5. Cf. P. Coward, *Environmental Law in Sydney*, p. 49.

212 *Stow v. Mineral Holdings (Australia) Pty Ltd* (1977) 51 ALJR 672; 14 ALR 397.

213 B. Davis, 'The Struggle for South-West Tasmania', in R. Scott (ed.), *Interest Groups and Public Policy*, p. 163.

214 See J. Brenner, 'Nuisance Law and the Industrial Revolution' (1973) 3 J Leg. Stud. 403.

215 M. McDougal, 'The Influence of the Metropolis in Concepts, Rules and Institutions Relating to Property' (1955) 4 J Pub. L 93, 113. See also A. Ogus & G. Richardson, 'Economics and the Environment: A Study of Private Nuisance' (1977) Cambridge LJ 284, 324–5; J. Bentil, 'Environmental Suits before the Courts' (1981) JP & EL 324, 337.

Conclusion

1 The argument, from a Marxist perspective, in K. Jones, *Law and Economy*.

2 There are many examples: for one, see J. Mackinolty, 'The Married Women's Property Acts', in J. Mackinolty & H. Radi (eds), *In Pursuit of Justice*, p. 73.

3 R. Cotterrell, *The Sociology of Law*, p. 287.

4 *Victoria v. Commonwealth* (1975) 134 CLR 338.

5 See G. Sawer, 'Political Questions' (1963) 15 U Toronto LJ 49.

6 *Winterbottom v. Wright* (1842) 152 ER 402, 405.

7 Australian Law Reform Commission, *Standing in Public Interest Litigation*, pp. 21–2.

8 Cf. R. Tomasic, 'Towards A Theory of Legislation' [1985] Statute Law Rev. 84, 102.

9 The courts generally only take judicial notice of what is notorious or clearly established.

10 Independently of provisions such as *Acts Interpretation Act* 1901 (Commonwealth), s.16A.

11 *Bank of New South Wales v. Commonwealth* (1948) 76 CLR 1.

TABLE OF CASES

Numbers in **bold italics** indicate references to the text; numbers in **bold** indicate references to the notes.

Commission (1977) 139 CLR 117
126

Kavvadias v. Commonwealth
Ombudsman (1984) 52 ALR 728
214

Kent v. Cavanagh (1973) 1 ACTR 43
218

Kent v. Johnson (1973) 21 FLR 177
220

Kentucky Fried Chicken Pty Ltd v.
Gantidis (1979) 140 CLR 675 **216**

Kidman v. Page [1959] Qd R 53 **220**

Kirmani v. Captain Cook Cruises Pty
Ltd (1985) 59 ALJR 265; 58 ALR
29 **201**

L'Estrange v. Brisbane Gas Co.
[1928] QSR 180 **220**

Lamb v. Moss (1983) 49 ALR 533 **214**

Levin v. Clark [1962] NSWR 686 **209**

Lloyd v. Robinson (1962) 107 CLR
142 **216**

Logan Downs Pty Ltd v. Federal
Commissioner of Taxation (1965)
112 CLR 177 **218**

Lomax v. Jervis (1885) 6 LR (NSW)
237 **221**

MacCormick v. Commissioner of
Taxation (1984) 58 ALJR 268; 52
ALR 53 **206**

Maguire v. Simpson (1977) 139 CLR
362 **205**

Majury v. Sunbeam Corporation Ltd
[1974] 1 NSWLR 659 **215**

Marsh v. Adamson (1985) 59 ALR
629 **193**

McKell v. Rider (1908) 5 CLR 480
219

McKinnon v. Grogan [1974] 1
NSWLR 295 **202**

McLeod v. Rub-A-Dub Car Wash
(Malvern) Pty Ltd 1972,
unreported **219**

Miles v. McIlwraith (1883) 8 AC 120
203

Miller Steamship Co. Pty Ltd v.
Overseas Tankship (UK) Ltd
[1963] NSWR 737 **221**

Miller v. Jackson [1977] QB 966 **220**

Minister for Immigration and Ethnic
Affairs v. Pochi (1980) 31 ALR
666 **198**

Mobil Oil Australia Ltd v. Brindle
(1985) 62 ALR 89 **211**

Moore v. Commonwealth (1951) 82
CLR 547 **206**

Moorgate Tobacco Co. Ltd v. Philip
Morris Ltd (No. 2) (1984) 59 ALJR
77; 56 ALR 193 **212**

Municipal Council of Sydney v.
Harris (1912) 14 CLR 1 **198**

Municipal Officers' Association of
Australia v. Lancaster (1981) 37
ALR 559 **214**

Munna Beach Apartments Pty Ltd v.
Kennedy (1982) 7 ACLR 257 **194**

Munro v. Southern Dairies Ltd [1955]
VLR 332 **219**

Murphyores Incorporated Pty Ltd v.
Commonwealth (1976) 136 CLR 1
198, 199, 215, 217

Myer Retail Investments Pty Ltd and
the Companies Act, Re (1983) 48
ACTR 41 **194**

Nalder v. Commissioner for
Railways [1983] 1 Qd R 620 **221**

National Commercial Banking Co. of
Australia Ltd v. Robert Bushby Ltd
[1984] 1 NSWLR 559 **195**

National Companies and Securities
Commission v. News Corporation
Ltd (1984) 58 ALJR 308; 52 ALR
417 **194**

National Trust of Australia (Vic.) v.
Australian Temperance and General
Mutual Life Assurance Society Ltd
[1976] VR 592 **217, 218**

New South Wales v. Bardolph (1934)
52 CLR 455 **205**

New South Wales v. Commonwealth
(1908) 7 CLR 179 **205**

New South Wales v. Commonwealth
(1975) 135 CLR 337 **92**

New South Wales v. Commonwealth
(No. 1) (1932) 46 CLR 155 **200**

News Corporation Ltd v. National
Companies and Securities

BIBLIOGRAPHY

PARLIAMENTARY AND GOVERNMENT PUBLICATIONS

Advisory Council for Inter-government Relations, *The Australian Loan Council and Inter-Governmental Relations*, AGPS, Canberra, 1982.

Attorney-General's Department, *Legal Aid Task Force*, AGPS, Canberra, 1985.

Attorney-General's Department, *Prosecution Policy of the Commonwealth*, AGPS, Canberra, 1982.

Australian Commissioner of Taxation, *Sixty-Third Report 1983–84*, Commonwealth Parliamentary Paper no. 77, 1984.

The Australian Constitution Annotated, AGPS, Canberra, 1980.

Australian Constitutional Convention, Standing Committee D, Special Report to Executive Committee, *The Senate and Supply*, 1977.

Australian Financial System, Report of the Review Group, AGPS, Canberra, 1984.

Australian Financial System, Final Report of the Committee of Inquiry, AGPS, Canberra, 1981.

——, *Commissioned Studies and Selected Papers*, AGPS, Canberra, 1982.

Australian Law Reform Commission, *Access to Courts—1. Standing: Public Interest Suits*, Working Paper no. 7, 1977.

——, *Standing in Public Interest Litigation*, AGPS, Canberra, 1985.

——, *Community Law Reform: Domestic Violence in the ACT*, AGPS, Canberra, 1984.

Commission of Inquiry into Land Tenures, Final Report, Commonwealth Parliamentary Paper no. 151, 1976.

Commonwealth Administrative Review Committee, *Report*, Commonwealth Parliamentary Paper no. 144, 1971.

Commonwealth Ombudsman, *Second Annual Report 1979*, AGPS, Canberra, 1979.

——, *Fourth Annual Report 1980–81*, AGPS, Canberra, 1981.

——, *Fifth Annual Report 1981–82*, AGPS, Canberra, 1983.

Commonwealth/State Transport Secretariat, *Report on the Development of a Long-Term National Motor Vehicle Emissions Strategy*, AGPS, Canberra, 1982.

Department of Employment and Industrial Relations, *Prices and Incomes Policy. The Third Progress Report on Government Initiatives*, AGPS, Canberra, 1985.

Department of Immigration & Ethnic Affairs, *Review of Activities 1983–84*, Parliamentary Paper no. 82, 1985.

Department of the Prime Minister and Cabinet, *Legislation Handbook*, AGPS, Canberra, 1983.

Department of the Special Minister of State, *Registration of Lobbyists, Guidelines*, 1985.

Economic Planning Advisory Council, *Tax Expenditures in Australia*, Canberra, 1986.

Estimates of Expenditure and Receipts of the Commonwealth Public Account 1985–86, Budget Paper no. 5, Commonwealth Parliamentary Paper no. 254, 1985.

Gyles, R., *Final Report to the Attorney-General for the Period 1 July 1984 to 21 September 1984*, Parliamentary Paper no. 12, 1985.

House of Representatives, *Standing Orders*, AGPS, Canberra, 1985.

House of Representatives Standing Committee on Environment and Conservation, *Administration of The Environment Protection (Impact of Proposals) Act 1974*, Commonwealth Parliamentary Paper no. 188, 1985.

Industries Assistance Commission Annual Report 1980–81, AGPS, Canberra, 1981.

Insurance Contracts. Treasury Submission to the Law Reform Commission, AGPS, Canberra, 1979.

Joint Committee on Pecuniary Interests of Members of Parliament, *Declaration of Interests*, AGPS, Canberra, 1975.

Joint Select Committee on Parliamentary Privilege, *Final Report*, Parliamentary Paper no. 219, 1984.

Law Reform Commission of Canada, *Crimes Against the Environment*, Working Paper no. 44, Ottawa, 1985.

Legal and Constitutional Committee (Parliament of Victoria), *Report on the Subordinate Legislation (Deregulation) Bill*, Melbourne, 1984.

Ministerial Statement, *Review of Commonwealth Functions*, 30 April 1981.

Ministry for Planning and Environment (Victoria), *Western Suburbs Planning and Environment Action Program Investigation Working Paper*, Melbourne, 1983.

New South Wales Law Reform Commission, *Accident Compensation*, 1984.

National Companies and Securities Commission, *Fifth Annual Report and Financial Statements 1st July 1983 to 30th June 1984*, AGPS, Canberra, 1985.

National Estate, Report of the Committee of Inquiry, AGPS, Canberra, 1975.

Office of Road Safety, *Summary of National Road Crash Statistics*, Department of Transport, Canberra, 1985.

Parliamentary Handbook on Commonwealth Government Financial Affairs, AGPS, Canberra, 1977.

Payments to or for the States . . . and Local Government Authorities 1985–86, Budget Paper no. 7, Commonwealth Parliamentary Paper no. 256, 1985.

Portfolio Program Estimates 1985–86, Budget Paper no. 6, Commonwealth Parliamentary Paper no. 255, 1985.

Public Duty and Private Interest. Report of the Committee of Inquiry, AGPS, Canberra, 1979.

Public Service Board, *Personnel Management Manual*, AGPS, Canberra, looseleaf.

——, *58th Annual Report 1981–82*, AGPS, Canberra, 1982.

Redlich, R., *Annual Report of The Special Prosecutor*, Commonwealth Parliamentary Paper no. 203, 1984.

Reform of the Australian Tax System, Draft White Paper, AGPS, Canberra, 1985.

Report of Inspectors Appointed to Investigate the Particular Affairs of Navillus Pty Ltd and 922 Other Companies, Government Printer, Melbourne, 1981.

Report of the Auditor-General Upon Audits, Examinations and Inspections..., Commonwealth Parliamentary Paper no. 64, 1985.

Report of the Royal Commission [on] Allegations of Corruption Relating to Dealings with Certain Crown Leaseholds in Queensland, Government Printer, Brisbane, 1956.

Report from the Joint Committee on Constitutional Review, Government Printer, Canberra, 1959.

Report to the Attorney-General for the Year Ended 30th June, 1984, Commonwealth Parliamentary Paper no. 258, 1984.

Reserve Bank of Australia, *Report and Financial Statements*, 30 June 1984.

Royal Commission on the Activities of the Federated Ship Painters and Dockers Union, *Final Report*, AGPS, Canberra, 1984.

Royal Commission into Australian Meat Industry, *Report*, AGPS, Canberra, 1981.

Royal Commission on Australian Government Administration, *Report*, AGPS, Canberra, 1976.

Royal Commission on Standards of Conduct in Public Life, Command Paper 6524, 1976.

Senate Select Committee on Air Pollution Part 1, Parliamentary Paper no. 91, 1969.

Senate Select Committee on Off-Shore Petroleum Resources, *Report*, Government Printing Office, Canberra, 1971.

Senate Select Committee on Private Hospitals and Nursing Homes, *Private Nursing Homes in Australia*, AGPS, Canberra, 1985.

Senate Select Committee on Securities and Exchange, *Australian Securities Markets and Their Regulation*, AGPS, Canberra, 1974.

Senate Standing Committee on Finance and Government Operations, *The Australian Dairy Corporation and its Asian Subsidiaries*, AGPS, Canberra, 1981.

——, *Statutory Authorities of the Commonwealth, Second Report*, AGPS, Canberra, 1979.

——, *Statutory Authorities of the Commonwealth, Fifth Report*, AGPS, Canberra, 1982.

Senate Standing Committee on Constitutional and Legal Affairs, *Reforming the Law*, AGPS, Canberra, 1979.

——, *The Constitutional Qualifications of Members of Parliament*, AGPS, Canberra, 1981.

Trade Practices Act Review Committee, *Report*, AGPS, Canberra, 1976.

Trade Practices Commission, *Annual Report 1980–1981*, AGPS, Canberra, 1981.

——, *Annual Report 1983–84*, AGPS, Canberra, 1984.

Western Australian Law Reform Commission, *Offices of Profit Under the Crown*, Report no. 14, 1971.

BOOKS

Ackerman, B. & Hassler, W., *Clean Coal Dirty Air*, Yale University Press, New Haven, 1981.

Aitken, H. (ed.), *The State and Economic Growth*, Social Science Research Council, New York, 1959.

Albon, R. & Lindsay G. (eds), *Occupational Regulation and the Public Interest*, Centre for Independent Studies, Sydney, 1984.

Aldred, J. & Wilkes, J. (eds), *A Fractured Federation?*, Allen & Unwin, Sydney, 1983.

Arens, R. & Lasswell, H., *In Defence of Public Order*, Columbia University Press, New York, 1961.

Armstrong, M., *Broadcasting Law and Policy in Australia*, Butterworths, Sydney, 1982.

Aronson, M. & Whitmore, H., *Public Torts and Contracts*, Law Book Company, Sydney, 1982.

Atiyah, P., *The Rise and Fall of Freedom of Contract*, Clarendon Press, Oxford, 1979.

Baram, M., *Alternatives to Regulation*, Lexington Books, Lexington, 1982.

Bardach, E. & Kagan, R., *Going by the Book*, Temple University Press, Philadelphia, 1982.

Barnes, S. & Blakeney, M., *Advertising Regulation*, Law Book Company, Sydney, 1982.

Barwick, G., *Sir John Did His Duty*, Serendip, Sydney, 1983.

Bates, G., *Environmental Law in Australia*, Butterworths, Sydney, 1983.

Becker, T. & Feeley, M. (eds) *The Impact of Supreme Court Decisions*, 2nd edn, Oxford University Press, New York, 1973.

Bell, J., *Policy Arguments in Judicial Decisions*, Clarendon Press, Oxford, 1983.

Black, D., *The Behaviour of Law*, Academic Press, New York, 1976.

—— (ed.), *Toward a General Theory of Social Control*, Academic Press, New York, 1984.

Blakeney, M., *Price Discrimination Law*, Legal Books, Sydney, 1983.

Bradbrook, A., *Solar Energy and the Law*, Law Book Company, Sydney, 1984.

—— & Neave, M., *Easements and Restrictive Covenants in Australia*, Butterworths, Sydney, 1981.

Braithwaite, J. & Grabosky, P., *Occupational Health and Safety Enforcement in Australia*, Australian Institute of Criminology, Canberra, 1985.

Braithwaite, J., *To Punish or Persuade: Enforcement of Coal Mine Safety*, SUNY Press, Buffalo, 1985.

Brennan, F., *Too Much Order With Too Little Law*, University of Queensland Press, Brisbane, 1983.

Breyer, S., *Regulation and Its Reform*, Harvard University Press, Cambridge, 1982.

—— & Stewart, R., *Administrative Law and Regulatory Policy*, Little, Brown & Co., Boston, 1979.

Brigham, J. & Brown D. (eds), *Policy Implementation*, Russell Sage, London, 1981 (reprint of (1980) 2 Law & Policy Q 3–128).

Brogden, S., *Australia's Two-Airline Policy*, Melbourne University Press, 1968.

Burman, S. & Harrell-Bond, S. (eds), *The Imposition of Law*, Academic Press, New York, 1979.

Butt, P., *Introduction to Land Law*, Law Book Company, Sydney, 1980.

Calabresi, G., *The Costs of Accidents*, Yale University Press, New Haven, 1970.

Cain, M. & Kulcsar, K. (eds), *Disputes and the Law*, Akademiai Kiado, Budapest, 1983.

Cannon, M., *Life in the Cities*, Nelson, Melbourne, 1975.

Chapman, R. & Roebuck, D., *The Court as the Public Conscience*, Environmental Law Reference Group, Hobart, 1976.

Clark, M., *A History of Australia*, vol. 4, Melbourne University Press, Melbourne, 1978.

Consultation and Government, Victorian Council of Social Service, Melbourne, 1981.

Cooray, L., *Conventions, The Australian Constitution and the Future*, Legal Books, Sydney, 1979.

Corbett, D., *Politics and the Airlines*, Allen & Unwin, London, 1965.

Cotterrell, R., *The Sociology of Law*, Butterworths, London, 1984.

Coward, P., *Environmental Law in Sydney*, Botany Bay Project, Canberra, 1976.

Craig, P., *Administrative Law*, Sweet & Maxwell, London, 1983.

Cranston, R., *Regulating Business*, Macmillan, London, 1979.

——, *Legal Foundations of the Welfare State*, Weidenfeld & Nicolson, London, 1985.

——, *Consumers and the Law*, 2nd edn, Weidenfeld & Nicolson, London, 1985.

—— & Schick, A. (eds), *Law and Economics*, Department of Law, Australian National University, Canberra, 1982.

——, Haynes, P. et al., *Delays and Efficiency in Civil Litigation*, Australian Institute of Judicial Administration, Canberra, 1985.

Creighton, B. & Gunningham, N. (eds), *The Industrial Relations of Occupational Health and Safety*, Croom Helm, Sydney, 1985.

Curnow, G. & Saunders, C., *Quangos*, Hale & Iremonger, Sydney, 1983.

Current Constitutional Problems in Australia, Centre for Research on Federal Financial Relations, Australian National University, Canberra, 1982.

Dalton, H., *Principles of Public Finance*, 10th edn, George Routledge, London, 1939.

Davis, K., *Discretionary Justice*, University of Illinois Press, Urbana, 1971.

de Smith, S., *Constitutional and Administrative Law*, 2nd edn, Penguin, London, 1973.

de Smith's Judicial Review of Administrative Action, 4th edn, Stevens, London, 1980.

Detmold, M., *The Australian Commonwealth*, Law Book Company, Sydney, 1985.

Dixon, O., *Jesting Pilate*, Law Book Company, Sydney, 1965.

Dolbeare, K., *Trial Courts in Urban Politics*, Wiley, New York, 1967.

Duggan, A., *The Economics of Consumer Protection*, Adelaide Law Review Association, Adelaide, 1982.

—— & Darvall, L. (eds), *Consumer Protection Law and Theory*, Law Book Company, Sydney, 1980.

Dworkin, R., *Taking Rights Seriously*, Duckworth, London, 1977.

Easton, D., *A Framework for Political Analysis*, University of Chicago Press, Chicago, 1979.

Eggleston, F., *State Socialism in Victoria*, P.S. King, London, 1932.

Eggleston, R., & St John, E., *Constitutional Seminar*, New South Wales University Press, Sydney, 1977.

Encel, S. (ed.), *Change the Rules!*, Penguin, Melbourne, 1977.

Evans, G. (ed.), *Labor and the Constitution 1972–1975*, Heinemann, Melbourne, 1977.

Evatt, H., Certain Aspects of the Royal Prerogative, LL.D. thesis, Sydney University, 1924.

——, *The King and His Dominion Governors*, 2nd edn, Frank Cass, London, 1967.

Finn, P., *Law and Government in Colonial Australia*, Oxford University Press, Melbourne, 1987.

Fisher, D., *Environmental Law in Australia*, University of Queensland Press, Brisbane, 1980.

Fisse, B. & Braithwaite, J., *The Impact of Publicity on Corporate Offenders*, SUNY Press, Albany, 1983.

Fitzgerald, R., *From 1915 to the Early 1980s*, University of Queensland Press, Brisbane, 1984.

Fleming, J., *The Law of Torts*, 6th edn, Law Book Company, Sydney, 1983.

Flint, D., *Foreign Investment Law in Australia*, Law Book Company, Sydney, 1985.

Fogg, A., *Australian Town Planning Law*, 2nd edn, University of Queensland Press, Brisbane, 1982.

Forbes, J., *The Divided Legal Profession in Australia*, Law Book Company, Sydney, 1979.

Forsey, E., *The Royal Power of Dissolution of Parliament in the British Commonwealth*, Oxford University Press, Toronto, 1943.

Fowler, R., *Environmental Impact Assessment, Planning and Pollution Measures in Australia*, AGPS, Canberra, 1982.

Freedman, J., *Crisis and Legitimacy*, Cambridge University Press, Cambridge, 1978.

Friedman, L., *The Legal System*, Russell Sage, New York, 1975.

—— & Macaulay, S., *Law and the Behavioural Sciences*, Bobbs-Merrill, Indianapolis, 1969.

Friedman, M., *Capitalism and Freedom*, University of Chicago Press, Chicago, 1962.

Friedmann, W. & Garner, J. (eds), *Government Enterprise*, Stevens, London, 1970.

Friedmann, W. & Kalmanoff, G., *Joint International Business Ventures*, Columbia University Press, New York, 1961.

Friedrich, C., *The Pathology of Politics*, Harper & Row, New York, 1972.

Fuller, L., *Anatomy of the Law*, Penguin, Harmondsworth, 1971.

——, *The Principles of Social Order*, Duke University Press, Durham, 1981.

Galligan, D. (ed.), *Essays in Legal Theory*, Melbourne University Press, Melbourne, 1984.

Gawler, J., *A Roof Over My Head*, Lothian, Sydney, 1963.

Gilbert, R., *The Future of the Australian Loan Council*, Centre for Research on Federal Financial Relations, Australian National University, Canberra, 1974.

Gilpin, A., *The Australian Environment*, Sun, Melbourne, 1980.

Goldring, J. & Maher, L., *Consumer Protection Law in Australia*, Butterworths, Sydney, 1983.

Grabosky, P. & Braithwaite, J., *Of Manners Gentle*, Oxford University Press, Melbourne, 1986.

Green, M. & Waitzman, N., *Business War on the Law*, Corporate Accountability Research Group, Washington, 1981.

Gribble; P., *What God Hath Wrought. The Story of the Electric Telegraph—Queensland*, Telecom, Brisbane, 1981.

Gruen, F. (ed.), *Surveys of Australian Economics*, Allen & Unwin, Sydney, 1978.

Gunningham, Neil, *Safeguarding the Worker*, Law Book Company, Sydney, 1984.

Hallam, H., *The Constitutional History of England*, John Murray, London, 1846.

Hambly, A. & Goldring, J. (eds), *Australian Lawyers and Social Change*, Law Book Company, Sydney, 1976.

Hancock, W., *The Battle of Black Mountain*, Dept Econ. History, Australian National University, Canberra, 1974.

Hanks, P., *Australian Constitutional Law*, 3rd edn, Butterworths, Sydney, 1985.

Harding, R., *Outside Interference*, Sun, Melbourne, 1979.

Harris, D., et al., *Compensation and Support for Illness and Injury*, Clarendon Press, Oxford, 1984.

Hart, H., *Punishment and Responsibility*, Clarendon Press, Oxford, 1968.

—— & Sacks, A., The Legal Process, unpublished, Harvard Law School, 1958.

Hawker, G., Smith, R. & Weller, P., *Politics and Policy in Australia*, University of Queensland Press, Brisbane, 1979.

Hawkins, K., *Environment and Enforcement*, Clarendon Press, Oxford, 1984.

Head, J. (ed.), *Taxation Issues of the 1980s*, Australian Tax Research Foundation, Sydney, 1983.

Heidenheimer, A., *Political Corruption*, Holt, Rinehart & Winston, New York, 1970.

Hickie, D., *The Prince and the Premier*, Angus & Robertson, Sydney, 1985.

Higley, J., Deacon, D. & Smart, D., *Elites in Australia*, Routledge & Kegan Paul, London, 1979.

Hobday, S., *Coulson and Forbes on the Law of Waters*, 6th edn, Sweet & Maxwell, London, 1952.

Holmes, J. & Sharman, C., *The Australian Federal System*, Allen & Unwin, Sydney, 1977.

Hopkins, A., *A Working Paper on White Collar Crime in Australia*, Australian Institute of Criminology, Canberra, 1977.

——, *Crime Law and Business*, Australian Institute of Criminology, Canberra, 1978.

——, *The Impact of Prosecutions under the Trade Practices Act*, Australian Institute of Criminology, Canberra, 1978.

Horne, D., *Money Made Us*, Penguin, Melbourne, 1976.

Hotop, S., *Principles of Australian Administrative Law*, 6th edn, Law Book Company, Sdyney, 1985.

Howard, C., *Australian Federal Constitutional Law*, 3rd edn, Law Book Company, Sydney, 1985.

——, *Australia's Constitution*, Penguin, Melbourne, 1978.

——, *Strict Responsibility*, Sweet & Maxwell, London, 1963.

Hughes, C., *The Government of Queensland*, University of Queensland Press, Brisbane, 1980.

Hughes, G. (ed.), *Law, Reason and Justice*, New York University Press, New York, 1969.

Hurst, J., *Dealing with Statutes*, Columbia University Press, New York, 1982.

James, M. (ed.), *The Constitutional Challenge*, Centre for Independent Studies, Sydney, 1982.

Jennings, I., *Cabinet Government*, 3rd edn, Cambridge University Press, Cambridge, 1969.

Jones, K., *Law and Economy*, Academic Press, London, 1982.

Jowell, J., *Law and Bureaucracy*, Dunellen, New York, 1975.

Kagan, R., *Regulatory Justice*, Russell Sage, New York, 1978.

Kahn, A., *The Economics of Regulation*, Wiley, New York, 1970–1.

Kapp, K., *The Social Costs of Business Enterprise*, Spokesman, Nottingham, 1978.

Kelly, P., *The Unmaking of Gough*, Angus & Robertson, Sydney, 1976 (subsequently published as *The Dismissal*).

Kercher, B. & Noone, M., *Remedies*, Law Book Company, Sydney, 1983.

Kerr, J., *Matters for Judgment*, Macmillan, Melbourne, 1978.

Keynes, J., *The General Theory of Employment, Interest and Money*, Macmillan, London, 1957.

Kirby, M., *Domestic Airline Regulation*, Centre for Independent Studies, Sydney, 1981.

Kirby, M.D., *Reform the Law*, Oxford University Press, Melbourne, 1983.

——, *The Judges*, Australian Broadcasting Commission, Sydney, 1983.

Kitto, F., *Judicial Essays*, Law Foundation of New South Wales and Victorian Law Foundation, n.d.

Kneese, A. & Schultz, C., *Pollution, Prices and Public Policy*, Brookings, Washington, 1975.

Kriegler, R., *Working for the Company*, Oxford University Press, Melbourne, 1980.

Land Degradation and Public Policy, Centre for Resource and Environmental Studies, Australian National University, Canberra, 1986.

Landis, J., *The Administrative Process*, Yale University Press, New Haven, 1938.

Lang, A. & Crommelin, M., *Australian Mining and Petroleum Laws*, Butterworths, Sydney, 1979.

Lang, J., *Why I Fight!*, Labor Publications, Sydney, 1934.

Leach, R., *Interstate Relations in Australia*, University of Kentucky Press, 1965.

Levin, M., *Urban Politics and the Criminal Courts*, University of Chicago Press, Chicago, 1977.

Lipsky, M., *Street-Level Bureaucracy*, Russell Sage, New York, 1980.

Loveday, P., *Promoting Industry*, University of Queensland Press, Brisbane, 1982.

Lumb, R., *The Constitutions of the Australian States*, 4th edn, University of Queensland Press, Brisbane, 1977.

Luntz, H., Hambly, A. & Hayes, R., *Torts*, Butterworths, Sydney, 1985.

Macaulay, S., *Private Government*, Disputes Processing Research Program, University of Wisconsin-Madison, Working Paper 1983–6.

MacAvoy, P., *The Regulated Industries and the Economy*, Norton, New York, 1979.

MacCormick, N., *Legal Reasoning and Legal Theory*, Clarendon Press, Oxford, 1978.

Mackinolty, J. & Radi, H. (eds), *In Pursuit of Justice*, Hale & Iremonger, Sydney, 1979.

Mannheim, H., *Criminal Justice and Social Reconstruction*, Routledge & Kegan Paul, London, 1946.

Marshall, G., *Constitutional Conventions*, Clarendon Press, Oxford, 1984.

Marx, K., *Capital*, vol. 1, Lawrence & Wishart, London, 1957.

Mathews, R., *The Australian Loan Council*, Centre for Research on Federal Financial Relations, Australian National University, Canberra, 1984.

——, *The Changing Pattern of Australian Federalism*, Centre for Research on Federal Financial Relations, Australian National University, Canberra, 1976.

—— (ed.), *Federalism and the Environment*, Centre for Research on Federal Financial Relations, Australian National University, Canberra, 1985.

—— (ed.), *Public Sector Borrowing in Australia*, Centre for Research on Federal Financial Relations, Australian National University, Canberra, 1982.

—— & Jay, W., *Federal Finance*, Nelson, Melbourne, 1972.

Max Weber on Law in Economy and Society, Simon & Schuster, New York, 1954.

Maxwell, J., *Commonwealth-State Financial Relations in Australia*, Melbourne University Press, Melbourne, 1967.

May, T., *The Law, Privileges, Proceedings and Usage of Parliament*, 17th edn, Butterworths, London, 1964.

Mayne, A., *Fever, Squalor and Vice*, University of Queensland Press, Brisbane, 1982.

McCallum, B., *The Public Service Manager*, Longman Cheshire, Melbourne, 1984.

McMillan, J., Evans, G. & Storey, H., *Australia's Constitution*, Law Foundation of NSW & Allen & Unwin, Sydney, 1983.

Melnick, R., *Regulation and the Courts*, Brookings, Washington, 1983.

Miers, D. & Page, A., *Legislation*, Sweet & Maxwell, London, 1982.

Morris, G. & Barker, M., *Planning and Environment Service (Victoria)*, Butterworths, Sydney, 1984.

Muir W., *Law and Attitude Change*, University of Chicago Press, Chicago, 1973.

Murphy, W., *Congress and the Court*, University of Chicago Press, Chicago, 1962.

Nader, L. & Todd, H. (eds), *The Disputing Process*, Columbia University Press, New York, 1978.

Nethercote, J., *Parliament and Bureaucracy*, Hale & Iremonger, Sydney, 1982.

Neutze, M., *Australian Urban Policy*, Allen & Unwin, Sydney, 1977.

——, *Urban Development in Australia*, 2nd edn, Allen & Unwin, Sydney, 1981.

Nieuwenhuysen, J. (ed.) *Australian Trade Practices*, Croom Helm, London, 1970.

—— & Norman, N., *Australian Competition and Prices Policy*, Croom Helm, London, 1976.

—— & Williams-Wynn, M., *Professions in the Marketplace*, Melbourne University Press, Melbourne, 1982.

Niland, J. & Isaac, J. (eds), *Australian Labour Economics Readings*, Sun, Melbourne, 1975.

Nott, A., *Environmental Planning and Development Law (NSW)*, Penman, Sydney, 1982.

O'Malley, P., *Law, Capitalism and Democracy*, Allen & Unwin, Sydney, 1983.

Oakes, L., *Crash Through or Crash*, Drummond, Melbourne, 1976.

Odgers, J., *Australian Senate Practice*, 5th edn, AGPS, Canberra, 1976.

Olson, M., *The Logic of Collective Action*, Harvard University Press, Cambridge, Mass., 1975.

Parsons, R., *Income Taxation in Australia*, Law Book Company, Sydney, 1985.

Pearce, D., *Commonwealth Administrative Law*, Butterworths, Sydney, 1986.

——, *Statutory Interpretation in Australia*, 2nd edn, Butterworths, Sydney, 1981.

——, *Delegated Legislation*, Butterworths, Sydney, 1977.

Pettifer, J., *House of Representatives Practice*, AGPS, Canberra, 1981.

Poole, W., *Management of Kangaroo Harvesting in Australia (1984)*, Australian National Parks and Wildlife Service, Canberra, 1984.

Porter, C., *Environmental Impact Assessment*, University of Queensland Press, Brisbane, 1985.

Poulton, H., *Law, History and Politics of the Australian Two Airline System*, H.W. Poulton, Melbourne, 1982.

Powell, J., *Environmental Management in Australia, 1788–1914*, Oxford University Press, Melbourne, 1976.

Power in Australia: Directions of Change, Centre for Continuing Education, Australian National University, Canberra, 1982.

Provost, D., Inter-Governmental Co-operation in Australia, Ph.D. thesis, University of Queensland, 1955.

Prowse, A. & Morey, E., *The Financial Agreement and the Future of the Loan Council*, Centre for Research on Federal Financial Relations, Australian National University, Canberra, 1976.

Pullan, R., *Guilty Secrets*, Methuen, Sydney, 1984.

Pullen, J., Young, N. & Geddes. S., *Court Surveys and Studies 1978–1984*, Civil Justice Committee, Melbourne, 1985.

Public Interest Research Group, *Legalized Pollution*, University of Queensland Press, Brisbane, 1973.

Puri, K., *Australian Government Contracts. Law and Practice*, Commercial Clearing House, Sydney, 1978.

Purvis, R., *Corporate Crime*, Butterworths, Sydney, 1979.

Quick, J. & Garran, R., *The Annotated Constitution of the Australian Commonwealth*, Angus & Robertson, Sydney, 1901.

Radi, H. & Spearritt, P. (eds), *Jack Lang*, Hale & Iremonger, Sydney, 1977.

Renfree, H., *The Executive Power of the Commonwealth of Australia*, Legal Books, Sydney, 1984.

Richardson, G., Ogus,A. & Burrows, P., *Policing Pollution*, Clarendon Press, Oxford, 1982.

Robinson, G., Gellhorn, E. & Bruff, H., *The Administrative Process*, 2nd edn, West, St Paul, 1980.

Roddewig, R., *Green Bans*, Hale & Iremonger, Sydney, 1978.

Ross, H., *Deterring the Drinking Driver*, Lexington Books, Lexington, 1984.

——, *Settled Out of Court*, Aldine, Chicago, 1970.

Ross, S., *Politics of Law Reform*, Penguin, Melbourne, 1982.

Rowley, C. & Peacock, A., *Welfare Economics*, Martin Robertson, London, 1975.

Russ, P. & Tanner, L., *The Politics of Pollution*, Visa, Melbourne, 1978.

Sawer, G., *Australian Federal Politics and Law 1929–1949*, Melbourne University Press, Melbourne, 1963.

——, *Federation Under Strain*, Melbourne University Press, Melbourne, 1977.

——, *Modern Federalism*, 2nd ed., Pitman, Melbourne, 1976.

Sawer, M. (ed.), *Program for Change—Affirmative Action in Australia*, Allen & Unwin, Sydney, 1985.

Schubert, G., *The Judicial Mind*, Northwestern University Press, Evanston, 1965.

Scott, R., *The Australian Loan Council and Public Investment*, Centre for Research on Federal Financial Relations, Australian National University, Canberra, 1983.

—— (ed.), *Interest Groups and Public Policy*, Macmillan, Melbourne, 1980.

Shapiro, M., *Courts*, University of Chicago Press, Chicago, 1981.

Sigler, J. & Beede, B., *The Legal Sources of Public Policy*, Lexington Books, Lexington, 1977.

Sornarajah, M. (ed.), *The South West Dam Dispute*, University of Tasmania, Hobart, 1983.

Stanford, J., *Money, Banking and Economic Activity*, Wiley, Sydney, 1973.

Stein, L., *Urban Legal Problems*, Law Book Company, Sydney, 1974.

Stewart, R. & Krier, J., *Environmental Law and Policy*, 2nd edn, Bobbs-Merrill, Indianapolis, 1978.

Stone, A., *Economic Regulation and the Public Interest*, Cornell University Press, Ithaca, 1977.

Sydney Labour History Group, *What Rough Beast?*, Allen & Unwin, Sydney, 1982.

Sykes, E. & Glasbeck, H., *Labour Law in Australia*, Butterworths, Sydney, 1972.

Sykes, T., *The Money Miners*, Fontana, Melbourne, 1979.

Tay, A. & Kamenka, E. (eds), *Law-Making in Australia*, Edward Arnold, Sydney, 1980.

Tearle, W., *Debt Recovery and Insolvency: Research Paper no. 1: Default Summons Survey*, Australian Law Reform Commission, Sydney, 1982.

Tomasic, R., *Legislation and Society in Australia*, Allen & Unwin, Sydney, 1980.

—— (ed.), *Business Regulation in Australia*, Commercial Clearing House, Sydney, 1984.

Trindade, F. & Cane, P., *The Law of Torts in Australia*, Oxford University Press, Melbourne, 1985.

Troy, P. (ed.), *Equity in the City*, Allen & Unwin, Sydney, 1981.

Tullock, G., *Trials on Trial*, Columbia University Press, New York, 1980.

Vaughan, D., *Controlling Unlawful Organisational Behaviour*, University of Chicago Press, Chicago, 1983.

Venturini, V., *Malpractice*, Non Mollare, Sydney, 1980.

Walker, S., *Contempt of Parliament and the Media*, Adelaide Law Review, Research Paper no. 4, Adelaide, 1984.

Warhurst, J., *Jobs or Dogma?* University of Queensland Press, Brisbane, 1982.

Weaver, S., *Decision to Prosecute*, Massachusetts Institute of Technology Press, Cambridge, 1977.

Weller, P. & Cutt, J., *Treasury Control in Australia*, Novak, Sydney, 1976.

Weller, P. & Jaensch, D. (eds), *Responsible Government in Australia*, Drummond, Melbourne, 1980.

Wheare, K., *Federal Government*, Oxford University Press, London, 1946.

Whitlam, G., *On Australia's Constitution*, Widescope, Melbourne, 1977.

——, *The Truth of the Matter*, Penguin, Melbourne, 1979.

——, *The Whitlam Government 1972–1975*, Viking, Melbourne, 1985.

Wilson, J. (ed.), *The Politics of Regulation*, Basic Books, New York, 1980.

Wilson, P. & Braithwaite, J. (eds), *Two Faces of Deviance*, University of Queensland Press, Brisbane, 1978.

Wiltshire, K., *An Introduction to Australian Public Administration*, Cassell, Melbourne, 1975.

——, *Administrative Federalism*, University of Queensland Press, Brisbane, 1977.

Winterton, G., *Parliament, the Executive and the Governor-General*, Melbourne University Press, Melbourne, 1983.

Wright, D., *Shadow of Dispute*, Australian National University Press, Canberra, 1970.

Wynes, W., *Legislative, Executive and Judicial Powers in Australia*, 5th edn, Law Book Company, Sydney, 1976.

Zimring, F. & Hawkins, G., *Deterrence*, University of Chicago Press, Chicago, 1973.

Zines, L. (ed.), *Commentaries on the Australian Constitution*, Butterworths, Sydney, 1977.

——, *The High Court and the Constitution*, 2nd edn, Butterworths, Sydney, 1986.

INDEX